PROBLEM SOLVING

Problem solving

S. Ian Robertson
University of Luton, UK

First published 2001 by Psychology Press
27 Church Road, Hove, East Sussex, BN3 2FA

www.psypress.co.uk

Simultaneously published in the USA and Canada
by Taylor & Francis Inc
325 Chestnut Street, 8th Floor, Philadelphia, PA 19106

Psychology Press is part of the Taylor & Francis Group

© 2001 Psychology Press Ltd

British Library Cataloguing in Publication Data
A catalogue record for this book is available from the British Library

Library of Congress Cataloging in Publication Data
Robertson, S. Ian, 1951-
    Problem solving/S. Ian Robertson.
      p. cm.
    Including bibliographical references (p.) and index.
    ISBN 0-415-20299-X—ISBN 0-415-20300-7 (pbk.)
    1. Problem solving. I. Title
    BF449.R63 2001
    153.4'3—dc21   00-059071

    ISBN 0-415-20299-X (hbk)
    ISBN 0-415-20300-7 (pbk)

Cover design by Leigh Hurlock
Typeset in Times by Facing Pages, Southwick, West Sussex
Printed and bound in the United Kingdom by Biddles, Guildford and King's Lynn

For Kathryn, Poppy, and Aidan (and then there were three)

Contents

Illustrations

Preface

Despite the title, I'm afraid this book will not necessarily help you solve your personal problems. Instead it is about the psychological processes involved in problem solving—how we go about solving various types of problems, what kinds of things make it hard to solve problems, and how we learn from the experience of solving them.

Who is it for? The book was written mainly (but not exclusively) with undergraduate students of psychology in mind, and should be particularly relevant to courses in cognitive psychology, cognitive science and problem solving and thinking. Students of artificial intelligence and computer modelling should also find several parts that are relevant to their studies. A large section of the book concerns "transfer of learning". In other words a lot of the book is about the effectiveness or otherwise of certain teaching contexts. As a result there is much here that would be of interest to educationalists including classroom teachers. Business, industry, and even spin doctors are interested in how to solve problems and how to present information in an effective way. Part Two of the book shows that the way information is presented can influence how well it is understood, and hence reflects the likelihood or otherwise of solving a particular problem.

Although the book was originally written for a particular audience, I have tried to ensure that it is accessible to the interested lay reader. Some concepts and phrases that are familiar to students of psychology are therefore explained, and there is a glossary at the back of the book to remind you of what these concepts mean.

What's in it? I should make it clear right away that this book does not cover such topics as models of deductive reasoning, or judgement and decision making under uncertainty. It sticks to a fairly restricted conception of problem solving mainly from an information-processing perspective.

There are two implicit themes throughout the book. The first is simply the question of what kinds of things make it difficult to solve problems. The second is that problem solving and thinking in general involve processing the information given—that is, we are strongly influenced by the way information is presented and by those aspects of a problem or situation that appear to be salient.

The book contains 10 chapters divided in turn into four parts. Part One and Chapter 1 introduce the subject and some of the main concepts that will be dealt with in the rest of the book. Part Two includes an overview of the subject, some of the history of problem-solving research, mainly by Gestalt psychologists, and how this research developed into the modern information-processing account. It deals with how we represent problems mentally and the kinds of processes we use as we go about solving them. Part Three deals with research into how we apply what we learn in one situation to another situation. Common sense tells us that we must be able to transfer our learning from one context (learning French in a classroom) to another (going on holiday to France). However, research suggests that evidence of such transfer is sometimes very hard to come by. Part three goes on to cover analogical problem solving, the creative use of analogy, and the pedagogical role of analogies as a means of teaching or explaining new concepts. It ends with a look at textbook problem solving, as a great deal of what we learn at school and college in science, mathematics, and computer programming comes in the form of textbooks. Part Four includes two chapters on learning from examples and the eventual development of expertise. The penultimate chapter looks at writing as a complex problem-solving task with the aim of integrating many of the themes that have come up in the book. It also includes a general summary and conclusion.

Throughout the book there are "Activities" to get you to think about the material presented. It is the role of a teaching text to teach, and, in the absence of a human teacher, the text itself must do what it can to help the student learn. I hope you find these activities and questions fun to do. There are also "Study Boxes" that provide detailed information about specific studies, and "Information Boxes" explaining some concepts in more detail. The aim of these is to cover certain studies and concepts in more depth than might otherwise be possible, and to prevent the flow of the text from being interrupted.

ACKNOWLEDGEMENTS

I am indebted to those who commented on early drafts of parts of this book. My thanks go to Thom Baguley, Norma Pritchett, Jill Cohen, Stephen Payne, Kathryn, and several anonymous reviewers for keeping me on the straight and narrow.

The quotation by S. Mithen is taken from *The prehistory of the mind*. © 1996, Thames and Hudson. Reprinted with permission of the publishers.

Quotations from Newell, A. are reprinted by permission of the publisher from *Unified Theories of Cognition* by Allan Newell, Cambridge, Mass: Harvard University Press. © 1990, by the President and Fellows of Harvard College.

S. Ian Robertson
University of Luton

PART ONE

Introduction

CHAPTER ONE

Introduction to the study of problem solving

We face problems of one type or another every day of our lives. Two-year-olds face the problem of how to climb out of their cot unaided. Teenagers face the problem of how to live on less pocket money than all their friends. Students have mathematics problems to do for homework. We have problems thinking what to have for dinner, how to organise a dinner party, what to buy Poppy for Christmas, how to fix the vacuum cleaner when it seems to have stopped sucking. Problems come in all shapes and sizes, from the small and simple to the large and complex, and from the small and complex to the large and simple. In some cases at least it is fairly obvious to those with experience what people *should* do to solve the problems. This book deals with what people *actually* do in their attempts to solve them.

To help get a handle on the issues involved in the psychology of solving problems, we need a way of defining our terms—what is a problem, exactly, and what is involved in problem solving? Are there useful ways of classifying problems that would help in working out how they are typically dealt with? What methods are used in studying problem solving? What issues are raised by the study of human (and machine) problem solving?

The aim of this introduction is to touch on some of these questions and to explain how this book is structured and the kinds of things you will find in it. To begin with we will look at what constitutes a "problem"—a number of definitions and concepts that recur throughout the book are introduced here.

WHAT IS A PROBLEM?

You have a problem when you are sitting at home in Manchester and you want to be on the beach at St Tropez, or when you read a section of a textbook and then try an exercise problem at the end of the section and haven't a clue how to do it. In these examples there is a difference between where you are now (e.g., in Manchester) and where you want to be (e.g., in St Tropez). In each case "where you want to be" is an imagined (or written) state that you would like to be in. In other words, a distinguishing feature of a problem is that there is a *goal* to be reached and how you get there is not immediately obvious. To put it at its simplest, you have a problem when you are required to act but you don't know what to do. However, perhaps a fuller definition might be more appropriate (Duncker, 1945, p. 1):

> A problem arises when a living creature has a goal but does not know how this goal is to be reached. Whenever one cannot go from the given situation to the desired situation simply by action, then there is recourse to thinking ... Such thinking has the task of devising some action which may mediate between the existing and the desired situations.

What this definition highlights is that if you know exactly what action (or series of actions) to take in a given situation, then you don't really have a problem. It's only when you don't know exactly what steps to take to get to the goal and have to take some mediating action that you have a problem. Figure 1.1 illustrates in an abstract form what is involved in a problem, and two forms of mediating action. The first action (Figure 1.1b) is to try to take steps along a path that seems to lead

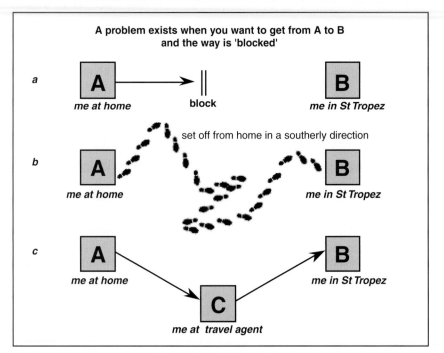

A problem exists when you want to get from A to B and the way is 'blocked'

a   **A** — block — **B**
me at home   block   me in St Tropez

set off from home in a southerly direction

b   **A**   **B**
me at home   me in St Tropez

c   **A**   **B**
me at home   me in St Tropez
C
me at travel agent

Figure 1.1. Problem solving.

in the direction of the goal. This is not a particularly sensible thing to do if your problem is how to get to St Tropez. The second is to perform some other action that will make it easier to get to the goal (Figure 1.1c). This is a reasonable thing to do, as you will probably get everything you need to know from the travel agent.

> **Activity 1.1**
>
> According to the definition just given would you class the following as problems:
>
> a. 2 + 3= ?
> b. 237 x 38 = ?
>
> If so, why? If not, why not?

In Activity 1.1, (a) is not a real problem because all you need to do is retrieve the answer directly from memory. It does not require a sequence of steps for its solution. For (b) things are a little bit trickier. You have a goal, but you probably *do* know what to do to achieve it, so in one sense you don't really have a problem. On the other hand, you would probably have recourse to thinking.

J.R. Anderson once wrote "Problem solving is defined as any goal-directed sequence of cognitive operations" (Anderson, 1980, p. 257). This definition does not distinguish between a sequence of actions that one *knows* will achieve a goal and a sequence of actions one undertakes when one does *not* immediately know how to reach the goal. The first is the result of experience and the second is the situation a novice faces. On the other hand, the view of problem solving emphasised in Duncker's quotation can be summarised by "What you do when you don't know what to do" (Wheatley, 1984, p. 1, cited in Frensch & Funke, 1995). More recently Anderson's definitions of problem solving have distinguished between early attempts at solving problems and the automated episodes that are still "no less problem solving" (Anderson, 2000a, p. 241; 2000b, p. 311).

Problem solving starts off from an initial given situation or statement of a problem (known as the **initial state** of the problem). Based on the problem situation and your prior knowledge you have to work towards a solution. When you reach it you are in the **goal state** of the problem. On the way from the initial state to the goal state you pass through a number of intermediate problem states. (This aspect is dealt with in more detail in Chapter 2.)

In some cases you don't know what the answer is in advance and you have to find it. *How* you find the answer might not be particularly relevant. In other problems it is precisely *how* you get the answer that is important: "I have to get back by six and my car's broken down"; "I have to get this guy into checkmate". The point of doing exercise problems in textbooks is to learn how to solve problems of a particular type. If the answer was all you were interested in, you could look that up at the back of the book. For example, in cases where you have to prove something, the "something" is given and it is the proof that is important.

Finally, you can have problems where you have only a vague idea what the answer is (although you could probably recognise it when you saw it) and an even vaguer idea of how to get there. Writing a 4000-word experimental report as an assignment is an example. The only thing you can be really sure of is whether you have written 4000 words or not. Another example might be finding a compromise in the domain of organising holidays. The travel agent would be rather confused if your problem was what to eat at a dinner party.

Some of the problems in Activity 1.2 have a simple structure. Problems 3 and 4 have simple rules and a clear description of how everything is set up at the beginning of the problem—the *initial state* of the problem—and what the problem should look like at the end—in the *goal state*. There are also some restrictions on what you are allowed to do in such problems. For example in problem 4 you cannot move more than three matches. Puzzle problems such as these are examples of **knowledge-lean** problems that require very little knowledge to solve them. Problems 1 and 5, on the other hand, are **knowledge-rich** problems. Problem 1 requires a lot of knowledge of Lisp programming. If you have that knowledge then it may be quite simple. If you are a novice Lisp programmer it might be quite difficult. If you have no knowledge of Lisp the question is completely meaningless. Similarly problem 5 requires a lot of knowledge of the causes of crime that may involve politics, sociology, criminal law, psychology, and so on.

Different types of goal

As mentioned earlier, some of the problems explicitly state what the goal "looks like". The task is to find a means of getting there. The Dots problem explicitly gives the goal. The problem here is: how do you get to it? The goal in problem 6 in Activity 1.3 is slightly different. Here the goal is to come up with an answer (a certain number of francs) but you won't necessarily know if it is correct (see next section). In problem 7, although you can probably readily evaluate whether you have reached your goal or not, there appear to be very few limits on how you get to it. You would probably impose your own constraints, however: getting caught might not be a good idea. Problem 8 has an infinite number of solutions that are probably rather hard to evaluate—it may well be an insoluble problem, unfortunately.

Activity 1.3

If you managed to achieve the goal in the Dots problem in Activity 1.2 and the three problems below, how confident would you be that the solution was adequate?

6. A tourist in St Tropez wants to convert £85 to French francs. If the exchange rate is 28FF to the pound how many francs will she get?
7. "Your task is in two parts ... One, to locate and destroy the landlines in the area of the northern MSR [main supply route, Iraq]. Two, to find and destroy Scud ... We're not really bothered how you do it, as long as it gets done." (McNab, 1994, p. 35)
8. How do I write a textbook on problem solving that everyone will understand?

Well-defined and ill-defined problems

Problems such as the Dots problem contain all the information needed to solve them, in that they describe the problem as it stands now (the initial state), what the

---

Activity 1.4

Try this problem:

9. The tale is told of a young man who once, as a joke, went to see a fortune-teller to have his palm read. When he heard her predictions, he laughed and exclaimed that fortune telling was nonsense. What the young man did not know was that the fortune-teller was a powerful witch, and, unfortunately, he had offended her so much that she cast a spell on him. Her spell turned him into both a compulsive gambler and also a consistent loser. He had to gamble but he never ever won a penny. The young man may not have been lucky at cards but it turned out that he was exceedingly lucky in love. In fact, he soon married a wealthy businesswoman who took great delight in accompanying him every day to the casino. She gave him money, and smiled happily when he lost it all at the roulette table. In this way, they both lived happily ever after. Why was the man's wife so happy to see him lose?

---

situation should be when you have solved the problem (the goal state), and exactly what actions you have to take to solve it (the **operators**). In the Dots problem the operation is MOVE (move a single dot). You are also told exactly what you are not allowed to do (the **operator restrictions**). Because thinking is done in your head, the operations are performed by mental operators. Although multiplication, say, is an arithmetic operator, you still have to know about it in order to apply it. Operators are therefore knowledge structures. (A useful mnemonic is to remember that the acronym from Initial state, Goal state, Operators, and Restrictions spells IGOR.)

A problem that provides all the information required to solve it is therefore **well-defined**. Actually, although you know where you are starting from, where you are going to, and what actions to perform to get there, it is not quite true to say that you have been given all the necessary information, as you are not told what objects to perform the action on. For example, in algebra (e.g., problem 2) there are four possible basic arithmetic operations—multiplication, division, addition and subtraction—but you might not know how to apply those operators or in what order to apply them to get the answer.

Problem 9 in Activity 1.4 is different. The initial state of the problem is given, and the goal is to find a reason why the man's wife is apparently happy to watch him lose money, but you are not told what operators to apply to solve the problem or what the restrictions are, if any. Since these two elements are missing this problem is **ill-defined**.

Activity 1.5

Is problem 2 (repeated below) well-defined or ill-defined?

Solve: $3(x + 4) + x = 20$

In Activity 1.5, if you thought problem 2 was well-defined then you are assuming that the solver knows what operators are available. You would also have to assume that the solver has a rough idea what the goal state should look like. This is a knowledge-rich domain—you have to write an essay in sociology. Chapter 4 deals with some of the general issues involved in transfer.

If we are to use one example to help solve another, there must be some kind of similarity between the two problems. Chapter 5 examines in some depth how we can characterise different types of similarity. Problems can be similar for several reasons—they may be superficially similar (for example, they may seem to be about the same kinds of objects); on the other hand, they may be similar because of some abstract quality (for example, they may be German verbs with separable prefixes); more importantly, they may be similar because they have the same solution structure (that is they are **structurally similar**).

Chapter 6 deals with the processes involved in analogical problem solving. If you are faced with a new problem and something about it reminds you of an earlier one, the chances are that this reminding is based on **surface similarities** between problems. Surface similarity is like saying that one book is similar to another because they both have blue covers. When a new problem shares few surface similarities with one you already know, the chances are you won't be reminded of the earlier one. In fact, we are not very good at recognising the analogy between a problem we have done in the past and a current one unless we are explicitly reminded of the earlier one or told that they are in some way the same. In analogical problem solving the analogue is presumed to be in long-term memory and the problem is mostly one of retrieving it. The other difficulty in analogical problem solving is adapting the analogue to solve the current problem. Chapter 6 also looks at the role of analogies as powerful teaching devices.

Chapter 7 looks at how analogies can be used to enhance teaching textbooks. The kind of analogical problem solving that one finds in teaching texts is different from the kind examined in Chapter 6, which concentrates on analogies in different domains. Textbooks use examples that students are supposed to use to solve exercise problems. This is within-domain analogising. When students are learning something for the first time they are unlikely to have an earlier problem in long-term memory that they can retrieve in the first place. Instead they have a textbook. Textbooks usually have examples to explain a solution procedure, but because students are novices they are unlikely to have a complete understanding of the examples, so adapting them to solve an exercise problem can be particularly difficult.

How do we ever manage to learn anything

Part Four follows on from the section on transfer and textbook problem solving by looking at how we learn from examples. Chapter 8 concentrates on two interrelated aspects of problem solving and learning:

- how we manage to abstract out a problem structure from experience. This problem structure (or **problem schema**) allows us to identify new problems of the same type and to access potentially useful solution strategies;

- how we abstract out general rules from specific examples. This is known as **rule induction**.

It also covers artificial intelligence (AI) models of problem solving and learning, and cognitive architectures.

The ultimate goal of learning, at least for some people, is to become an "expert". Chapter 9 therefore discusses studies of experts and novices, and looks at what distinguishes them. The chapter also discusses complex problem solving—the kind that experts engage in and that is far removed from the puzzle-like problems with which the study of problem solving began. The chapter ends with a brief look at writing expertise.

SUMMARY

1. Problem solving involves finding your way towards a goal. Sometimes the goal is easy to see and sometimes you will recognise it only when you see it.
2. Problems can be categorised as being:

   - *Knowledge-lean,* where little prior knowledge is needed to solve them; you may be able to get by using only domain-general knowledge—general knowledge of strategies and methods that apply to many types of problem.
   - *Knowledge-rich,* where a lot of prior knowledge is usually required; such knowledge is domain-specific—it applies only to that domain.
   - *Well-defined,* where all the information needed to solve it is either explicitly given or can be inferred.
   - *Ill-defined,* where some aspect of the problem, such as what you are supposed to do, is only vaguely stated.
   - *Semantically lean,* where the solver has little experience of the problem type.
   - *Semantically rich,* where the solver can bring to bear a lot of experience of the problem type.
   - *Insight* problems, where the solution is usually preceded by an "Aha!" experience.

3. Methods of investigating problem solving include:

   - "Laboratory" experiments, where variables are controlled, and the nature of the problem to be solved is under the control of the researcher.
   - Analysis of verbal protocols, where people talk aloud while solving problems and the resulting protocol is then analysed.
   - Artificial intelligence models, where theories of human problem solving are built into a computer program and tested by running the program. Different types of "architecture" can model different aspects of human thinking.

4. Three important issues in relation to how people solve problems are addressed throughout the book. These are:

Part Two: Introduction

Imagine for a moment that you are a parent and that you normally drop your daughter off at school on your way to work. One day you both pile into the car and discover that the car won't start. What do you do?

Let's suppose, for the sake of argument, that it is important you get to work and your daughter gets to school as soon as possible. However, you have to get your car fixed. You decide to call a taxi and phone a garage from work to ask them to go out and look at the car. You then realise the garage will need a key for the car. While you are waiting for the taxi you call the garage and explain the situation. You say you will drop the keys off at the garage on your way to work. Okay so far. The next problem is how to get home and pick your daughter up from school in the evening. You decide that the simplest thing would be to take a bus from work that stops close to the garage and pick up the car (assuming there's nothing seriously wrong with it). You can then go and pick up your daughter in the car. She may have to wait in school for a while but, with a bit of luck, she shouldn't have to wait longer than about quarter of an hour.

Five minutes later, the taxi arrives.

The point of this little story is that all you have done to solve the problem is to stand beside the telephone and think. It is exceedingly useful to be able to imagine— to think about—the results of an action or series of actions before you actually perform them. But what exactly does it mean to think? Thinking involves reasoning about a situation, and to do that we must have some kind of dynamic "model" of the situation in our heads. Any changes we make to this mental model of the world should ideally mirror changes in the real world. So where does this mental model or **mental representation** come from?

Before engaging in any kind of conscious problem-solving activity the solver needs to understand the problem in the first place. Understanding a problem means building some kind of representation of the problem in one's mind, based on what the situation is or what the problem statement says and on one's prior knowledge. It is then possible to reason about the problem within this mental representation. Generating a useful mental representation is therefore the most important single factor for successful problem solving.

What kind of representation do we form of a problem? When we talk of a mental representation we are referring to the way that information is encoded. The word "rabbit" can be represented visually as a visual code, and by what it sounds like as a phonological code. We also know what "rabbit" means, so there must be a semantic code (a "meaning code"). The way we encode information from a problem situation is often based on what we are told or what we read. When we read a piece of text, for example, we not only encode the information that is explicitly stated, but we also have to make inferences as we read to make sense of the text. Most of these inferences are so automatic that we are often unaware that we have made any inferences at all. Bransford, Barclay, and Franks (1972) presented people with the following sentence:

1. Three turtles rested on a floating log and a fish swam beneath them.

They later gave a recognition test to some of the subjects that included the sentence:

2. Three turtles rested on a floating log and a fish swam beneath it.

Bransford et al. had hypothesised that subjects would draw the inference that the fish swam beneath the log (notice that this is not stated in the original sentence). Indeed, the subjects who were presented with the second sentence on the recognition task were as confident that it had been presented originally as those subjects who had been given the original sentence on the recognition task. The point here is that one's memory of a situation, based on a reading of a text, may include the inferences that were drawn at the time the representation of the text was constructed or retrieved.

Problem solving, then, involves building a mental representation of a problem situation, including any inferences you make on reading the problem, that will allow you to carry out some action. In other words, for the mental representation to be of any use it has to include some idea of what you can do that will allow you to move from the initial problem situation to the goal. Now it follows that if you don't know much about the domain, or you have never attempted this kind of problem before, then your understanding of the problem is unlikely to be all that good. Glaser (1984, p. 93) explains why:

> At the initial stage of problem analysis, the problem solver attempts to 'understand' the problem by construing an initial problem representation. The quality, completeness, and coherence of this internal representation determine the efficiency and accuracy of further thinking. And these characteristics of the problem representation are determined by the knowledge available to the problem solver and the way the knowledge is organised.

This does not mean that the representation has to be "complete" before any problem solving can take place. If you had a "complete" representation of a problem then you wouldn't have a problem, as you would know exactly how to get from where you are now to where you want to be. A problem only exists when it is not immediately obvious how to get from where you are now to your goal. An adequate representation should at least allow you to see what moves you can possibly make and allow you to start heading towards your goal. Chapter 2 deals with how we build mental representations of problems and how we use them to work towards a solution. (The topic is revisited in Chapter 7.)

However, there is also the case of those problems where our initial representation gets us nowhere. The difficulty here lies in finding a different way of representing the problem (this is sometimes referred to as "**lateral thinking**", although the concept of re-representing problems in order to find a solution goes back long before the term was invented). Unfortunately, knowing that you should find a new way of representing the problem does not in fact help you very much—you still have to find this "new way of representing" it. Nevertheless when a new representation comes to mind a solution is often immediately obvious; or, at least, you often know what to do so that a solution can be reached very quickly. The kind of problem solving that involves being stuck for a while until you suddenly see what to do is called insight, and is the subject of Chapter 3.

Insight is not confined to so-called "insight problems". The same phenomenon may occur when solving typical textbook algebra problems, for example, or in solving simple everyday problems. Here again the initial representation may be extremely unhelpful, and only when a new representation is found can the poor student or DIY enthusiast apply the solution procedure that is made obvious by the new representation. The study of insight problems can therefore tell us something about everyday problems and textbook problems.

CHAPTER TWO

Characterising problem solving

As mentioned in Chapter 1, some types of problems can be solved by following a clear and complete set of rules that will allow you, in principle, to get from the situation described at the start of the problem (the initial state) to the goal. Many of them are also knowledge-lean; that is, very little domain knowledge is needed to solve them. It was also pointed out that such problems are rare in everyday life, yet these are the types of problems that information-processing psychologists have spent a lot of time studying in the past. So why study them?

First of all, the experimenter knows in advance all the possible paths that a "fully rational" solver can take to solve the problem. The experimenter can therefore concentrate on what strategies people use, rather than on the nature of the problem. One can also examine how people improve after repeated attempts at solving the problem. Indeed, if you are prepared to wait long enough you can watch the emergence of *expertise*.

Second, the subjects in experiments using well-defined puzzle problems generally tend to know nothing in advance about the knowledge-lean problems they are usually presented with. This allows the psychologist to examine how someone builds up a useful representation of the problem. Furthermore, to get at the heart of the processes involved in solving problems it is often necessary to control for individual subject variables, and knowledge is a variable that bedevils experiments in problem solving.

Third, as the problem structure is usually fairly clear, psychologists can examine the generalisation of transfer of learning from one problem to another by presenting two problems with identical structures (known as **isomorphs**) but a different **cover story**. For example, there are several isomorphs of the Tower of Hanoi puzzle (see Figure 2.1) involving acrobats, monsters with globes, a Himalayan tea ceremony, and so on. The description of each of these problems involves a different cover

25

story. Thus, we can look at how people differ in how well they understand (represent) problems with different cover stories; or we can look at the circumstances under which we can apply what we learn in one problem to another problem of the same type.

THE INFORMATION-PROCESSING APPROACH

The information-processing approach to thinking and problem solving owes a very great deal to the work of Alan Newell and Herb Simon, and is described in detail in their book *Human Problem Solving* (Newell & Simon, 1972). Indeed, their model of human and computer problem solving could be termed the *modal model* of problem solving, given that it is used to explain a wide variety of studies of thinking (see, e.g., Ericsson & Hastie, 1994). This would be the problem-solving equivalent of the modal model of memory (Atkinson & Shiffrin, 1968).

To understand Newell and Simon's model we shall take a simple example of thinking. Take a few moments to do Activity 2.1. As you solve the problem, try to be aware of how you go about doing it; that is, try to imagine the individual steps you would go through.

Activity 2.1

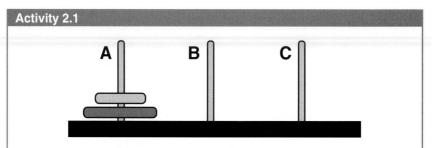

Figure 2.1 A trivial version of the Tower of Hanoi puzzle.

Look at the fairly trivial Tower of Hanoi problem in Figure 2.1. *Using only your imagination,* how would you get the two rings from peg A to peg C in three moves bearing in mind that:

- you can move only one ring at a time from one peg to another and;
- you cannot put the large ring on top of the small one.

Your mental solution to the problem may have been something like that represented in Figure 2.2. Using the diagram in Figure 2.1 you probably formed a mental image similar to that in "thought 1" in Figure 2.2. Activity 2.1 describes the "state" of the problem at the start (the initial state) and "thought 1" is simply a mental representation that is analogous to this initial state of the problem. The state of the problem at the end (the goal state) can be represented as in "thought 4". Notice here that there is no diagram given in Activity 2.1 to correspond to "thought 4". Instead you had to construct the representation from the verbal

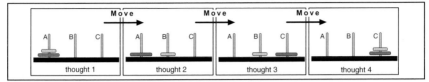

Figure 2.2.   The sequence of imagined moves in solving the two-ring Tower of Hanoi puzzle.

description of the goal. In between there are intermediate states, "thought 2" and "thought 3", which you reach after moving one ring each time. All of these thoughts are not states in the real world, but states inside your head. You created a *model* of the problem in your head and solved the problem within that model. When we read a statement of a problem, such as the one in Activity 2.1, we put together what we think are the relevant bits of information to construct this internal model of the problem situation. An internal model corresponds to a specific concrete situation in the external world and allows us to *reason* about the external situation. To do so you used information about the problem presented in the problem statement. The process of **understanding**, then, refers to constructing an initial mental representation of what the problem is, based on the information in the problem statement about the goal, the initial state, what you are not allowed to do, and what operator to apply, as well as your own personal past experience. Past experience, for example, would tell you that moving the small ring from peg A to peg C, then moving it to peg B, is a complete waste of time. As your knowledge of the problem at each state was inside your head, each "thought" corresponds to a **knowledge state**.

A second aspect of your thought processes that you may have noticed is that they were *sequential*. This simply means that you had one thought after another, as in Figure 2.2. One consequence of the fact that much of our thinking is conscious and sequential in nature is that we can often easily verbalise what we are thinking about. You may have heard a voice in your head saying something like "okay, the small ring goes there … no, there. And then the large ring goes there …" and so on. In fact, for many people saying the problem out loud helps them to solve it, possibly because the memory of hearing what they have just said helps to reduce the load on working memory (that part of memory that briefly stores and manipulates information). The fact that a lot of problem solving is verbalisable in this way provides psychologists with a means of finding out how people solve such problems (Ericsson & Simon, 1993).

Next, notice that you moved from one state to another as if you were following a path through the problem. If you glance ahead at Figures 2.3 and 2.4 you will see that harder versions of the problem involve a number of choices. Indeed, in the simple version you had a choice to start with of moving the small ring to peg B or peg C. As such problems get harder it becomes less obvious which choices you should make to solve the problem in the smallest number of moves. In this case the ideal path through the problem is unclear and you have to **search** for the right path.

One further aspect you may have noticed was the difficulty you may have had keeping all the necessary information in your mind at once. Try

Activity 2.2

Try to multiply 243 by 47 in your head.

Activity 2.2 and keep a mental watch on your thought processes as you do so.

Tasks such as the one in Activity 2.2 are tricky because the capacity of our working memory is limited—we can only keep so much information in our heads at any one time; overload it and we forget things or lose track of where we are in the problem. Other examples of the limits to our capacity to process information are given in Information Box 2.1.

Information Box 2.1

Processing limits and symbol systems

The information-processing account of problem solving sees it as an interaction between the information-processing system (the problem solver; either human or computer) and the **task environment** (the problem in its context). By characterising the human problem solver as an **information-processing system** (IPS), Newell and Simon saw no qualitative distinction between human information processors and any other kind, the digital computer being the most obvious example. An IPS processes information in the form of symbols and groups of symbols, and a human IPS has built-in limitations to how well it processes information. This Information Box gives a very brief sketch of some of the processing limits of human problem solving and what is meant by **symbols**, **symbol structures**, and **symbol tokens**.

Processing limitations

The human information-processing system has certain limitations. It is limited in:

- how much it can keep active in working memory at any one time;
- its ability to encode information—we may not be able to recognise what aspects of a task are relevant; we don't have the capacity to encode all the information coming through our senses at any one time;
- its ability to store information—memories laid down at one time can suffer interference from memories laid down later, or may be distorted in line with prior expectations (see e.g., Brewer & Treyens, 1981);
- its ability to retrieve information—human memory, as you may have noticed, is fallible;
- its ability to maintain optimum levels of motivation and arousal—we get bored, we get tired.

Symbols, symbol structures, and tokens

Newell and Simon regarded the human problem solver as an information-processing system. An IPS encodes individual bits of information as symbols. In other words a symbol is a representation of something. Symbols include things like words in sentences, objects in pictures, numbers and arithmetic operators in equations, and so on. These symbols are grouped into patterns known as symbol structures. Knowledge is stored symbols and symbol structures. Here is an example of a symbol structure for "cat".

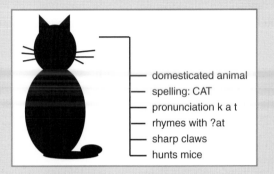

A specific occurrence of the word "cat" in the phrase "the cat sat on the mat" is known as a *symbol token*. A symbol token refers the information processor to the symbol itself. As you read the phrase "the cat sat on the mat", you process the individual words. Processing the word "cat" means accessing your stored knowledge associated with the word "cat" and retrieving something that permits the processing (also referred to as "computation") to continue:

> *...when processing 'the cat sat on the mat' (which is itself a physical structure of some sort) the local computation at some point encounters 'cat'; it must go from 'cat' to a body of (encoded) knowledge associated with 'cat' and bring back something that represents that a cat is being referred to, that the word 'cat' is a noun (and perhaps other possibilities), and so on. Exactly what knowledge is retrieved and how it is organized depend on the processing scheme. In all events, the structure of the token 'cat' does not contain all the needed knowledge. It is elsewhere and must be accessed and retrieved.*

(Newell, 1990, p. 74)

ANALYSING WELL-DEFINED PROBLEMS

In order to investigate the processes used in problem solving we first need to find a way to characterise or analyse the task. We will begin with well-defined problems such as the Tower of Hanoi that conform to the IGOR format—that is, they have a well-defined initial state, a clear goal state, and the operators that should be applied are given as well as the restrictions that apply. The initial state, goal state, operators, and restrictions for the Tower of Hanoi problem are given in Figure 2.3.

Figure 2.4 shows the different states that can be reached when the move operator is applied twice. In state 1 only the smallest ring can move and there are two free pegs it can move to. If the solver places it on peg C then the problem is now in state 2. In state 2 there are three moves that can be made. The smallest ring can

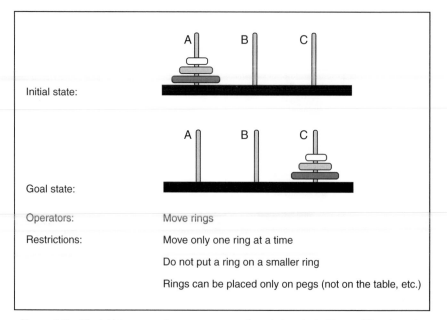

Figure 2.3.   The initial state, goal state, operators and restrictions in the Tower of Hanoi puzzle.

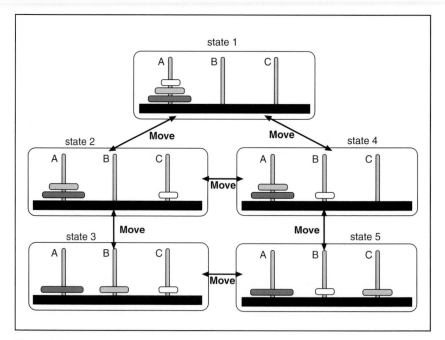

Figure 2.4.   The possible states that can be reached after two moves in the Tower of Hanoi puzzle.

move from peg C back to peg A which takes the solver back to the initial state, state 1. Alternatively the smallest ring can move from peg C to peg B leading to state 4, or the middle-sized ring can move to peg B leading to state 3. If you carry on this type of analysis then you end up with a diagram containing all possible states and all possible moves leading from one state to another. Although the only action you need to perform in the Tower of Hanoi is "move", other problems may involve a variety of mental operators. For this reason the diagram you end up with is known as a **state–action diagram** or **state space diagram**.

State–action spaces

Thinking through a problem can be a bit like trying to find a room in an unfamiliar complex of buildings such as a university campus or hospital. Suppose you have to get to room A313 in a complex of buildings. Initial attempts to find your way may involve some brief exploration of the buildings themselves. The initial exploration, where you are trying to gather useful information about your "problem environment", can be characterised as an attempt to understand the problem. You discover that the buildings have names but not letters. However, one building is the Amundsen Building. As it begins with an "A" you assume (hypothesise) that this is the building you are looking for, so you decide to find out (test this hypothesis). You enter and look around for some means of getting to the third floor (accessing relevant operators). You see a stairway and a lift next to it. You take the lift. When you get out on the third floor you see swing doors leading to corridors to the right and left. Outside the swing doors on the left is a notice saying "301–304, 321–324" and outside the one on the right is the sign "305–308, 317–320". You want 313, so now what do you do? (The answer, by the way, is on page 235.)

The room-finding analogy likens problem solving to a search through a three-dimensional space. Some features of the environment in which the problem is embedded are helpful, and some less so, leaving you to make inferences. The room numbers are sequential to some extent, although it's not clear why there are gaps. Furthermore, in trying to find your way through this space you call on past knowledge to guide your search. The problem of finding the room is actually fairly well-defined—you know where you are, you know where you want to be, you know how to get there (walk, take the lift, take the stairs) even if you don't actually know the way.

Activity 2.1 showed that problem solving can be regarded as moving from one "place" in the problem to another. As you move through the problem your knowledge about where you are in the problem has to be updated; that is, you go through a sequence of knowledge states. If you carry on the analysis of what choices are available at each state of the Tower of Hanoi problem, as in Figure 2.4, you end up with a complete **search graph** for the problem (Figure 2.5). In the Figure you can see that each state is linked to three others except at the extremities of the triangle where there is a choice of only two moves: at states 1, 15, and 27.

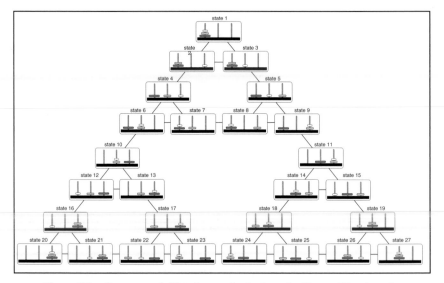

Figure 2.5.   State space of all legal moves for the three-ring Tower of Hanoi puzzle.

Figure 2.5 constitutes a **state–action space**, or more simply **state space**, of all legal moves (actions) for the three-ring Tower of Hanoi problem, and all possible states that can be reached. In tree diagrams of this sort, the points at which the tree branches are called **nodes**. All of the numbered states are therefore nodes of the state space diagram. The Dots problem introduced earlier has some dead ends, as well as a goal state from which no other legal moves are possible. These would therefore constitute **terminal nodes** or leaf nodes.

The space of all possible states in a problem, as exemplified in Figure 2.5, "represents an omniscient observer's view of the structure of a problem" (Kahney, 1993, p. 42). For instance, there are hundreds of possible states you can reach in the Dots problem in Activity 1.2. No system, human or computer, can encompass the entire state space of a game of chess, for example. Indeed the size of the problem space for a typical chess game is estimated to be 10^{120}. This means that our mental representation of the problem is likely to be impoverished in some way, which in turn means that the path through the problem may not be all that clear. Newell and Simon (1972) referred to the representation we build of a problem as the **problem space**.

A person's mental representation of a problem, being a personal representation, cannot be "pointed to and described as an objective fact" (Newell & Simon, 1972, p. 59). Various sources of information combine to produce a problem representation. The main sources of information are:

The task environment.   The problem itself is the main source of information about how to construct a relevant problem space. It defines the initial state and goal state, and may provide information about possible operators and restrictions. People are also particularly influenced by parts of the problem statement that appear particularly salient. In addition, the problem is embedded in a context that may also influence how a task is carried out.

Inferences about states, operators, and restrictions.   Any information missing from the problem statement may have to be inferred from the person's long-term memory. For a problem such as "Solve: $(3x + 4) + x = 20$" no operators are provided and the solver has to access the necessary arithmetic operators from memory. It is also left to the solver to infer what the final goal state is likely to look like, so it can be recognised when it is reached.

Text-based inferences.   Other inferences may have to be generated from the text of a problem. For example, if the problem involves one car leaving half an hour after another and overtaking it, the solver will (probably) infer that both cars have travelled the same distance when they meet (see also Kintsch, 1998 on understanding text; Nathan, Kintsch, & Young, 1992).

Previous experience with the problem.   The solver may have had experience with either the current or a similar problem before, and can call on this experience to help solve it.

Previous experience with an analogous problem.   The solver may recognise that the structure of an earlier problem that, superficially at least, seems unrelated to the current one is actually relevant to the solution of the current one. For example, the equation in a problem involving the distance covered by a car travelling at a certain speed may be identical to one involving currency exchange rates, even though both problems are from different domains. The likelihood of this happening is usually fairly low. When it does happen it may constitute an "insight" (see Chapter 3).

Misinformation.   The solver may construct a problem space based on a misapprehension of some aspect of the problem. According to Newell and Simon (1972, p. 76):

> States represented by nodes of the search space need not correspond with realizable states of the outside world but can be imaginable states—literally so since they are internal to the problem solver. These states, in turn, may be generated, in turn, by operators that do not satisfy all the conditions for admissibility

For example, someone might decide to move all three rings of the three-ring Tower of Hanoi problem at once, not realising or remembering that there is a restriction on the number of rings that can be moved at the same time.

Procedures for dealing with problems. From general problem-solving experience the solver has a number of procedures for combining information in the external environment (e.g., the written statement of the problem, the state of the rings and pegs of the Tower of Hanoi problem) with information in LTM. Thus the solver might generate context-specific heuristics for dealing with the problem. For example, in a crossword puzzle the solver may pick out the letters believed to form an anagram and write them down in a circle to make it easier to solve.

External memory. The external environment may contain clues to the particular state a problem is in. The Tower of Hanoi, for example, provides constant information about the state of the problem, as it changes to a visibly new state each time you move a ring. Similarly the little scribbles or 1s one might write on a subtraction or addition problem serve as an **external memory** to save us having to try to maintain the information in working memory. These days, diaries, palmtops, electronic organisers, telephone numbers stored in mobile phones, etc., all serve as forms of external memory.

Instructions. Newell (1990) further argued that problem spaces come from instructions. In a psychological experiment involving reaction times, for example, there are liable to be trial-specific instructions a participant would be given immediately before a particular trial of the experiment. There may also be prior general instructions before the experiment begins, and introductory instructions when the participant walks through the door that provide the general context for the experiment and what the participant is expected to do.

All these sources of information together constitute the "space" in which a person's problem solving takes place. Together they allow us to define the nodes (the states) of a problem and links between them along with a possible strategy for moving from node to node. Hayes (1989a, p. 53) provides the following analogy for a problem space:

> As a metaphor for the problem solver's search for a solution, we imagine a person going through a maze. The entrance to the maze is the initial state of the problem and the exit is the goal. The paths in the maze, including all its byways and blind alleys, correspond to the problem space—that is, to all the possible sequences of moves available to the solver.

According to Newell and Simon, problem solving involves finding your way through this problem space (searching for a way through the maze). Because of the limits of working memory we can only see a very few moves ahead and may not remember all the states that have been visited before. Figure 2.6 attempts to capture some of the information an individual might access when trying to understand a novel problem. The shading in the figure represents the fact that we can only see a few moves ahead and are likely to have only a couple of previous

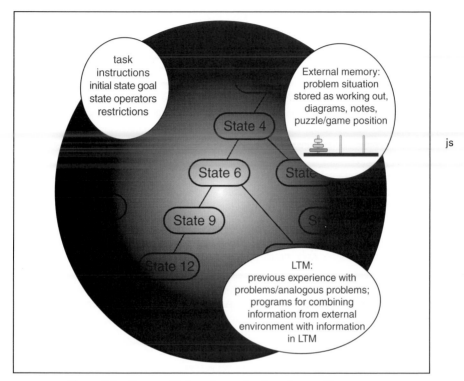

Figure 2.6.   Sources of information used to determine a problem space.

states in working memory at one time. The state of the problem that is in focal attention is the currently active knowledge state.

Although I have made a distinction between a **state space** as the space of all possible moves in a problem, and a **problem space** as the individual representation a person has of the problem, you will often see the term "problem space" used to describe something like a search tree such as the one in Figure 2.5. Reed, Ernst, and Banerji (1974), for example, refer to their version of Figure 2.5 as the problem space of legal moves. Similarly, Hunt (1994, p. 221) describes the game of chess thus: "In chess the starting node is the board configuration at the beginning of the game. The goal node is any node in which the opponent's king is checkmated. The (large) set of all legal positions constitutes what Newell and Simon call the *problem space*". The kind of problem space referred to in both cases is the *objective problem space*—the set of all possible paths and states a solver could theoretically reach given the initial state, operators, and some way of evaluating when the goal has been reached. The solver (Newell and Simon refer to the information-processing system) "incorporates the problem space, not in the sense of spanning its whole extent, but in possessing symbol structures and programs that provide access to that space via the system's processes for generating, testing and so on" (Newell & Simon, 1972, p. 78).

Apart from being unable to encompass the sheer size of some state spaces, people are usually just not aware of them. As VanLehn points out (1989, pp. 531–532):

> An incontestable principle of cognition is that people are not necessarily aware of the deductive consequences of their beliefs, and this principle applies to problem spaces as well. Although the state space is a deductive consequence of the initial state and operators, people are not aware of all of it

The actual path solvers take through a state space does not depend on them being aware of all of it. People usually manage to find ways of limiting the search space in some way, and that is what problem-solving research is interested in.

THE INTERACTION OF THE PROBLEM SOLVER AND THE TASK ENVIRONMENT

Newell and Simon stressed two main processes involved in solving unfamiliar problems: *understanding* and *search*. As mentioned earlier, understanding is the process that allows you to construct a representation of the problem from a combination of what it says in the problem statement, what inferences you can draw from the problem statement based on general knowledge, and your past problem-solving experience. Armed with this representation the information-processing system engages in a search to find a path through the problem that will lead to a solution.

Concentrating on the task environment sounds as though an analysis of the task itself is enough to show how a person can perform the task (i.e., solve the problem). This, of course, is not the case. People are not perfectly rational, and analysing the task in detail does not necessarily tell us how or if the solver can actually solve the problem. Nor does a task analysis tell us that the solver will use that particular representation (problem space) to solve the problem. So what is the point of such analyses?

Laird and Rosenbloom (1996) refer to the "principle of rationality", ascribed to Newell, that governs the behaviour of an intelligent "agent" whereby "the actions it intends are those that its knowledge indicates will achieve its goals" (p. 2). Newell and Simon argue that behaviour is usually *rational* in the sense that it is adaptive. This means that people's problem-solving behaviour is an appropriate response to the task, assuming that they are motivated to achieve the goal demanded by the task. Gigerenzer and Todd (1999) would also add that we have developed problem-solving short-cuts ("fast and frugal heuristics") that achieve our goals with the least computational effort. Newell and Simon (1972) make the point that "if there is such a thing as behavior demanded by a situation, and if a subject exhibits it, then his [*sic*] behavior tells us more about the task environment than about him"

(p. 53). If we want to know about the psychology of problem-solving behaviour, then examining behaviour that is entirely governed by the task environment tells us nothing. If, on the other hand, our problem analysis reveals (as far as such a thing is possible) how a perfectly rational person would solve the problem and we then compare this to what a subject actually does when confronted with the problem, then the difference between the two tells us something about the psychology of the solver.

The first thing an IPS (solver) does is generate an internal representation of the task environment based on the problem statement. This representation involves the selection of a problem space. The choice of a problem space can be influenced by manipulating the salience of objects in the task environment or the givens in a problem statement. The selection of a problem space results in the system choosing appropriate problem-solving methods. A method is "a process that bears some rational relation to attaining a problem solution" (Newell & Simon, 1972, p. 88). Problem-solving methods come in two general types: "strong" and "weak". **Strong methods** are domain-specific, learned methods that are pretty much guaranteed to get a solution; that is, strong methods are used when you already know how to go about solving the problem. Of course if, as a result of reading a problem, you already know what to do (you have an available strong method), then you don't really have a problem. **Weak methods** are general-purpose problem-solving strategies that solvers fall back on when they don't know what to do directly to solve the problem. These methods are discussed in the next section.

The particular method chosen controls further problem solving thereafter. The outcome of applying problem-solving methods is monitored; that is, there is feedback about the results of applying any particular step in the application of the method. This feedback may result in a change in the representation of the problem. Suppose you are trying to find the video channel on a television with which you are unfamiliar. There are two buttons marked –P and +P, and you can't work out what they stand for. Lacking any "strong" method for finding the correct channel, you fall back on weak methods. There are three choices facing you. You can either press –P, press +P or press both together. Past experience might tell you that pressing both together is probably not a good idea—at best they may just cancel each other out. That reduces the choice to two. What you are left with is a trial and error method, which is about as weak a method as you can get. You decide to press +P and a recognisable channel appears along with the channel number on the top left of the screen. As a result, you may infer that pressing +P steps through the channels in an ascending order, and –P in a descending order. Applying a trial and error method once may therefore be enough to allow you to re-represent the problem based on monitoring the result of your action. On the other hand, if the button-pressing strategy fails and nothing appears on the screen you may have to change the problem space to one that involves searching for a remote control, or finding someone who knows how this television works.

HEURISTIC SEARCH STRATEGIES

Searching for a solution path is not usually governed by trial and error, except in a last resort or where the search space is very small. Instead people try to use **heuristics** to help them in their search. Heuristics are rules of thumb that help constrain the problem in certain ways (in other words they help you to avoid falling back on blind trial and error), but they don't guarantee that you will find a solution. Heuristics are often contrasted with **algorithms** that will guarantee that you find a solution—it may take forever, but if the problem is algorithmic you will get there. However, heuristics are also algorithms. The clearest description of the two has been made by Dennett (1996, p. 210):

> There is ... a tradition within computer science and mathematics of *contrasting* heuristic methods with algorithmic methods: heuristic methods are risky, not guaranteed to yield results, whereas algorithms come with a guarantee. How do we resolve this "contradiction"? There is no contradiction at all. Heuristic algorithms are, like all algorithms, mechanical procedures that are guaranteed to do what they do, but what they do is engage in risky search! They are not guaranteed to *find* anything—or at least they are not guaranteed to find the specific thing sought in the time available. But, like well run tournaments of skill, good heuristic algorithms *tend* to yield highly interesting, reliable results in reasonable amounts of time.

Examples of both are provided in Information Box 2.2.

Heuristics serve to narrow your options and thus provide useful constraints on problem solving. However, there are other, more general heuristics that a solver might apply. When you don't know the best thing to do in a problem, the next best thing is to choose to do something that will reduce the difference between where you are now and where you want to be. Suppose you have a 2000-word essay to write and you don't know how to go about writing a very good introductory paragraph. The next best thing is to write down something that seems vaguely relevant. It might not be particularly good, but at least you've only got 1800 words left to write. You are a bit nearer your goal. In the Tower of Hanoi problem this means that solvers will look at the state they are in now, compare it with where they want to be (usually the goal state), and choose a path that takes them away from the initial state and nearer to the goal state. This general type of heuristic is called **difference reduction**, the most important examples of which are known as **hill climbing** and **means–ends analysis**.

Hill climbing

The term hill climbing is a metaphor for problem solving in the dark, as it were. Imagine that you are lost in a thick fog and you want to climb out of it to see where you are. You have a choice of four directions: north, south, east and west. You take

Information Box 2.2

Algorithms and heuristics

To illustrate the difference between algorithms and domain-specific heuristics, imagine how you might go about solving a jigsaw puzzle.

Algorithmic approach:

Starting off with a pile of jigsaw pieces, an algorithm that is guaranteed to solve the jigsaw might proceed as follows:

1. Select piece from pile and place on table.
2. Check > 0 pieces left in pile;
   IF YES go to 4
   ELSE go to 3
3. Check > 0 pieces in discard-pile
   IF YES discard-pile becomes pile; Go to 2
   ELSE go to 7
4. Select new-piece from pile.
5. Check whether new-piece fits piece (or pieces) on table
   IF YES go to 6
   ELSE put new-piece on discard-pile; go to 2
6. Check colour-match
   IF YES go to 2
   ELSE put new-piece on discard-pile; go to 2
7. FINISH

Heuristic approach:

Divide pieces into categories in terms of: colour, straight edges, pieces belonging to same object.

Assemble categorised pieces.

Look for specific pieces that are required to fill perceived gaps, etc.

a step north—it seems to lead down, so you withdraw your foot and turn 90° to the east and take another step. This time it seems to lead upwards, so you complete the step and try another step in the same direction. It also seems to lead upward so you complete the step and try again. This time the path leads downwards, so you withdraw your foot, turn 90° and try again. You carry on doing this until there comes a time when, no matter which direction you turn, all steps seem to lead down. In this case you are at the top of the hill.

This kind of problem-solving heuristic is useful if, say, the revs on your car seem to be too high and you try to adjust the petrol/air mixture. You make fine adjustments by turning a screw one way; if the revs increase then you start turning it the other way. If the revs slow down so much that the car is in danger of stalling then you turn the screw back the other way. You continue in this way until the engine sounds as if it is running neither too fast nor too slow.

Although hill climbing will eventually take you to the top of a hill, there is no guarantee that it is the top of the highest hill. You may emerge from the fog only to find you are in the foothills and the mountain peaks are still some way off. That is, in some cases you do not necessarily know if the solution you have arrived at is the correct one, or the optimal one. (Dennett, 1996, has argued that this "local" selecting of the next step is how Darwinian selection operates.) Another problem with the method is that it only applies if there is some way of measuring whether you are getting closer to the goal. If no matter which way you step the ground remains flat, then any direction is as good as any other and your search for a way out of the fog will be random. Anyone who has ever got lost in the middle of an algebra problem will know what this feels like. You might end up multiplying things, subtracting things, and nothing you do seems to be getting anywhere near the answer.

A puzzle that has been often used to examine hill climbing is the so-called Missionaries and Cannibals problem. Subjects tend to use hill climbing as their main strategy to reduce the difference between where they are in the problem and where they want to be. The basic version of the problem is shown in Activity 2.3. Have a go at it before reading on to see the complete problem space of legal moves.

Activity 2.3

Three missionaries and three cannibals, having to cross a river at a ferry, find a boat but the boat is so small that it can contain no more than two persons. If the missionaries on either bank of the river, or in the boat, are outnumbered at any time by cannibals, the cannibals will eat the missionaries. Find the simplest schedule of crossings that will permit all the missionaries and cannibals to cross the river safely. It is assumed that all passengers on the boat disembark before the next trip and at least one person has to be in the boat for each crossing.

(Reed et al., 1974, p. 437)

There are a number of variations of the basic problem including: the Hobbits and Orcs problem (Greeno, 1974; Thomas, 1974) where Orcs will gobble up Hobbits if there are fewer Hobbits than Orcs; book-burners and book-lovers (Sternberg, 1996a) where book-burners will burn the books of the book-lovers if they outnumber them; and scenarios where, if there are fewer cannibals than missionaries, the missionaries will convert the cannibals (Eisenstadt, 1988; Solso, 1995). The structure of the problem is interesting because there are always two legal moves. One will take you back to the previous state and one will take you nearer the solution (Figure 2.7).

Figure 2.7 contains a pictorial representation and a state–action graph of the Hobbits and Orcs problem to make it a little easier to see what the graph represents.

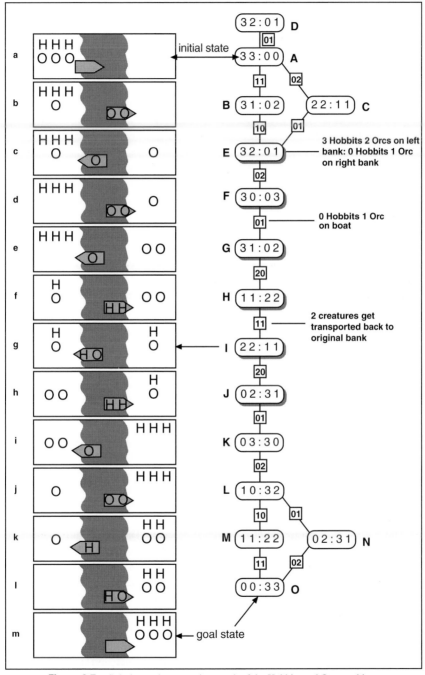

Figure 2.7.   Solution and state–action graph of the Hobbits and Orcs problem.

The figures divided by a colon represent the numbers of Hobbits and Orcs in that order on both banks at any one time (the figure on the left always refers to the number of Hobbits and the figure on the right always refers to the number of Orcs). Thus 33:00 means that there are 3 Hobbits and 3 Orcs on the left bank (left of the colon) and 0 Hobbits and 0 Orcs on the right bank (right of the colon). On the lines linking the ovals containing these, there are figures representing who is in the boat. Thus, on the line linking state B to state E, the 10 means that there is 1 Hobbit and no Orcs on the boat. From the initial state (state A) there are three legal moves that will lead you to states B, C, or D. If one Orc were to take the boat across from the initial state then there would be 3 Hobbits and 2 Orcs on the left bank and no Hobbits and 1 Orc on the right bank as in state D. This is a pointless move, as the only possible next move is for the Orc to take the boat back to the left bank (i.e., back to state A). It makes more sense for two persons to take the boat, either two Orcs (leading to state C) or one Hobbit and one Orc (leading to state B).

It looks from Figure 2.7 that, if you avoid illegal moves and avoid going back to an earlier state, you ought to get straight to the solution. So what makes this problem hard? If hill climbing is the method used to solve this task then one can make some predictions about where people will have difficulty. If you are standing in a metaphorical fog at night and you are trying to take steps that will lead you uphill, and if you get to a "local maximum" (where every step you take seems to take you downhill), then you are stuck. If the same thing happens in the middle of a problem then problem solving will be slowed down or you will make mistakes.

The Hobbits and Orcs problem was also studied by Thomas (1974) and by Greeno (1974). Thomas' study is described in Study Box 2.1. If you look back at state H in Figure 2.7 you will see that there are two Hobbits and two Orcs on the right bank. If the subjects are using some form of hill-climbing strategy, and trying to reduce the difference between where they are at state H and where they want to be (*increase* the number of people on the right bank), then state H poses a problem. To move on in the problem, one Hobbit and one Orc have to move *back* to the left bank, so the subject seems to be moving away from the goal at this point. This is equivalent to taking a step that seems to lead downhill when trying to climb uphill using a hill-climbing strategy.

There was also another point at which subjects in Thomas's study seemed to get stuck. At state E in Figure 2.7, there are three legal moves leading to states F, B, and C. It is the only place in the problem where subjects can move backwards without returning to an earlier problem state. In fact subjects may find themselves caught in a loop at this point, moving, for example, from B to E to C to A to B then back to E.

Another difficulty subjects seemed to come up against was not realising that a particular move would lead to an error. In other words their Hobbits kept getting eaten by the Orcs. Again the problems centred around states E and H where subjects made an average of 4 errors compared with between 0 and 1 error elsewhere.

Study Box 2.1

Thomas' Hobbits and Orcs Study

Thomas (1974) used two groups of subjects. The control group were asked to solve the problem on a computer and the times taken to solve the first half and second half of the problem were noted. A second group (known as the "part–whole" group) were given prior experience of the *second* part of the problem starting from state H and were then asked to solve the whole problem.

Results

TABLE 2.1

Average number of moves in each part of the Hobbits and Orcs task

Group	First part of task	Second part of task	First attempt (part–whole group)
Control	13.0	15.5	—
Part–whole	10.8	14.3	12.0

Discussion

The part–whole group performed significantly better than the control group on the first half of the task but there was no significant difference between them on the second part. This suggests that the prior experience the part–whole group had on the second half of the problem benefited them when they came to do the first part of the whole problem afterwards. However, the fact that there was no difference between the groups on the second half suggests that there was a strong context effect when they came to state H and were reluctant to make a "detour". The results show that means–ends analysis exerts a strong influence on problem solving, making subjects reluctant to choose moves that seem to be leading them away from the goal.

Figures showing delays before making a move (the latencies) at each state follow a very similar pattern, with states E and H once again causing difficulties for the subjects. The longest response time occurs at state A where subjects are thinking about the problem and planning how to move. On successive attempts at the problem this delay is greatly reduced.

What these studies show us is that you don't need to have a complicated state space for problem solving to be hindered. If the main method used is hill climbing, then you are likely to experience difficulty when you have to move away from the goal state to solve the problem. There is, however, a more powerful difference-reduction strategy for searching through a problem space.

Means–ends analysis

The most important general problem-solving heuristic identified by Newell and Simon was means–ends analysis. In means–ends analysis the solvers also try to reduce the difference between where they are in a problem and where they want to be. They do so by choosing a mental operator or choosing one path rather than another that will reduce that difference, but the difference between this heuristic and hill climbing is that the problem solver is able to break the problem down into sub-problems. For instance, if you have a 2000-word essay to write and an essay title in front of you then, rather than starting to write immediately, you might generate the sub-goal of planning what you are going to say in your introduction first. In order to write the introduction you need to have some idea of the issues, the pros and cons, and how you are going to deal with them, so you generate a sub-goal of generating an essay plan, and so on. Here is a further example to illustrate this.

Suppose you want to go on holiday to Georgioúpoli in Crete. Let's assume for the sake of the example that you like to organise holidays by yourself and avoid package holidays as much as possible. You can begin to characterise the problem in the following way:

> *initial state:*   *you at home in Milton Keynes (well, somebody has to live there)*
> *goal state:*   *you at Georgioúpoli*

There are several *means* (operators) by which you normally travel from one place to another. You can go: on foot, by boat, by train, by plane, by taxi, and so on. However, your general knowledge of the world tells you that Crete is a long way away and that it is an island. This knowledge allows you to restrict your choice of operators.

> *restrictions:*   *Crete is a long way away*
> *You want to get there as quickly as possible*

Your general knowledge tells you that the fastest form of transport over land and sea is the plane. So,

> *operator:*   *go by plane*

Unfortunately your problem is not yet solved. There are certain preconditions to travelling by plane, not the least of which is that there has to be an airport to travel from and there is no airport in Milton Keynes. You are therefore forced to set up a *sub-goal* to reduce the difference between you at home and you at the airport. Once again you have to search for the relevant *means* to achieve your *end* of getting to the airport. Some operators are not feasible due to the distance (walking), others you might reject due to your knowledge of, say, the cost of parking at airports, the cost of a taxi from home to the airport, and so on. So you decide to go by train.

initial state:	*you at home*
sub-goal:	*you at the airport*
restrictions:	*you don't want to spend a lot of money*
	you don't want to walk
operator:	*go by train*

Once again the preconditions for travelling by train are not met, as trains don't stop outside your house, so you set up a new sub-goal of getting from your home to the station; and so on.

Means–ends analysis therefore involves breaking a problem down into its goal–sub-goal structure and should provide a chain of operators that should eventually lead you to the goal. This method of problem solving is also known as **sub-goaling**. It can also be applied to the Tower of Hanoi problem. Simon (1975) outlined three different strategies that involved decomposing the goal into sub-goals. One of them is the "goal recursion strategy". If the goal is to move all three rings from peg A (see Figure 2.8) to peg C, then first move the two top rings from peg A to peg B so that the largest ring can move to peg C (Figure 2.8b). Then set up the sub-goal of moving the two-ring pyramid on peg B to peg C. Another more "trivial" sub-goal involves moving the two-ring pyramid from one peg to another. If the goal is to

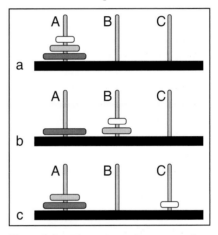

Figure 2.8.   The goal recursion strategy of solving the Tower of Hanoi puzzle.

move two rings from peg A to peg B then first move the smallest ring from peg A to peg C (Figure 2.8c).

This form of sub-goaling is also known as **working backwards** because you are analysing the problem by starting off from the goal state and working backwards from it to see what needs to be done (i.e., what sub-goals need to be achieved). The reason why it's called a "**recursion**" strategy is because the procedure for moving entire pyramids of rings (e.g., three rings, five rings, 64 rings) involves moving the entire pyramid *minus one* ring. And the procedure for moving the pyramid-minus-one-ring involves moving the pyramid-minus-one-ring *minus one* ring, and so on. A diagrammatic representation of the recursion strategy can be found in Figure 4.1 in Chapter 4. The recursive procedure can be written as follows (Simon, 1975, p. 270):

To move Pyramid(k) from A to C
    Move Pyramid($k - 1$) from A to B
    Move Disk(k) from A to C
    Move Pyramid($k - 1$) from B to C

where k is an (odd) number of rings (the substructure of the Tower of Hanoi problem is illustrated in Figure 4.1 in Chapter 4). The difficulty with this strategy for solving the problem is the potential load on short-term memory. "For a subject to use this recursive strategy, he must have some way of representing goals internally, and holding them in short-term memory while he carries out the sub-goals. How large a STM this strategy calls for depends on how many goals have to be retained in STM simultaneously" (Simon, 1975, p. 270).

The idea that we have a "stack" of goals that we keep in mind as we solve some types of problem comes from computer science. Some computer programs are hierarchically ordered so that in order to achieve goal A you first have to achieve goal B and to achieve goal B you have to achieve goal C, and so on. Newell and Simon (1972) give the example of driving a child to school (the main goal), but the car doesn't work so you have to fix the car first (a new goal) and to fix the car you have to call the garage (a new goal), and so on. Notice that these goals and sub-goals are interdependent, each one depending on the next one "down". When you embark on a new goal—when a new goal comes to the top of the **goal stack** —this is called *pushing* the stack. When the goal is satisfied (for example, when you have made the phone call to the garage), the goal of phoning is dropped from the stack—known as *popping* the stack—and you move to the next goal down: in this case waiting for the mechanic to repair the car.

The psychological reality of human beings using such a goal stack as they solve problems is discussed in Anderson (1993). Aspects of which are discussed in Information Box 2.3.

Newell and Simon's theory of human problem solving has had a profound influence on our understanding of human and machine thinking. Their model of a limited-capacity information-processing system operating in an environment that provides the system with information still influences current models of problem-solving behaviour. The notion that there are general problem-solving heuristics such as means–ends analysis explains how we can often solve problems that we have never before encountered, and allows this kind of behaviour to be modelled on a computer.

SUMMARY

1. Information-processing accounts of problem solving emphasise the interaction of the problem solver and the environment (in this case the problem). Newell and Simon (1972) suggested that problem solving involved two co-operating processes called *understanding* and *search*. Understanding refers to the process of building a representation of a problem, initially by reading the text of the problem. This representation constitutes a "problem space". Search is the process whereby the solver attempts to find a solution within this problem space.
2. Search and understanding interact. The search process might lead to the solver revising the mental representation, or the solver may re-read the problem or parts

Information Box 2.3

The psychological validity of goal stacks

Anderson (1993) argues that much of our behaviour can be described as arising from a hierarchy of goals and sub-goals. For example, a subject in a laboratory experiment "may be trying to solve a Tower of Hanoi problem in order to satisfy a subject participation requirement in order to pass a psychology course in order to get a college degree in order to get a job in order to earn social respect" (1993, p. 48). This hierarchy of goals is modelled in the ACT-R model of cognition (see Chapter 8) as a goal stack. The goals, as in the example of the laboratory subject, are interdependent, but one can only make progress by dealing with the currently active goal—the one at the top of the goal stack. Because of this interdependency of goals, and the logic of having to deal with the currently active one, "goal stacks are a rational adaptation to the structure of the environment" (1993, p. 49). As goal stacks are an "adaptation to the environment" Anderson argues that: (a) we have evolved cerebral structures that co-ordinate planning (the pre-frontal cortex); and (b) we can find evidence of hierarchical planning in other species. "The decision to design a tool is a significant sub-goal (a means to an end), and the construction of a tool can involve complex co-ordination of sub-goals under that. Neither hierarchical planning nor novel tool use are uniquely human accomplishments and they are found to various degrees in other primates" (1993, p. 49).

There is an argument that certain types of forgetting are not dealt with adequately in this scenario. For example, people sometimes forget to remove the original from a photocopier after making photocopies. This can be explained by arguing that making and collecting the photocopies is the goal and this does not include removing the original. Byrne and Bovair (1997, p. 36) argue that, when the super-goal of making and getting copies is satisfied, it is popped from the stack along with its associated sub-goals, and so forgetting the original should happen every time.

Although this explanation has intuitive appeal, it does not make entirely plausible predictions. According to this account, people should make this error every time—the goal structure for tasks like the photocopier never changes, so the error should persist indefinitely.

On the other hand, if the "post-completion" step (removing the original) is always placed on the stack as part of the overall goal then the error should *never* happen.

of it (an aspect of problem understanding) which in turn may suggest ways in which the search for the solution can continue.

3. To guide search through a problem space people tend to use strategies called heuristics. The main types involve trying to find a way of reducing the difference between where you are now and where you want to be. One such fairly blind method is called hill climbing, where the solver heads in a direction that seems to lead to the solution. A more powerful method is means–ends analysis which can take into account the goal–sub-goal structure of problems.

4. Working memory can be seen as a "goal stack". A goal stack means that behaviour involves making plans, which in turn involves breaking plans down into goals and sub-goals. Goal stacks are a rational adaptation to a world that is structured and in which we can identify causes and effects.
5. The modern sense of rationality implies that (a) our ways of thinking are the product of evolutionary processes, (b) as far as we can we use our knowledge in pursuit of our goals, (c) our thinking is likely to be biased by the knowledge we have available.

CHAPTER THREE

Problem representation:
The case of insight

My favorite example of problem solving in action is the following true story. When I was a graduate student, I attended a departmental colloquium at which a candidate for a faculty position was to present his research. As he started his talk, he realized that his first slide was projected too low on the screen. A flurry of activity around the projector ensued, one professor asking out loud, "Does anyone have a book or something?" Someone volunteered a book, the professor tried it but it was too thick—the slide was now too high. "No, this one's too big. Anyone got a thinner one?" he continued. After several more seconds of hurried searching for something thinner, another professor finally exclaimed, "Well, for Pete's sake, I don't believe this!" He marched over to the projector, grabbed the book, opened it halfway, and then put it under the projector. He looked around at the lecture hall and shook his head, saying, "I can't believe it. A roomful of PhDs, and no one knows how to *open a book*!"

(Ashcraft, 1994, p. 576)

This chapter is about why a roomful of PhDs (bar one) could not solve this problem. In particular it elaborates on the point made in the last chapter that we often do not represent a problem completely. That is, there is often something missing from our representation of a problem, such as the fact that you can open a book; or, indeed, that our representation of a problem may be totally inappropriate. Another point to be made is that intelligence does not necessarily guarantee successful problem solving. In examples such as the one above, the answer is "obvious", there is no missing bit of knowledge that prevents people from solving it. Finally, this everyday example of problem solving is one where one can imagine a lightbulb lighting up above someone's head as the person suddenly realises what to do. This lightbulb blinking on—the "Aha!" experience—is known as **insight**.

BUILDING A PROBLEM REPRESENTATION

In the real world we are rarely faced with problems where all the relevant information is provided. Usually we need to supplement what the problem says with information from long-term memory, so that we can make inferences and possibly choose operators that will allow us to make changes to our mental model that reflect what would happen if we manipulated the concrete world. The difficulty facing us when we have to make inferences is two-fold. First, we may build entirely the wrong mental model from the information we read or hear. If you hear, for example, that a man walked into a bar and fell on the floor, the chances are that you have some kind of image in your head about the man's position and surroundings and so on. If you then hear that it was an iron bar, whatever mental model you had built will probably have to be changed. You probably know that the word "bar" has at least two meanings, yet I would guess that you picked on only one of them and did not consider any other—at least, not consciously. Our habit of sticking to one mental model once we have built it is the reason we find some types of problem hard to solve, as the next few sections will show.

The second difficulty facing us is that we may well build a reasonably correct initial representation of a problem, but this representation may be impoverished in some way because we have no idea what inferences are relevant, such as the fact

---

Activity 3.1

Imagine that you have a normal chequer board containing 64 black and white squares.

You also have 32 dominoes each one of which exactly covers two squares on the chequer board. It is therefore possible, and quite straightforward, to cover the entire board with all 32 dominoes.

Now suppose that the chequer board were "mutilated" in such a way that two squares were removed from diagonally opposite corners as in Figure 3.1. You now have 62 squares. How can you cover those 62 squares with 31 dominoes?

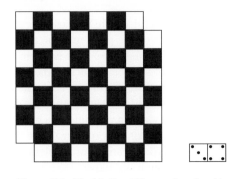

Figure 3.1. The Mutilated Chequer Board problem.

that a book can be opened; or, indeed, in the worst case we may be unable to make any inferences. This makes the problem hard. An example of this can be found in Activity 3.1.

RE-REPRESENTING PROBLEMS

You may have tried to solve the Mutilated Chequer Board problem by mentally trying to place dominoes on the board. After a while you will have realised that there are just so many possible permutations of pieces—758,148, in fact—that you can't keep track of them all. You can't solve the problem that way because your limited-capacity working memory rapidly becomes overloaded. The solution can be found a lot more easily if you can change your representation of the problem. Here are three ways in which you might try to re-represent the Mutilated Chequer Board problem.

Focus on a different aspect of the problem

First, you may notice that a domino has to cover *both a black square and a white square*. If you have 31 dominoes then they *have* to cover 31 black squares and 31 white squares. However, there are only 30 black squares and there are 32 white ones, so it is impossible for 31 dominoes to cover them.

Look at extreme cases

A second way of re-representing the problem is to think of a much simpler version of it. Any conclusions you reach may be scaled up to apply to the full-scale version of the problem. This technique, however, is not always guaranteed to work. It is therefore a heuristic. The simplified version of the Mutilated Chequer Board in Figure 3.2 works for the same reason as the one given in the last paragraph. In this

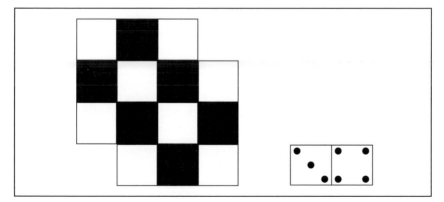

Figure 3.2.   A simplified version of the Mutilated Chequer Board problem.

version you can probably imagine placing dominoes on the squares and you can easily see that it is impossible to cover them all no matter how they are arranged. Nevertheless, you can't really be sure that the same applies to the full-size version unless you understand why.

Another example is the Dots problem introduced in Activity 1.1 (Chapter 1). If you start with the simplest form of the puzzle (Figure 3.3) and see what's involved in solving that, then look at a slightly more difficult version and see what's involved in solving that, then you can build up a picture of the strategies that are needed to solve the full-size Dots problem.

Find an analogous solution

Activity 3.2

In the dance floor problem there are 32 dancing couples—32 men and 32 women. If two of the women leave, can the remaining 62 people form heterosexual dancing couples? Explain your answer.

(Source: Gick & McGarry, 1992)

The third way of re-representing the problem is to use an appropriate analogy, although the likelihood of your thinking of one spontaneously is vanishingly small (see Chapter 6). A problem that is identical in structure to the Mutilated Chequer Board problem is the dance floor isomorph given in Activity 3.2.

The answer to the dance floor isomorph is obviously no. There are two spare men with no dancing partners. The same reasoning can be applied to the Mutilated Chequer Board problem where there are two spare white squares. If you want to make people really suffer, you can make the Mutilated Chequer Board problem much more difficult by having only white squares.

GESTALT ACCOUNTS OF PROBLEM SOLVING

It was the question of how we represent problems and how we might re-represent them that interested the Gestalt psychologists. The Gestalt school is well-known for its study of perceptual processes. For Gestalt psychologists, the relationships between elements in the visual field gave rise to "wholes". In Figure 3.4 the viewer sees a square rather than a series of black dots with chunks cut out.

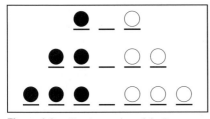

Figure 3.3. Simpler version of the Dots problem.

Figure 3.4. A square "emerges" from the configuration of black dots.

As with their study of perceptual phenomena, the Gestalt school provided a description of a number of problem-solving phenomena and also some useful labels for them. With the rise of the behaviourist school, however, the study of problem solving and such inaccessible mental events as insight declined in the middle part of the twentieth century. As we saw in Chapter 2, the emergence of cognitive science has recently seen a strong interest in problem solving, including the study of insight, within the information-processing framework.

Gestalt psychologists laid great stress on how we "structure" problems. When we have difficulties solving a problem, insight into its solution can come about by **restructuring** the problem. Nowadays we would talk of having the wrong, or at least an unhelpful, initial representation of a problem. A solution comes about after we have "re-represented" it correctly. Activity 3.3 gives an example of the types of mathematical problems that Gestalt psychologists were interested in.

> **Activity 3.3**
>
> Is the following number divisible by 9?
>
> 1,000,000,000,000,000,000,000,008

The initial way in which you may have approached the question in the activity was probably to try to divide the number by 9 to see what happens. This would be a perfectly natural approach to what appears to be a division problem. Our past experience of division problems predisposes us to attempt it by applying the procedure we have learned for dealing with division problems. However, sometimes a learned procedure is not the easiest way of solving the problem. In Activity 3.3, notice what happens when you subtract 9 from the number. Now can you say whether it is divisible by 9?

It is always possible that you tried to solve the problem by the "method of extreme cases". If you did so, you will have noticed that the simple case of 18 is divisible by 9, 108 is divisible by 9, 1008 is divisible by 9, and so on. You may have boldly extrapolated to the number in the Activity and assumed it was divisible by 9 as well. You may even have worked out why.

Another example of this kind of restructuring can often be found on the walls of mathematics classrooms in secondary schools. You may sometimes find a poster there describing how the 6-year-old Karl Gauss, who later became a prominent mathematician (the Gauss, a unit of magnetic flux, is named after him), solved a tedious arithmetic problem very quickly by reconstruing the problem. His teacher, thinking to give himself a few minutes' peace, had asked the class to add up the numbers $1+2+3+4$ etc. up to 100. Hardly had the class begun laboriously to add up all the numbers when Gauss put his hand up with the answer. How had he done it so quickly?

Gauss had seen the problem structured in a way similar to Figure 3.5. The figure looks a bit like a rectangle with a side 100 units long cut diagonally in half. All Gauss did was to complete the rectangle by imagining Figure 3.5 duplicated, flipped over and added to itself as in Figure 3.6. You end up with a rectangle 100×101 giving an area of 10,100. Adding the series $1+2+3+4+5$

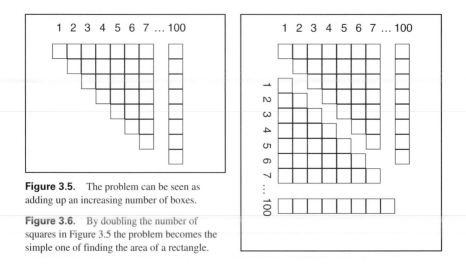

Figure 3.5.   The problem can be seen as adding up an increasing number of boxes.

Figure 3.6.   By doubling the number of squares in Figure 3.5 the problem becomes the simple one of finding the area of a rectangle.

up to 100 is therefore the same as taking half of 10,100; that is, 5050 (see also Gilhooly, 1996).

The young Gauss was able to see relationships between the parts of the problem that the other children in the class were unable to see. In other words he had understood the underlying structure of the problem. Wertheimer (1945) referred to the kind of thinking exhibited by Gauss as **productive thinking**. This can be contrasted with **reproductive thinking** where the solver attempts to solve the problem according to previously learned methods—in this case by simply adding up the numbers 1 to 100. Reproductive thinking of this latter kind is **structurally blind**. There appears to be no real understanding of the underlying structure of the problem.

Lack of understanding of a problem (or a concept, or a system of relations) can lead to superficial answers to problems, as well as to blindly following a procedure. Peter Hughes, chief examiner in the public awareness of science for the University of Cambridge Local Examinations Syndicate, bemoans the fact that answers to science questions in an English A-Level science exam showed too great a reliance on factual knowledge and little understanding. For example, students "assumed that electric cars would be greener without considering the relative efficiency of petrol and electric vehicles, or exploring other ways of generating electricity, say, by wind or nuclear power" (Hughes, 1996, p. 45).

Set effects

As Wertheimer's analysis showed, one of Gestalt psychology's achievements in the study of problem solving was to point out the difficulties people often have in solving problems because of the inappropriate use of prior knowledge. Using our knowledge can sometimes make us psychologically set in our ways. Applying a learned rule or procedure for doing something when there is a simpler way of doing it is therefore called a **set effect**. The Gestalt term for using a learned method for solving problems, where a simpler method might be quicker and more appropriate, is **Einstellung**. Einstellung can be regarded as "the blinding effects of habit" (Luchins & Luchins, 1950). Learned procedures for doing things are extremely useful most of the time. We wouldn't get on too well if we didn't apply the rules we had learned in the past to new occurrences of the same situation. Just how many novel ways are there of making a cup of tea or of doing multiplication problems? Do we need to think up novel ways of doing them? Nevertheless, Luchins (1942, p. 93) argued that a mechanised procedure for solving a particular problem type ceases to be a tool "when … instead of the individual mastering the habit, the habit masters the individual".

Another type of mental set is **functional fixedness** (or **functional fixity**) where we are unable to see how we might use an object as a tool to help us solve a problem, because that is not the normal function of the object. To get an idea of what functional fixedness means, have a go at Activity 3.4 before reading on.

Activity 3.4

Imagine you and a friend are on a picnic and you have brought along a bottle of wine. Having found a convenient spot and cooled the wine in a nearby babbling brook, you are ready to eat and drink. At this point you realise you have forgotten to bring a corkscrew. You both frantically empty your pockets looking for something you can use. You find you have a £10 note, a cigarette lighter, a piece of string, a £20 note, some coins of various denominations, a pen, and a box of matches. With a flash of insight you realise how you can completely remove the cork from the bottle. How do you do it?

The point here is that the objects you have found in your pocket all have specific functions, none of which has anything to do with removing corks from bottles. Functional fixedness is being unable to forget for a moment the normal function of an object to be able to use it for a totally novel purpose. In doing Activity 3.4 you may have realised that you can force the cork into the bottle using the pen. You may even have done so in the past. However, the cork is still in the bottle and tends to get in the way when you are pouring the wine. If you tie a fairly large knot in the string and push it into the bottle below the cork, you can then pull on the string which causes the knot to pull the cork out of the bottle.

Restructuring, Einstellung and functional fixedness can be illustrated by three classic experiments conducted by Maier (1931), Luchins and Luchins (1959), and Duncker (1945). Study Box 3.1 describes Maier's account of restructuring in an insight problem; Study Box 3.2 describes Luchins and Luchins' study of Einstellung; and Study Box 3.3 describes studies by Duncker into functional fixedness.

Study Box 3.1

Maier's Two-string problem

Rationale

The aim of the study was to see how people can solve insight problems by "restructuring" the problem, and how they might be led to do so.

Method

In Maier's (1931) experiment subjects were brought into a room with the experimenter where there were two strings hanging from the ceiling and some objects lying around on the floor (pliers, poles, extension cords). The subjects' task was to tie the two strings together. However, the subjects soon found out that if they held onto one string, the other was too far away for them to reach (Figure 3.7).

Figure 3.7. Maier's Two-string problem.

The only way to solve the problem is to use the objects lying around on the floor. In particular, Maier was interested in how the subjects might use the pliers. After the subjects had been trying to solve the problem for a while, Maier gave one of two hints.

- The experimenter "accidentally" brushed against one of the strings, causing it to swing.
- If the first hint failed, after a few minutes the subject was handed the pliers and told that the problem could be solved using them.

Discussion

According to Maier, apparently accidentally brushing against the string often led to a "restructuring" of the problem. Interestingly, very few of the participants who needed a hint to solve the problem seemed to be aware that they had been given any kind of hint at all. They also seemed to fall into two categories based on what they reported afterwards. There were those who reported that the solution "just came to me", and those who seemed to go through a series of stages: "Let's see, if I could move the cord", "throw things at it", "blow at it", "swing it like a pendulum", "aha!". Using these failed attempts at solving the problem to help refine what the problem is, and thereby to work towards a solution, is known as **solution development** (Duncker, 1945; Gick & Holyoak, 1980).

The Water Jars problem (Luchins & Luchins, 1959)

Rationale
The aim of much of Luchins' work was to examine the effects of learning a solution procedure on subsequent problem solving, particularly when the subsequent problems can be solved using a far simpler procedure. In such cases learning actually impedes performance on subsequent tasks

Method
In these studies subjects are given a series of problems based on water jars that can contain different amounts of water. Using those jars as measuring jugs, the participants had to end up with a set amount of water. For example, if jar A can hold 18 litres, jar B can hold 43 litres, and jar C can hold 10 litres, how can you end up with 5 litres?

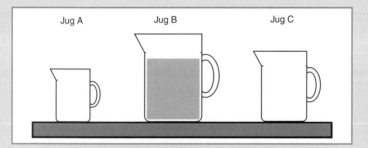

Figure 3.8. Luchins' Water Jars problem.

The answer is to fill jar B with 43 litres, from it fill jar A and pour out the water from A, then fill C from B twice, emptying C each time. You end up with 5 litres in jar B.

After a series of such problems, subjects begin to realise that pouring water from one jar to another always follows the same pattern. In fact, the pattern or rule for pouring is $B - A - 2C$ (from the contents of jar B take out enough to fill A, and enough to fill C twice; e.g., $43 - 18 - (2 \times 10) = 5$). Examples 1, 2, and 3, below all follow that rule (try 2, 3, and 4 for yourself).

Study Box 3.2 (continued)

	Jug A	Jug B	Jug C	Goal
1	18	43	10	5
2	9	42	6	21
3	14	36	8	6
4	28	76	3	25

Results and discussion

When subjects reached problems at the very end of the series, the rule changed as in example 4. Subjects who had induced the rule B – A – 2C did much worse than control subjects on this problem. In fact, it can be solved very easily following the rule A – C, which is pretty trivial. Not only that, but when the problem could be solved by either rule (i.e., B – A – 2C *or* A – C), subjects who had learned the complicated rule applied it without noticing that the simpler rule applied. For example, both rules will work in example 3. Did you notice the easier solution in 3?

The results showed the effects of Einstellung. Having learned a rule that worked, participants followed it blindly and thus failed to see that a simpler solution could be used. Furthermore, those who had learned a rule got stuck on problems such as example 4 for far longer than those who had not learned a rule showing the deleterious effects of reproductive thinking.

Study Box 3.3

The Candle Holder problem (Duncker, 1945)

Rationale

The aim here was to examine the effects of the "functional fixedness of real solution-objects". Can people ignore the usual function of objects in order to use them for a different function to solve a particular problem?

Method

In this study, subjects were presented with the items shown in Figure 3.9. Their task was to fix three candles to a door so that when lit the wax would not drip onto the floor. The experiment was repeated using a number of conditions. In one condition subjects were asked to fix three candles to a door. On the table before them were three matchbox-size boxes, tacks, and candles "among many other objects" (Figure 3.9a). In the second condition, the boxes were filled with candles, matches, and tacks. As the boxes were being used to hold objects, and subjects would have to empty the boxes before using them, this condition was known as the "after pre-utilisation" condition (Figure 3.9b). The other condition was known as the "without pre-utilisation" condition, as the boxes were not used for anything beforehand.

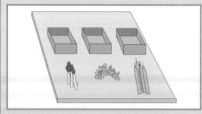

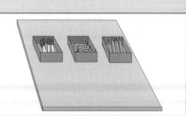

Figure 3.9a. Duncker's Candle Holder problem: the "without pre-utilisation" condition.

Figure 3.9b. The "after pre-utilisation" condition (Source: Robertson, 1999, pp. 85–86).

Results

All subjects solved the problem in the "without pre-utilisation" condition but only three out of seven solved it in the "after pre-utilisation" condition. In a third condition the boxes were filled with "neutral" objects such as buttons. Here only one subject solved the problem..

Discussion

Subjects could not reconceptualise a box containing matches, for example, as a candle holder, due to "fixating" on its function as a matchbox. In Duncker's words: "the crucial object [the box] is embedded in a particular context, in a functional whole, which is to some degree dynamically segregated" (1945, p. 100). If the functional whole disintegrates, as in Figure 3.9a, the elements (boxes, candles, tacks) are "released from its grasp".

While the Gestalt psychologists provided descriptions of the situations in which insight occurred or failed to occur, as well as useful methods for examining problem solving (such as the use of verbal protocols), they were less precise about the processes underlying insight. Explanations such as "short-circuiting" normal problem-solving processes don't tell us how or why such a short-circuit takes place. More recently, therefore, information-processing explanations have been put forward to explain insightful problem solving.

INFORMATION-PROCESSING ACCOUNTS OF INSIGHT

Insight poses a problem for modern information-processing accounts of problem solving. Why should working away at a problem produce no results, whereas a complete answer can sometimes suddenly pop into one's head? According to Ohlsson (1992, p. 2):

Insight poses a particularly severe challenge to information-processing theories of thinking. If thinking is a species of symbol manipulation (Newell, 1980), then it follows that problem solutions are constructed piecemeal, through heuristic search, means–ends analysis, planning or other step-wise processes. Also there is little reason to believe that extensive problem-solving can happen outside consciousness, in parallel with deliberate efforts, because the capacity of human beings for processing information is limited. The sudden appearance of a complete solution within consciousness constitutes an anomaly, which cannot be accommodated within a computational theory without auxiliary assumptions.

Ohlsson then goes on to explain just how insight might readily be plugged in to an information-processing framework (see page 65). Nevertheless, there are some disagreements among modern-day psychologists about just how special insight is.

Insight as a special property

Does solving the following two types of problem involve the same basic cognitive processes, or is there something special about the first one?

1. A stranger approached a museum curator and offered him an ancient bronze coin. The coin had an authentic appearance and was marked with the date 544 BC. The curator had happily made acquisitions from suspicious sources before, but this time he promptly called the police and had the stranger arrested. Why? (From: Metcalfe, 1986, p. 624)
2. $(3x^2 + 2x + 10)(3x) = ?$ (From: Metcalfe & Wiebe, 1987, p. 245)

Some psychologists argue that solving these two problems involves the same sorts of processes. For example, the argument that restructuring in Gestalt insight problems comes about through the same type of search process as described by Newell and Simon was put forward by Weisberg and Alba (1981, 1982). They argued that insightful problem solving involved both a search through the problem space and a search through memory. "Restructuring of a problem comes about as a result of further searches of memory, cued by new information accrued as the subject works through the problem. This is in contrast to the Gestalt view that restructuration is spontaneous"' (Weisberg & Alba, 1982, p. 328).

Janet Metcalfe, on the other hand, argued that, if the same memorial processes were at work in insightful as in non-insightful problem solving, then one should find that the metacognitive processes would also be the same. **Metacognition** (also sometimes referred to as "metamemory" or "metaknowledge") means "knowing what you know". If you have played "Trivial Pursuit" you may well have experienced the tip-of-the-tongue phenomenon, where you are sure you know the answer but just can't quite get it out. It has been shown that people are quite good at estimating how likely they are to find an answer to a question that produces a tip-of-the-tongue state, given time or a hint such as the first letter (Cohen, 1996; Lachman, Lachman, & Thronesberry, 1979). In fact you can produce a gradient of "feeling-of-knowing" (FOK) from "definitely do not know" to "could recall the answer if given more hints and more time". If, therefore, insight problems involved a search through memory using the current state of the problem as a cue, one might reasonably expect that one could estimate one's FOK (in this case feeling that you know how close you are getting to an answer) just as readily for insight problems as for trivia knowledge or even algebra problems.

Metcalfe (1986) found that there was a significant positive correlation between subjects' estimates of FOK for trivia questions but not for insight problems. Furthermore, as subjects solved algebra problems, deductive reasoning problems, or the Tower of Hanoi problem, they were able to produce "warmth" ratings as they got closer to a solution—the closer they were to a solution the "warmer" they were (the more confident that they were close to a solution) (Metcalfe & Wiebe, 1987). Indeed, these types of problems showed gradual increases in the subjects' warmth ratings from 1 ("cold") to 7 ("very warm") every 15 seconds. For insight problems, on the other hand, there were hardly any increases in feelings of warmth until immediately before a solution was found. Metcalfe and Wiebe therefore concluded that "insight problems … require a sudden illumination for their solution" (p. 292). They also argued that their study "shows an empirically demonstrable distinction between problems that people thought were insight problems and those that are generally considered not to require insight such as algebra or multistep problems" (p. 243). They even argue that such "warmth protocols" might be used to diagnose problem types.

Insight as nothing special

Despite Metcalfe's conclusion, there have been several attempts at explaining Gestalt insight problems in "classical" information-processing terms. Most of the accounts have a lot in common, as they appeal to a number of cognitive processes usually involved in other forms of problem solving such as retrieval of information from long-term memory, search through a problem space, search for relevant operators from memory, problem understanding, and so on.

Kaplan and Simon's account of insight

The title of Kaplan and Simon's (1990) paper *In Search of Insight* is intended to show that search is part of insightful problem solving. The difference is that, rather than developing a representation of a problem and then searching through that representation (the problem space), the solver has to search for the appropriate representation. Kaplan and Simon use the metaphor of searching for a diamond in a darkened room to illustrate insight. At first you might grope blindly on your hands and knees as you search for the diamond. After a while, though, you may feel that this is getting you nowhere fast. You therefore look for a different way of trying to find the diamond and decide to start searching for a light switch instead. If you find one and turn it on, the diamond can be seen almost at once.

Kaplan and Simon used variants of the Mutilated Chequer Board problem to examine the process of search in insightful problem solving. If you re-read the statement of the problem in Activity 3.2, the most obvious apparent solution is to try covering the squares with dominoes. This method of searching for a solution is equivalent to groping in the dark for the diamond. The reason why this strategy is likely to fail is that the *search space* is too big (one graduate student spent over 18 hours trying to solve it this way). Another way of looking at it is that there are not enough **constraints** on the problem—there are too many possible paths to search. A problem constraint allows you to "prune the search tree". Figure 3.10 makes this idea a little clearer.

Kaplan and Simon argued that the problem was hard because there were not enough constraints. The only way to find a solution is to stop searching through the initial representation (the problem space of covering squares with dominoes) and search for a representation that provides more constraints. Figure 3.11 depicts this switch from a search through a single representation to a search through a meta-representation (the problem space of problem spaces). Figure 3.11 also contains some of the problem spaces used by subjects and identified from think-aloud protocols. All subjects at first searched for a solution by "covering" squares with dominoes. When this failed to work they eventually switched to another representation of the problem. Some attempted to search for a mathematical solution; some attempted to manipulate the board by, for example, dividing it into separate areas; some sought an analogy or another similar problem. Eventually all tried to find a solution based on parity (that is, a solution based on the fact that the dominoes had to cover two squares of different colours).

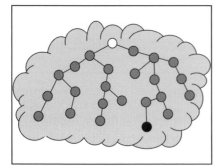

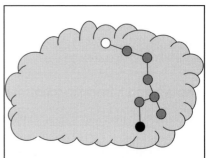

Figure 3.10a.   This depicts an imaginary problem showing all possible stages (grey circles) and paths you can follow (lines) from the start (white circle) to the goal (black circle).

Figure 3.10b.   This depicts the effects of pruning the search tree. Constraints thereby allow you to concentrate on fewer paths and steps through the problem space.

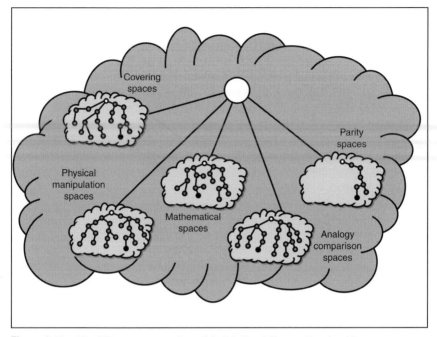

Figure 3.11.   The different representations of the Mutilated Chequer Board problem
(Source: Robertson, 1999, p. 50).

In sum, Kaplan and Simon argued that insight is not a special type of problem-solving phenomenon, but involves the same processes as other forms of problem solving, "The same processes that are ordinarily used to search within problem space can be used to search for a problem space (representation)" (Kaplan & Simon, 1990, p. 376). Subjects' difficulty in solving the problem was mainly due to an inappropriate and underconstrained representation.

Keane's information-processing explanation of functional fixedness

Another reinterpretation of Gestalt insight problems in information-processing terms comes from Mark Keane. According to Keane (1989a) the difficulties in solving "construction" problems (such as Maier's Two-string problem and Duncker's Candle Holder problem) are due to (a) the subjects not having a complete representation of the properties of the objects involved, and (b) consequently failing to access a suitable solution plan from memory.

The failure to represent completely the properties of objects leads to functional fixedness. When we think of objects and categories, we access **context-independent information** about those objects and categories. When we think of a *skunk* we think of a *bad smell*; when we think of *pliers* we think of *something for gripping small objects* and *made of metal*; when we think of a *box* we think of a *container*; and so on. This context-independent information represents an object's **conceptual core** (Barsalou, 1989). However, our knowledge of an object or category may include **context-dependent information** under the right circumstances. As Barsalou (1989) puts it, "When people *read* frog in isolation, for example, *eaten by humans* typically remains inactive in memory. However, *eaten by humans* becomes active when reading about frogs in a French restaurant" (p. 77). Furthermore, you might more readily retrieve such context-dependent information if it was mentioned or encountered recently. For example, *edible* may be retrieved when someone thinks of frogs if that person had recently eaten frogs' legs in a restaurant.

Applying this idea of how we recall the properties of objects to the Gestalt "construction" problems, Keane points out that it is the *salience* of these context-independent properties that either cues or fails to cue a solution plan. If you see a pair of pliers next to an electrician's toolbox, the property of gripping tightly would be salient and hence incorporated into your representation of the tool. If, on the other hand, you saw the pliers beside the bleeding head of a corpse, you might represent the tool in terms of its *heaviness* because that property is salient in this context. In Maier's Two-string problem the context-independent properties of the pliers (*gripping tightly, made of metal*) are likely to be represented, and the pliers' heaviness may not be seen as salient. In Duncker's Candle Holder problem the salience of the boxes as containers is emphasised because they contain tacks, matches, etc. Other possible properties of the box are therefore not immediately represented.

The second aspect of Keane's theory involves seeing the process of problem solving as attempting to access relevant solution plans from long-term memory. The objects lying around the room in Maier's and Duncker's problems are "bad cues" for retrieving relevant solution plans. "This view of problem solving as a sort of memory recall task conflicts with the traditional view of problem solving; that it is something more than simply remembering. However, remembering the right thing at the right time is not a trivial task; in fact, it could be viewed as the very basis of human intelligence" (Keane, 1989b, p. 4).

In summary, Keane's view of solving certain types of Gestalt insight problems involves looking at the solution process in terms of the way we represent the objects and the kinds of retrieval processes that come in to play based on those object representations. To the extent that our representations of objects and categories are **unstable** (Barsalou, 1989) (that is, the information about an object or category that we deem to be relevant may vary from context to context) we are often unable to pick out the salient properties of the objects. This leads to functional fixedness, for example, when only context-independent properties are represented. However, the salience of an object's properties can be manipulated, to make it more likely that it will cue a relevant solution plan. Thus, in Duncker's Candle Holder experiment, when subjects were given the candles, matches, and tacks inside boxes, the container property of the boxes was seen as salient. When all the objects including the boxes were presented separately, the "container" property of the boxes was less salient and made it more likely that subjects would find a solution.

Ohlsson's theory of insight

One of the features of insight problems is that, once you have read the problem and made a few incorrect attempts at solving it, you get stuck. Problem solving grinds to a halt. Getting stuck in the course of problem solving is usually referred to as reaching an **impasse** (e.g., Laird, Newell, & Rosenbloom, 1987; Newell, 1990; VanLehn, 1990). A second aspect of insight problems is that people are usually able to solve them but they don't realise it. The answer is often obvious once you hear it. Understanding how to solve an insight problem is therefore a bit like getting a joke (Koestler, 1970). Jokes often rely on the listener generating a typical, but in this case wrong, interpretation of a situation. One could turn the statement "a man walked into a bar and fell on the floor" into an insight problem by adding the question "Why?" The answer (the punch line) is that it was an iron bar. The point here is that you could have solved the problem (got the joke) if you had accessed the relevant meaning of "bar". It is not that you didn't know that bar had two meanings, it's just that you didn't realise which one was relevant. Thus, "insight occurs in the context of an impasse, which is unmerited in the sense that the thinker is, in fact, competent to solve the problem" (Ohlsson, 1992, p. 4). The corollary of this is that if you do not have a particular competence then you cannot have an insight. You are "terminally stuck" as Ohlsson puts it. Once again a joke can illustrate this point:

Question: How many Heisenbergs does it take to change a light bulb?
Answer: If you knew that you wouldn't know where the light bulb was.

Activity 3.5

The Radiation problem

Suppose you are a doctor faced with a patient who has a malignant tumour in his stomach. It is impossible to operate on the patient, but unless the tumour is destroyed the patient will die. There is a kind of ray that can be used to destroy the tumour. If the rays reach the tumour all at once at sufficiently high intensity, the tumour will be destroyed. Unfortunately, at this intensity the healthy tissue that the rays pass through on the way to the tumour will also be destroyed. At lower intensities the rays are harmless to healthy tissue, but they will not affect the tumour either. What type of procedure might be used to destroy the tumour with the rays, and at the same time avoid destroying the healthy tissue?

(Gick & Holyoak, 1980, pp. 307–308)

If you don't know anything about Heisenberg's Uncertainty Principle then you won't get the joke—you would be terminally stuck. Similarly if an insight problem requires for its solution knowledge that you do not have, then there is no way you can get out of the impasse.

A third aspect of insight problems is that, as Weisberg (1995) pointed out, you can have an "Aha!" experience on problems that would not normally be classed as insight problems. One might suddenly have an insight into how to solve an algebra problem. Furthermore, an insight may well be completely wrong. Some of these and other points made by Ohlsson will be illustrated with the Radiation problem originally used by Duncker (1945). The version here (Activity 3.5), however, is taken from Gick and Holyoak (1980).

Ohlsson's theory is based on five problem-solving principles.

1. Reading a problem generates a mental representation of the problem's **givens** (the situation described by the problem) and some solution criterion.
2. Based on this mental representation we access a set of mental operators that we think might apply. Associated with the operators is information about pre-requisites and the effects of applying them. The solver can "see" what happens in his or her mind's eye when an operator is applied.
3. Problem solving is sequential, hence only one operator can be selected and applied at a time from those retrieved from memory. On the basis of some heuristic or plan, an operator is chosen from the ones retrieved from memory. Any operators not retrieved naturally cannot be executed.
4. Retrieving a relevant operator from the vast number in memory is not trivial. It comes about through **spreading activation** (bits of information in a semantic network that are related to the current context are activated, some more strongly than others). Activation spreads from information currently in working memory or in the goal stack. Spreading activation is an unconscious process.
5. The mental representation we form of the problem situation acts as a memory probe for relevant operators in long-term memory. The operators retrieved will have some semantic relationship with the problem situation and goal. Operators that have no such semantic relationship will not be retrieved. Notice that this aspect of the theory resembles Keane's, in which salient features of the problem activate related operators.

When a problem is unfamiliar we may not interpret it in an optimal way. We therefore encounter an impasse when we generate a representation based on an interpretation that does not allow us to retrieve relevant operators from memory. When solvers hit an impasse, the only way out is to construct a new representation of the problem (we "restructure" the problem). The new representation generates a different spread of activation.

In the Radiation problem any interpretation that involves rays projected at full power is not going to work. Firing the rays down the oesophagus, for example,

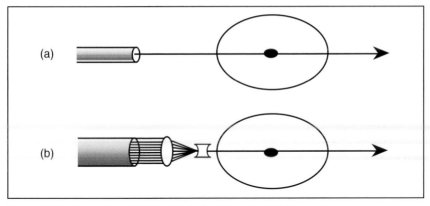

Figure 3.12.   Diagrams used by Duncker in describing the Radiation problem
(adapted from Duncker, 1945).

won't work as there is no straight path that way to the tumour. Opening the
stomach to clear the way for the rays is expressly forbidden. However providing
hints or rephrasing the problem statement can have an effect by acting as different
memory probes, allowing different mental operators and hence different solutions
to be attempted. Duncker gave two diagrams with the Radiation problem to two
groups of people (Figures 3.12a and 3.12b). Figure 3.12b was more effective at
generating a solution. He also tried rephrasing the problem statement causing the
participants to focus on different aspects of the problem:

1. How could one prevent the rays from injuring…
2. How could one protect the healthy tissues from being injured.

Giving different diagrams and presenting the question in different ways
influenced the representation subjects formed of the problem. There are, according
to Ohlsson, three ways that one can change an initial representation:

Elaboration.   The solver might notice features of the problem that he or she
had not noticed before. This might enrich or extend the representation of the
problem. In the Mutilated Chequer Board problem, for example, the solver might
notice that the domino *has* to cover one square of each colour, so if two squares
of the same colour are missing then the Chequer Board cannot be entirely covered
by dominoes. Elaboration can also come about by retrieving relevant information
from long-term memory

Re-encoding.   The representation of the problem may be mistaken rather than
incomplete. In Duncker's Candle Holder problem, the solver has to re-encode the
boxes from *containers* to *platforms*. Similarly the thinker has to re-encode the pliers
in Maier's Two-string problem as a pendulum weight.

Constraint relaxation.   Sometimes the solver may have assumed that there were constraints placed on the problem that were not in fact there. In the Radiation problem there is nothing to stop you using more than one ray machine or changing the intensity of the rays. To solve it you have to relax any constraints you may have imposed about the number of ray machines at the doctor's disposal.

Completing the solution

If an impasse is successfully broken by forming a re-representation of the problem, a new set of operators becomes available. This leads to either a **partial insight** or **full insight**. A partial insight occurs when a new path through the problem can suddenly be seen. A full insight is where the answer is suddenly staring you in the face. The latter is hard to explain within an information-processing framework. Ohlsson suggests that a solution is constructed at the moment of insight. This process is fast, hence it seems immediate (the "Aha!" experience).

How such a construction process might come about can be seen from a new view of a well-known insight problem. The Nine Dots problem is an example of a problem where the difficulty seems to be in overcoming self-imposed constraints (Figure 3.13 in Activity 3.6).

A Gestalt explanation of the Nine Dots problem is that there is a perceptual constraint—subjects assume they have to stay within the square formed by the nine dots (Scheerer, 1963). However, there has been some argument over the exact nature of the constraints involved in this problem. Weisberg and Alba (1981) found that only 20% of their subjects produced a correct solution after being given a hint to go outside the dots. As so few people solved it despite the constraint being presumably "relaxed", Weisberg and Alba argued that the difficulty could not be due to a perceptual constraint. Lung and Dominowski (1985) argued that the constraint was that people felt that lines had to begin and end on dots.

In a series of studies, MacGregor, Ormerod, and Chronicle (in press; Chronicle, Ormerod, & MacGregor, in press; Ormerod, Chronicle, & MacGregor, 1997) argue that the self-imposed constraints are due to the information-processing demands of the problem. For example, Chronicle et al. found that, despite being given visual cues to guide them towards constraint relaxation, participants were still unlikely to solve the problem. MacGregor et al. therefore propose a model of performance on the Nine Dots problem based on two general problem-solving heuristics—a type of means–ends analysis, and progress monitoring based on some criterion. The Nine Dots problem is an abstractly defined problem, so there is no

Activity 3.6

Draw four straight lines that connect all nine dots without taking the pencil from the paper. There is a hint in the text (answer on page 235).

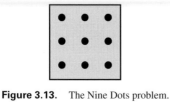

Figure 3.13.   The Nine Dots problem.

explicit goal state—no "end", as it were, that can readily be reached by difference reduction. Nevertheless, MacGregor et al. argue that, in abstractly defined problems, people try to use operators that are "locally rational". Such an operator would allow a solver to reduce the difference between where they are in a problem and some "local sub-goal state". Specifically, people try to cancel as many dots as possible in one move. This means–end strategy MacGregor et al. refer to as a "maximisation heuristic". The second strategy is to monitor progress through a problem. One way to do this is to look one or more moves ahead. Unfortunately, capacity limitations restrict our ability to do this. Another way to monitor progress is to evaluate prospective moves based on some kind of criterion: in this case, cancel an average of 2.25 dots per move.

MacGregor et al. argue that fixating on the square or failing to consider non-dot turning points are the *results* of applying the local means–end heuristic to the basic Nine Dots problem. It also explains the finding shown in Figure 3.14. In the Figure the first line provided in (a) was less likely to lead to a correct solution than the diagonal line in (b), despite the fact that the horizontal line seems to indicate a relaxation of a constraint that says you should stay within the square.

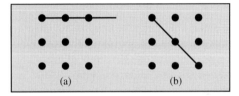

Figure 3.14.   Two variants of the Nine Dots problem presented in MacGregor et al. (in press).

The model also predicts that experience of criterion failure in problems of this kind—possibly brought about by various manipulations—may cause the problem space to be expanded and new operators sought that may in turn lead to an insightful solution (e.g., drawing a line outside the dot array). Such a move may produce a "promising state" that may in turn lead to a re-conceptualisation of the problem.

MacGregor et al. seem to have succeeded in building a detailed process model of success and failure on abstractly defined problems such as the Nine Dots problem. A traditional insight problem has yielded to an information-processing account that can predict success and failure on the problem and its variants. Not only that but their model also shows "how insight may be achieved incrementally through experience of one or many partial solutions".

THE RELATIONSHIP BETWEEN INSIGHT PROBLEMS AND OTHER PROBLEMS

The necessity to re-represent problems is not confined to those normally referred to as insight problems. All so-called "word" problems in algebra and physics

---

Activity 3.7

Rate problems

1. The Mad Bird problem

Two train stations are 50 miles apart. At 2 p.m. one Saturday afternoon two trains start towards each other, one from each station. Just as the trains pull out of the stations, a bird springs into the air in front of the first train and flies ahead at 100 mph to the front of the second train. When the bird reaches the second train it turns back and flies towards the first train. The bird continues to do this until the trains meet. If both trains travel at the rate of 25 miles per hour, how many miles will the bird have flown before the trains meet? (Posner, 1973, pp.150–151)

2. The River Current problem

You are standing by the side of a river which is flowing past you at the rate of 5 mph. You spot a raft 1 mile upstream on which there are two boys helplessly adrift. Then you spot the boys' parents 1 mile downstream paddling upstream to save them. You know that in still water the parents can paddle at the rate of 4 mph. How long will it be before the parents reach the boys? (Hayes, 1989a, p. 25)

(problems involving some kind of cover story rather than a simple sum) require the solver to represent the problem appropriately before a way of solving it (a solution procedure) becomes obvious. The study of insight problems therefore has important consequences for our understanding of how we solve all kinds of problems. Activity 3.7 contains two examples of *distance = rate x time* problems and ways of representing them.

There are two features of these kinds of algebra problems that are important. The first is that you often have to throw common sense out of the window (Birds don't fly at 100 mph and anyway why would it fly back and forth like that? How do the parents know their sons are adrift on a raft two miles away?). Common sense, or general world knowledge, can often interfere with such problem solving. Second, both problems are written in such a way that certain features are more salient than others—that is, they stand out. One effect of this is that you may be led into representing the problems in a certain way. In the first case you may be led to represent the problem from the point of view of the bird. In the second case you may be led to represent the problem from the point of view of the person on the bank. Both these representations of the problems make the solutions harder.

A representation of the Mad Bird problem from the bird's point of view, as in Figure 3.15, involves trying to add up how far the bird travels each time it flies from one train to the other. This makes the solution rather difficult. However, the problem is readily solved if we ignore the bird for the moment and concentrate on the trains as in Figure 3.16. All you need to find out to begin with is how long it takes the trains to meet. Both trains travel at a very sluggish 25 miles an hour and meet after travelling 25 miles so they take an hour to meet. The problem now

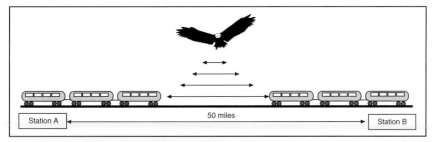

Figure 3.15. The Mad Bird problem from the bird's point of view.

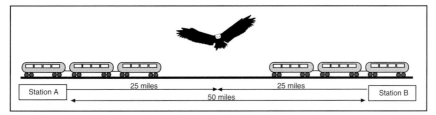

Figure 3.16. The Mad Bird problem from the trains' point of view.

becomes how far does the bird travel in an hour at a speed of 100 miles an hour. The answer is obviously 100 miles.

The River Current problem can be represented in two ways as in Figures 3.17 and 3.18. In Figure 3.17 the parents are paddling at 4 mph but the river current is 5 mph so they are actually heading away from the observer at 1 mph. The boys are travelling in the same direction at 5 mph so the difference between the two speeds is 4 mph. That is, the boys are approaching their parents at 4 mph. If they travel 4 miles in one hour then they will travel 2 miles in half an hour.

In Figure 3.18 we can forget about the observer and take the point of view of the boys on the raft. We can also forget about the river current, as it affects the

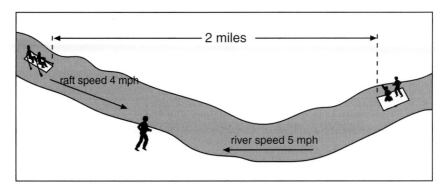

Figure 3.17. The River Current problem from the observer's point of view.

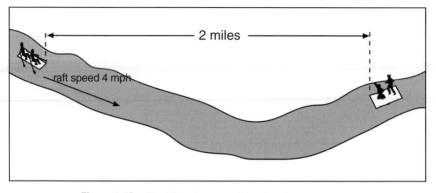

Figure 3.18.   The River Current problem ignoring the observer.

parents and the boys equally (similarly, if you are sitting on a train travelling at 80 mph you don't normally think of a ticket inspector as moving at 82 mph—you can ignore the train's speed as it affects you both equally and regard the inspector as moving at a much more sedate 2 mph). The only relevant figure therefore is the speed at which the parents are paddling, i.e., 4 mph. In which case they will reach the boys in half an hour.

INFLUENCING PROBLEM REPRESENTATIONS: THE EFFECT OF INSTRUCTIONS

The two examples just quoted illustrate how we are often "persuaded" to form a particular representation of a problem by the way a problem is worded. The Mad Bird problem is likely to generate a mental representation involving a bird flying between the two trains. The River Current problem invites you to represent the problem in terms of the speed of the river past an observer, so that's what you do. You are given information, some of which appears to be particularly salient by the way the problem is worded, and so the representation you form is based on that salient information.

The effect of instructions on the representations people form of problems was investigated by Hayes and Simon (1974; Simon & Hayes, 1976) using two variants of the Tower of Hanoi problem. When two problems have an identical underlying structure (as revealed, for example, by state-space analysis) they are said to be isomorphic (see also Chapter 4). The two isomorphs of the Tower of Hanoi problem used by Simon and Hayes are shown in Table 3.1. In the move isomorph, globes are transferred from one monster to another in much the same way that disks in the Tower of Hanoi are moved from one peg to another and with the same constraints—if a peg (monster) has more than one disk (globe) only the smallest can be transferred to another peg (monster); a large disk (globe) cannot be placed on a peg (moved to a monster) that has a smaller disk

TABLE 3.1

The Monster problem

A move isomorph

Three five-handed extraterrestrial monsters were holding three crystal globes. Because of the quantum-mechanical peculiarities of their neighbourhood, both monsters and globes come in exactly three sizes with no others permitted: small, medium, and large. The medium-sized monster was holding the small globe; the small monster was holding the large globe; and the large monster was holding the medium-sized globe. As this situation offended their keenly developed sense of symmetry, they proceeded *to transfer globes from one monster to another* so that each monster would have a globe proportionate to his own size. Monster etiquette complicated the solution of the problem as it requires:

1. *that only one globe may be transferred at a time,*
2. *that if a monster is holding two globes, only the larger of the two may be transferred;*
3. *that a globe may not be transferred to a monster who is holding a larger globe.*

By what sequence of transfers could the monsters have solved the problem?

A change isomorph

Three five-handed extraterrestrial monsters were holding three crystal globes. Because of the quantum-mechanical peculiarities of their neighbourhood, both monsters and globes come in exactly three sizes with no others permitted: small, medium, and large. The medium-sized monster was holding the small globe; the small monster was holding the large globe; and the large monster was holding the medium-sized globe. As this situation offended their keenly developed sense of symmetry, they proceeded *to shrink and expand the globes* so that each monster would have a globe proportionate to his own size. Monster etiquette complicated the solution of the problem as it requires:

1. *that only one globe may be changed at a time;*
2. *that if two globes are of the same size, only the globe held by the larger monster can be changed;*
3. *that a globe may not be changed by a monster who is holding a larger globe.*

By what sequence of changes could the monsters have solved the problem?

(Adapted from Simon & Hayes, 1976, pp. 168–169)

(globe). The change isomorph is trickier. It involves changing the sizes of globes, and the globes stay with a single monster. Actually what has happened is that the equivalent of pegs and disks have swapped round in the two representations. The equivalent of a disk in the move isomorph is actually a peg in the change isomorph.

Simon and Hayes developed a computer program called UNDERSTAND that would take as input the problem instructions and identify the goal, states, and operators that applied to the problem. This information was then fed to a general-purpose program called the General Problem Solver. The UNDERSTAND program predicted that the representations solvers would generate (in terms of states and operators) would be entirely determined by the problem instructions. For example, a move in the change isomorph would be represented as a particular monster changing the size of its globe. When Simon and Hayes (1976) analysed the verbal protocols of people attempting to solve the two variants, they found that their subjects were powerfully influenced by the version of the story they were given, as UNDERSTAND predicted.

This chapter has shown that our initial representation of a problem can often determine its difficulty, or even whether it is possible to solve it at all. In insight problems in particular we often hit an impasse early on that prevents further search for a solution. Whereas in well-defined problems a solution may be found by searching *through* a problem space, in insight problems a solution can only be found by searching *for* a useful problem space. Recently theorists have shown that the processes involved in trying to solve ill-defined or abstractly defined insight problems are essentially similar to those used in solving well-defined problems. We are now in a position to say much more precisely why such problems are difficult.

SUMMARY

1. The way we represent problems when we encounter them has a powerful influence on our ability to solve them. Occasionally, our representation of a problem is so poor that we get stuck—we reach an impasse.
2. It is sometimes possible to get out of an impasse by such means as:

   - focusing on a different aspect of the problem;
   - looking at extreme conditions;
   - trying to find an analogy;
   - re-encoding aspects of the problem—trying to see them in different ways;
   - relaxing constraints that we have inadvertently placed on the problem.

3. Gestalt psychologists were interested in how we represent and "restructure" problems. They viewed thinking as often either reproductive, where we use previously learned procedures without taking too much account of the problem structure, or productive, where thinking is based on a deep understanding of a problem's structure and is not structurally blind.

4. They were also interested in the failures of thinking due to:

   - functional fixedness, when we fail to notice that an object can have more than one use;
   - the effects of set, when we apply previously learned procedures when a simpler procedure would work.

5. Insight problems would appear to pose problems for information-processing theories of problem solving because they do not appear to involve sequential, conscious, heuristic search. Consequently some researchers have viewed insight as a special case of problem solving. Others have tried to fit insight into traditional information-processing accounts:

   - Kaplan and Simon saw insight as a search for a representation rather than a search in a representation.

- Keane pointed out that functional fixedness could be understood in terms of the salient properties of objects. That is, functional fixedness is due to the organisation of semantic memory.
- Ohlsson argued that we access one operator at a time based on our initial interpretation of a problem. Retrieving operators is an unconscious process involving spreading activation (and hence also depends on the organisation of semantic memory). When we cannot retrieve an operator based on our initial representation we reach an impasse and have to change the representation before we can access a relevant operator.

6. MacGregor et al. have produced a detailed model of the processes involved in solving abstractly defined insight problems such as the Nine Dots problem that incorporate heuristics such as means–ends analysis, and show how the conditions for an insightful solution might arise.

7. The study of insight problems is important because the processes involved are often the same as those involved in establishing an appropriate representation of a situation or word problem. Without an appropriate representation, no relevant operators can be accessed and problem solving reaches an impasse or becomes more difficult.

8. The way a problem is phrased can have a powerful effect on the representation that we form of it. Simon and Hayes showed how an initial representation can be formed from problem instructions and how it can be modelled.

Analogical problem solving

Part Three: Introduction

Very often the simplest way of solving a problem is to think of a similar one we have solved in the past and use that solution. The general term for using an earlier problem to solve a new one is **analogical problem solving**. Although we can often use an earlier problem as an analogy, the term analogy can be used to cover a wide range of phenomena. For example, if we are trying to explain an unfamiliar concept to someone it is common to use some kind of analogy with a concept the person already knows. Analogies in the form of metaphors can also provide a new way of looking at things with which we are already familiar, allowing us to see new and perhaps unforeseen relationships.

Analogies, then, come in all shapes and sizes. Because of their ubiquity, they are used for a variety of purposes. They can be found in:

Poetry: Shall I compare thee to a summer's day?

Pithy sayings: Experience is the comb nature gives us when we are bald.

Textbook explanations: Russian dolls can be used to explain recursion.

Explanations of systems: The heart can be seen as a pump.

Witty repartee:
  Unknown interlocutor: Ah, I see we are to have a battle of wits.
  Oliver Wendell Holmes: Sir, I never fight an unarmed man.

Aesthetic prose: "No bull ever abused a china shop as sex abuses the DNA archives" (Dawkins, 1995, p. 40).

Persuasive argument: President Johnson believed there would be a domino effect if Vietnam fell to the communists and therefore escalated the war in Vietnam.

Instructional texts: Science, mathematics, and computing textbooks usually contain example problems and exercise problems; the student uses the examples to solve the exercise problems.

Several important issues concerning using past examples or experience to solve a current problem or make sense of a current situation are dealt with over the next four chapters. Generally, the most important thing to bear in mind about the usefulness of analogies in solving new problems is that *you have to understand the analogue* if it is to be of any use. Similarly, if analogies are used to illustrate new concepts in teaching texts, the analogies have to be understandable, otherwise the new concepts may not be well understood. This aspect of analogical problem solving has important ramifications for teaching with analogies. Curtis and Reigeluth (1984) found a total of 216 analogies used in 26 science textbooks to elucidate scientific concepts. They are also particularly relevant to the kind of textbook problem solving discussed later in Chapter 7.

Another important aspect of analogies is that the similarity between the analogue and the problem you are trying to solve (or the concept you are trying to understand) can vary enormously. Bulls in china shops seem to have very little *on the surface* to do with genetic inheritance through sex. On the other hand, an example involving cars overtaking one another is very similar to an exercise problem involving trucks overtaking one another.

All analogies have to be adapted in some way in order to solve a new problem. As they need to be adapted in some way, there is always a point at which an analogy breaks down. The surface features of analogues and the need to adapt the analogue to solve the new problem have a powerful influence on analogical problem solving. For a novice, identifying the relevant similarities and ignoring the irrelevant differences can be tricky. Thus analogies may help novices by shifting their focus away from the surface features of problems to the underlying structure.

When we are presented with numerous examples of the same type of thing we normally eventually abstract out the commonalities between them. As toddlers we saw many examples of dogs and thereby learned to recognise new instances of dogs and to distinguish them from cats. Now, if we see a strange and unusual breed of dog for the first time, we can readily categorise it as a dog. The process of abstracting out the common features of things in this way is known as **induction**. Applying what we have learned—generalising from one or a few examples to a whole range of new examples—is known as **deduction**. Induction is the process of moving from the particular to the general, and deduction is the process of going from the general to the particular. Most of what we have learned about the world is through induction. For this reason a large part of this book is devoted to the inductive role of analogies and examples in learning.

CHAPTER FOUR

Transfer of learning

The two problems described in Activity 4.1 are different in their surface features (one is about currency exchange rates and the other is about a car's journey) and similar in their underlying structure—in both you get the answer by multiplying the two known quantities (both are therefore solved using the equation: $a = b \times c$). The elements (45 mph, 5 hours) or surface features of a problem are related to each other, and the set of relations (represented here by the structure of the equation) constitutes the problem's structure. As the examples in Activity 4.1 show, the set of relations may indicate a procedure that has to be followed. Over the next few chapters you will find that the emphasis is sometimes on the relational structure and sometimes on the procedure that derives from it, although the two are intertwined.

Activity 4.1

In what ways are these two problems similar and different?

A. A tourist in St Tropez wants to convert £85 to Euros. If the exchange rate is 1.8€ to the pound how many Euros will she get?

B. A car travelling at an average speed of 40 mph reaches its destination after 5 hours. How far has it travelled?

1. How likely is it that learning to do problem A will make it easier to do problem B?

2. Suppose you have just exchanged pounds for Euros and are idly motoring through the French countryside pondering question B; how likely are you to be reminded of problem A?

3. If so, why; and if not, why not?

4. Under what conditions are you likely to use A to solve B?

---

were to compare the time it took you to learn the original word processor for the first time with the time taken to learn the new one you would probably find that you learned the new one faster than the old one despite the initial confusion (Singley & Anderson, 1985; VanLehn, 1989). Whether this is true of the windscreen wiper/indicator scenario is a moot point.

SET AND EINSTELLUNG AS EXAMPLES OF NEGATIVE TRANSFER

Some of the difficulties in problem solving identified by the Gestalt psychologists can be classified as negative transfer. The most obvious example is Einstellung. In Luchins and Luchins' Water Jar experiments subjects learned a rule for generating a solution that prevented them from seeing a simpler solution to a later example of the same type of problem. Similarly functional fixedness prevents you from seeing a solution to a problem. Learning that a tool such as pliers is used for grasping things tightly may prevent you from seeing that the tool can be used as a pendulum weight. What you have learned in one context prevents you from solving a problem in a different context using the same tool.

HYPOTHESIS TESTING THEORY

To try to make sense of why human problem solving is affected by negative and positive transfer, John Sweller (1980; Sweller & Gee, 1978) conducted a series of neat little experiments to show how the same set of training examples could produce both positive and negative transfer. According to Sweller (1980) positive transfer accounts for the *sequence* effect (Hull, 1920). The sequence effect means simply that if there is a series of similar problems graded in complexity, then it is easier to solve them in an easy-to-complex sequence than in a complex-to-easy sequence. A solver's experience of solving the early examples speeds up the solution to the later ones. Furthermore, a modification of Levine's (1975) hypothesis testing theory can account for this type of positive transfer as well as for the kind of negative transfer produced by Einstellung (Luchins, 1942).

I should point out that the following discussion uses "hypotheses" and "rules" almost interchangeably. This is because they can both be framed in the same way. "If you do X then Y will happen" can be both a rule and a hypothesis.

The hypothesis testing theory involves three assumptions:

1. "If people perceive a series of problems as being related, they tend to begin each problem by testing hypotheses as closely related as practicable to their previously correct hypotheses … the corollary is that to the extent that people do not perceive a series of problems as being related, their choice of hypotheses on subsequent problems will not be influenced by previous problems" (Sweller, 1980, p. 234).

So if you have a rule (or closely related rules) that worked on similar problems before, then use it. The more these or similar rules have worked in the past, the more likely they will work again. On the other hand, if you don't see any similarity between the problem you are working on and one you did in the past, then you are hardly likely to use the earlier one as a basis for solving the current one for the simple reason that is does not occur to you to do so.

2. A hypothesis that is fairly simple and has few similar related hypotheses will be more salient than a complex hypothesis or one that has a number of similar related hypotheses (see Activity 4.3). In other words a simple rule will appear more obvious than a complex one.

3. Assumption number 1 overrides 2 if there is a conflict between them. For example, you are more likely to retrieve and use a rule or hypothesis that has been successful with similar problems in the past, *no matter how complex*, than to retrieve a rule that is simple rather than complex.

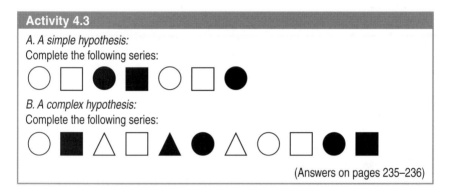

Activity 4.3

A. A simple hypothesis:
Complete the following series:

B. A complex hypothesis:
Complete the following series:

(Answers on pages 235–236)

When we learn something new we generally start off with simple examples. With learning and practice the examples can get harder and harder until eventually we can solve complex problems in that domain. When we have learned to solve problems of a certain type, features of a new problem will trigger the relevant procedure. As we saw in the Water Jars problem, features of the problem can trigger a complex procedure when a much simpler one exists. A simple problem whose features resemble a complex one can therefore trigger the complex learned procedure.

Sweller's experiment into transfer effects is shown in Study Box 4.1. The results show that you can solve a difficult problem if you have had experience with similar problems involving related rules. With experience of related rules people can make successful hypotheses about a new problem that is similar to earlier ones, on condition that the sequence of problems starts off with one requiring a relatively simple hypothesis and becomes increasingly complex. The downside to this effect is that a simple problem can be made difficult for the same reason. The same rule-learning ability that makes an otherwise insoluble problem soluble produces

Sweller's (1980) study of transfer effects

Rationale

The assumptions of the hypothesis testing theory predict that there will be different transfer effects (both positive and negative) despite very similar learning conditions in problems where subjects have to induce a rule. The same "training set" of problems can therefore turn a simple problem into a hard one (due to the effects of negative transfer) and a hard problem into a simple one (due to the effects of positive transfer and the sequence effect).

Method

Subjects were given a two-digit number such as 49 and told to give a number in response. They were then given the correct answer. This was repeated until the subjects got the answer correct 6 out of 7 times, or until they had 40 trials. There were two types of possible response. A simple *Add* response where the correct answer was simply the sum of the two digits. So, for example, the two digit number 49 should elicit the answer 13 (by adding 4 and 9). The second type of response was based on a set of increasingly complex rules. The first problem was very simple. No matter what two-digit number was given to the participant the answer was *always* 10. In the second problem two responses alternated. For the first two-digit number the answer was 12, for the second two-digit number it was 7, for the third 12 again, and so on. The third problem required the subject to pick out a sequence of three numbers, and so on.

Results

None of the subjects who had learned the increasingly complex procedure were able in 10 attempts to solve the problem requiring them simply to add the numbers. All bar one (12 out of 13) subjects in the control group who had had no training managed to solve the simple Add problem within 10 attempts. No one managed the complex problem without practice.

Einstellung when a new problem is presented that requires a different although simpler hypothesis. As Sweller puts it, "Identical variations in preliminary problems either can transform a normally simple problem into an insoluble one or alternatively an insoluble problem into a simple one with the only alteration being in the degree of similarity between the hypotheses required for the initial problems and the critical problem" (1980, p. 237).

Sweller's studies are important for the light they cast on human thinking. Sweller regards the process by which we induce rules from experience as a natural adaptation. As a result positive and negative transfer are two sides to the same coin. Einstellung is not an example of human rigid or irrational thinking, but a consequence of the otherwise rather powerful thinking processes we have evolved to induce rules that in turn make our world predictable.

TRANSFER IN WELL-DEFINED PROBLEMS

Using the methods described in Chapter 2 to analyse problem structures, we can tell if two problems have the same structure or not. If there are differences in people's ability to solve two problems that share the same structure then the difficulty must lie in some aspect of the harder problem other than the structure itself. As stated in Chapter 3, problems that have an identical structure and have the same restrictions are known as *isomorphs*. The Monster problems in Table 3.1 described two such isomorphs. Have a look now at Activity 4.4.

Activity 4.4 illustrates one further variant of the Tower of Hanoi problem. The only difference between the Tower of Hanoi problem and the three isomorphs you have seen is in their *cover stories*. Because the problems look so different on the surface you may not have realised that the underlying structure was identical with the Tower of Hanoi problem. All four problems therefore differ in terms of their surface features but are similar in their underlying structural features. As pointed out in Chapter 3, despite their underlying similarity, it is the surface features that most influence people. The Himalayan Tea Ceremony is an example of a "Transfer

---

Activity 4.4

The Himalayan Tea Ceremony

In the inns of certain Himalayan villages is practised a most civilised and refined tea ceremony. The ceremony involves a host and exactly two guests. When his guests have arrived and have seated themselves at his table, the host performs three services for them. These services are listed below in the order of the nobility that the Himalayans attribute to them:

> stoking the fire,
> fanning the flames,
> passing the rice cakes.

During the ceremony, any of those present may ask another, "Honoured Sir, may I perform this onerous task for you?"

However, a person may request of another only the least noble of the tasks that the other is performing. Furthermore, if a person is performing any tasks, then he may not request a task that is nobler than the noblest task he is already performing. Custom requires that by the time the tea ceremony is over, all of the tasks will have been transferred from the host to the most senior of his guests.

How may this be accomplished?

(Adapted from Simon & Hayes, 1976)

problem" where tasks are transferred from one participant to another, like the first Monster problem in Table 3.1. Simon and Hayes (1976) used 13 isomorphs of the Tower of Hanoi problem, all of which were variations of the Monster problem with two forms: Change and Transfer. They found that subjects were strongly influenced by the way the problem instructions were written. None of their subjects tried to map the Monster problem onto the Tower of Hanoi to make it easier to solve, and "only two or three even thought of trying or noticed the analogy" (1976, p. 166).

Activity 4.5

The Jealous Husbands problem

Three jealous husbands and their wives having to cross a river at a ferry find a boat, but the boat is so small that it can contain no more than two persons. Find the simplest schedule of crossings that will permit all six people to cross the river so that none of the women shall be left in company with any of the men, unless her husband is present. It is assumed that all passengers on the boat disembark before the next trip, and at least one person has to be in the boat for each crossing.

The problem in Activity 4.5 should, however, be recognisable. It was used by Reed et al. (1974) in their study of transfer between similar problems. The Jealous Husbands and Hobbits and Orcs problems both have an identical structure (see Figure 2.7). However, notice that there is one further restriction in the Jealous Husbands problem. A woman cannot be left in the company of other men unless her husband is present. "Moving two missionaries corresponds to moving any of three possible pairs of husbands since all husbands are not equivalent. But only one of the three possible moves may be legal, so there is a greater constraint on moves in the Jealous Husbands problem" (Reed et al., 1974, p. 438). This added constraint means that the Missionaries and Cannibals and the Jealous Husbands problems are not exactly isomorphic but are **homomorphic**. That is the problems are similar but not identical. Reed, Ernst, and Banerji's experiments are outlined in Study Box 4.2.

Reed et al. found a number of things. First the extra constraint imposed by the Jealous Husbands problem made it harder to ensure that a move was legal or not. The effect of this was to increase the length of time subjects took to make a move and the number of illegal moves made. Second, transfer was asymmetrical; that is, there was transfer only from Jealous Husbands to Missionaries and Cannibals but not the other way round. Third, there was no transfer between the two different problems unless the subjects were explicitly told to use the earlier problem (e.g., "whenever you moved a husband previously, you should now move a missionary, etc."). Fourth, subjects claimed to make little use of the earlier problem even when a hint was given to use it. No one claimed to remember the correct sequence of moves from the earlier problem. Instead subjects must have remembered the earlier

Reed, Ernst, and Banerji (1974)

Rationale

The aim of Reed and co-workers' experiments was "to explore the role of analogy in problem solving". They examined under what circumstances there would be an improvement on a second task.

Method

In Experiment 1 subjects were asked to solve both the Missionaries and Cannibals (MC) problem and the Jealous Husbands (JH) problem. Approximately half did the MC problem before doing the JH problem and approximately half did them in the reverse order. No transfer was found between the two problems. The next two experiments were therefore designed to find out how transfer could be produced. Experiment 2 looked for signs of improvement between repetitions of the same problem. Half the subjects did the MC problem twice and half did the JH problem twice. Experiment 3 tested whether being told the relationship between the problems would produce transfer. The independent variables were: the time taken, the number of moves, and the number of illegal moves made by the subjects.

Results and discussion

In all cases there was no significant difference in the number of moves made, but in some conditions there was a reduction in time to solve the problem and a reduction in the number of illegal moves in the second presentation of a problem. As one might expect there was some improvement on the same problem presented twice. However, the only evidence for any transfer was from the Jealous Husbands to the Missionaries and Cannibals problem, and then only when there was a hint that the two problems were the same. Some transfer of learning took place from the harder to the simpler problem only.

problem at a "more global level". That is, they remembered some general strategies ("balance missionaries and cannibals, move all missionaries first", etc.).

One other point emerges from Reed and co-workers' experiments. As with Simon and Hayes' (1976) Tower of Hanoi isomorphs, it was not the problem structure that was the source of the difficulty in problem solving. The main difficulty was knowing whether a particular move was legal or not. This aspect was examined further by Luger and Bauer (1978). They found no transfer asymmetry between the Tower of Hanoi (TOH) and Himalayan Tea Ceremony (HTC) problems—there was a transfer of learning no matter which of the two problems was presented first. One reason they give for the difference between their results and those of Reed et al. is that the TOH has "an interesting substructure of nested isomorphic subproblems" (p. 130) (see Figure 4.1). What this means is that learning to solve one of the two variants involves decomposing the problem into sub-problems, the solution of which can be used in the other isomorphic problem. The Missionaries and Cannibals variants lack this kind of problem substructure.

We will look first at studies that have examined the extent to which domain-specific knowledge can be transferred. By representing procedures as IF–THEN rules (known as production rules) some researchers claim to be able to predict the extent to which the rules that apply in one area can transfer to another. We will then look at the kinds of domain-general knowledge that can be transferred. This generally refers to strategic knowledge; metacognitive skills such as time, mood, and task management; and learning to learn.

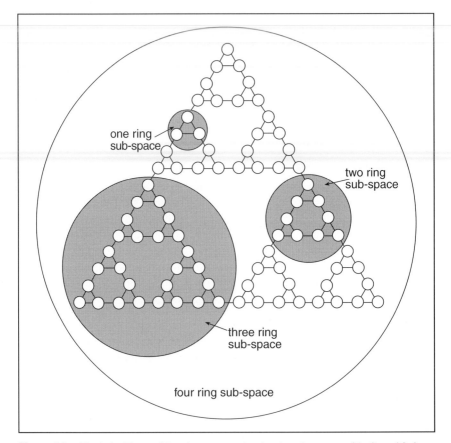

Figure 4.1.   The 4-ring Tower of Hanoi state space showing the substructure of 1-, 2-, and 3-ring sub-spaces. Smaller sub-spaces embedded within larger sub-spaces illustrate the recursive nature of the problem. (Reprinted from *Acta Psychologica*, 1978, Luger and Bauer. "Transfer effects in isomorphic problem situatios," pp. 121–131. © 1978, reprinted with permission from Elsevier Science.)

SPECIFIC TRANSFER

The persistent failure to find transfer effects in many studies of learning unless some kind of hint is given seems to fly in the face of our everyday experience. We are constantly faced with new situations and we constantly use our past experience to deal with these new situations, mostly successfully. We must therefore have learned something from the past and we must be able to use what we learned to cope in the present.

To examine what aspects of past experience we can readily apply to new situations we need a way to characterise or represent that past experience. As mentioned at the beginning of the chapter, one way to think of the similarity between one problem or bit of knowledge is in terms of their shared "elements". When Thorndike referred to identical elements he had in mind a set of stimulus–response associations. Some aspect of the environment would lead to a specific behaviour learned in one context; when the same (perceptually similar) aspect of the environment was encountered later the same behaviour would be elicited even if aspects of the task were slightly different. However, the contexts would have to be awfully similar for the behaviour to be elicited in both. As a result we should expect very little transfer of learning from one situation to another unless the two situations were very similar.

A more recent version of this theory of transfer has been developed by Singley and Anderson (Anderson & Singley, 1993; Singley & Anderson, 1985, 1989). This modified version of the identical elements theory of transfer is known as the identical productions theory of transfer. The emphasis here is on the transfer of skill where a skill can be broken down into individual bits or productions. Before looking at the theory in more detail, the next section gives some background on types of knowledge.

Declarative and procedural knowledge

Assume for the moment that you are learning to drive a car for the first time (or think back to a time when you did not know how to drive). In order to know what to do inside a car you either have to be told or you have to read the instructions for driving this particular car. You might *know that* you have to change from second to third gear but you might not *know how* to do it. *Knowing that* is called **declarative knowledge**. Somehow or other you have to convert that declarative knowledge into a set of actions that will perform a gear change—a procedure for changing gear. Knowledge of how to do something is called **procedural knowledge** (see Information Box 4.1).

Notice that procedural knowledge is not so much either right or wrong as more or less useful (as in the last rule given in Information Box 4.1). The difference between declarative and procedural knowledge can be seen in the example of driving a car. You can memorise the instructions for driving a car so that you are

Information Box 4.1

Declarative and procedural knowledge

Declarative knowledge ("knowing that") is our knowledge of facts, and includes general knowledge about the world as well as episodic and autobiographical knowledge. Examples include:

- Rome is the capital of Italy
- We are coming out of recession
- $e = mc^2$
- Instructions for driving a car or a bike
- I am going to have chicken for dinner

Generally declarative knowledge tends to be either true or false.

Procedural knowledge ("knowing how") is our knowledge of how to do something. This knowledge underlies our skilled performance and is often not accessible to consciousness. That is we can't get back the declarative knowledge from which our procedural knowledge was originally built. Declarative knowledge can be turned into procedural knowledge by stating it as a rule for action: compare the declarative version $e = mc^2$ above with the procedural version below. Examples include:

- How to drive a car or ride a bike
- IF you want to find out the energy (e) in a system
  THEN multiply its mass (m) by the square of the speed of light (c^2)
- IF you want to know if PERSON is a man or a woman
  THEN check to see if PERSON has long hair

word perfect, but this won't make you a skilled driver. In fact, if you have never driven before then you'd be lucky to pull away from the kerb without stalling.

Declarative knowledge can be of three types (Ohlsson & Rees, 1991):

1. **Factual knowledge** such as the instructions for driving a car or any other form of general knowledge. Factual knowledge consists of assertions about specific objects or events such as "The gear lever is currently in second gear".
2. **Episodic knowledge**, in fact a subset of (1), which is knowledge of personal experiences. This kind of knowledge consists of assertions about a specific spatio-temporal context: "The last time I tried to change gear the car stalled".
3. **Abstract knowledge** or general principles. This kind of knowledge can be applied to an infinite number of cases. For example, the arithmetic principle: *A set of numbers always yields the same sum, regardless of the order in which they are added* applies to any set of numbers you like: 3 + 7 + 2956 + 675 will give the same result as 7 + 2956 + 3 + 675.

Procedural knowledge specifies the actions that are to be taken under certain conditions. It often refers to the ability to perform skilled actions. The learner driver may have a great deal of declarative knowledge about the sequences of actions involved when changing gear, but this does not mean that he or she will be able to execute that sequence smoothly when called upon to drive a car for the first time. Procedural knowledge comes about through *practice* at performing the actions of driving. In many theories of problem solving and skill acquisition declarative knowledge is a necessary precursor to procedural knowledge (Anderson, 1983; Byrnes, 1992).

Another distinction that can be made between declarative and procedural knowledge is in terms of the use that can be made of them. The general semantic and episodic forms of declarative knowledge are goal-independent. They can be used in a variety of circumstances and can serve a variety of goals—there is no "commitment" as to how they should be used. Furthermore, declarative knowledge can be true or false: "We are coming out of the recession", "Italy is the capital of the Ukraine", "The button on top of the gear lever operates the ejector seat". Procedural knowledge, on the other hand, can only be understood in terms of the goals one is trying to achieve. It involves the knowledge of what to do given a certain set of circumstances. Rather than being strictly true or false, procedural knowledge is more or less effective in achieving one's goals:

IF the goal is to get to the city centre by 5.00 p.m.
THEN look up the bus timetable
AND walk to the bus stop
AND get on the bus
AND buy a ticket
etc.
IF the goal is to change from second into third gear
AND the car is currently in second gear
THEN put your foot down on the clutch pedal
AND push the gear lever into the neutral position
AND move the gear lever to the right
AND push the gear lever forward into the third position
AND take your foot slowly off the clutch pedal

Note that in these examples, the procedures are ones that have already been learned. In the second example the declarative knowledge has been incorporated into a procedure and a number of individual procedures have been chained together. How declarative knowledge is turned into procedural knowledge in this way is dealt with in Chapter 8 on learning.

Not everyone accepts that there is a rigid distinction between declarative and procedural knowledge (Laird et al., 1987; Newell, 1990; Silver, 1986). Silver (1986), for example, points out that procedural fluency (driving a car) does not have to rest on conceptual fluency (knowledge of internal combustion). He argues that conceptual knowledge is neither necessary nor sufficient for procedural knowledge, but rather that the two are interrelated. Nevertheless, conceptual knowledge can be equated with abstract knowledge, and this type of declarative knowledge may not be the relevant type when considering procedural learning. Procedural learning may still need a solid base of factual and episodic knowledge. Declarative knowledge of the type "Put your hand on the gear lever and push it forward" would be more appropriate.

Identical productions theory of transfer

If we look at learning to drive a car or learning to solve a problem as the acquisition of procedures, then we can begin to look at the question of how knowledge can transfer from one situation to another. Going back again to the infamous car you have been learning to drive, suppose now that it is a left-hand-drive car. Once you have learned to drive this car it should be relatively easy for you to go off and drive another left-hand-drive car. You might find it a bit more difficult to drive a truck, however, or a right-hand-drive car. In each case there are going to be similarities and differences between the new vehicle and the one you learned to drive. The similarities should make it easier to learn to drive the new vehicle. In other words there will be positive transfer from the old context to the new one. Where there are differences between the vehicles in terms of the procedures for driving them you will have to start from scratch to learn some new procedures. Finally, as pointed out near the beginning of the chapter there may even be differences (reversed position of windscreen wiper and indicator levers) that will produce a degree of negative transfer to the new vehicle.

If we can characterise the similarities and differences in terms of specific procedures, can we predict how much will be transferred from one situation to another? Indeed, we can, according to Singley and Anderson (Anderson & Singley, 1993; Singley & Anderson, 1985, 1989). They argued that the theory of identical elements was a useful way of explaining various aspects of transfer, although not quite in the stimulus–response terms that Thorndike proposed. Rather, if one looks at transfer as the overlapping of shared productions (see VanLehn, 1989) then one can make predictions about the effects of learning one task on how well one learns another (Figure 4.2).

Singley and Anderson (1985, 1989) performed a number of experiments looking at text-editing skill. Their subjects learned various screen editors and Singley and Anderson were interested in seeing the effect learning one text editor would have on learning a different one, or the same one with certain changes made to the commands that could be performed. The text-editing tasks were also modelled as a production system. Singley and Anderson found that the number of productions involved in using one text editor could predict the time saved by subjects learning a second text editor. For example, two "line editors" ED and EDT shared a great many productions and there was a consequent high level of transfer from one to the other. However, they shared relatively few productions with a third editor, EMACS, and there was relatively little transfer between the line editors and EMACS. The structure of the experiments is shown Table 4.1.

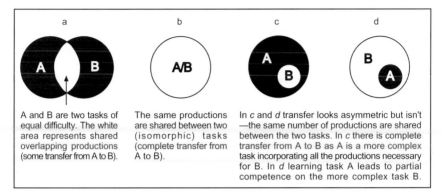

a

A   B

A and B are two tasks of equal difficulty. The white area represents shared overlapping productions (some transfer from A to B).

b

A/B

The same productions are shared between two (isomorphic) tasks (complete transfer from A to B).

c

A
B

In c and d transfer looks asymmetric but isn't —the same number of productions are shared between the two tasks. In c there is complete transfer from A to B as A is a more complex task incorporating all the productions necessary for B. In d learning task A leads to partial competence on the more complex task B.

d

B
A

Figure 4.2.   Four cases where two tasks (A and B in each case) share a number of productions.

TABLE 4.1

Conditions in the text-editing experiments of Singley and Anderson
(Adapted from Anderson & Singley, 1993, p. 189)

	Day		
	1 & 2	*3 & 4*	*5 & 6*
Experiment 1			
One editor	EMACS	EMACS	EMACS
Two editors	ED	ED	EMACS
	EDT	EDT	EMACS
Three editors	ED	EDT	EMACS
	EDT	ED	EMACS
Control	type	type	EMACS
Experiment 2			
Negative transfer	EMACS	Perverse EMACS	EMACS

On day 3 the three-editor group switched from one editor to another. Nevertheless there was no difference in times to perform a number of edits compared to the two-editor groups. In fact the scores for the three-editor group and the two-editor groups remained the same throughout the experiment. There was therefore almost total transfer from one line editor to another. On day 5 all groups switched to EMACS. There was a significant difference between the line-editor groups and the EMACS group, with the latter performing better. However, they were still faster than the EMACS group on day 1 so there had been a small amount of positive transfer.

One of the things to notice from these results is that there seems to be nowhere for negative transfer to fit. Either some productions are shared between task A and task B, in which case there will be at least some speed-up in learning task B, or there isn't. There appears to be no mechanism for negative transfer to take place. Singley and Anderson tested this prediction (Experiment 2 in Table 4.1). They created a version of EMACS where the key assignments were changed round. For example, in EMACS the key combinations Ctrl-D erased a letter, Esc-D erased a word, and Ctrl-N moved down one line. In "Perverse EMACS" Ctrl-D moved down one line and Esc-R erased a letter. There were two groups of subjects: one learned pure EMACS for six days, whereas the other learned EMACS for the first two days, Perverse EMACS on days 3 and 4, and EMACS again on days 5 and 6. Although the performance of the Perverse EMACS group was worse on Day 3, when they switched to Perverse EMACS, then on Day 2, it was still better than on Day 1. In other words what looked like negative transfer was in fact positive, just as the identical elements theory of transfer would predict.

Anderson argues that his ACT-R production system (or indeed most other production-system models) can represent the use of knowledge in a more flexible way than Thorndike's fairly strict theory of identical elements (Singley & Anderson, 1989, p. 112):

> The analysis of transfer in the text-editing experiment has implications for the identical productions model of transfer. The very high level of positive transfer observed between text editors that shared few commands reinforces the position that superficial identical elements models of the type that Thorndike advocated are inadequate.

In other words it is not useful to look at transfer in terms of superficial identical elements but rather in terms of identical productions.

A similar study of transfer effects was carried out by Kieras and Bovair (1986). They examined how their participants converted declarative knowledge, in the form of instructions for carrying out a sequence of actions, into procedural knowledge. They then looked at how well the participants were able to learn new procedures. Their study is covered in Study Box 4.3 and Information Box 4.2.

If a procedure can be broken down and described in detail, that is in terms of specific production rules, then any effort required to learn a new related procedure depends on how different a new production is from previously learned ones. As was mentioned earlier, declarative knowledge is not "committed". Once embedded in a production it is committed because it is used to achieve a specific goal. If the *use* of the knowledge changes then there is likely to be very little transfer even if the use of knowledge in the two situations relies on the same basic facts (declarative knowledge) (Pennington & Rehder, 1996).

Given the identical productions view of transfer, how can we account for the effects of Einstellung described, for example, by Luchins and Luchins and Sweller (see Study Box 3.2 and Study Box 4.1). One way of explaining aspects of negative transfer is by assuming that the features of a problem remind one of a procedure that worked in the past. Set effects are caused by accessing irrelevant procedures. They persist either because there is no feedback about what they should do to get a correct answer, or because they get a correct answer albeit in an unnecessarily laborious way. Singley and Anderson did not find negative transfer because their subjects were not kept in the dark about what they should do.

Study Box 4.3

Kieras and Bovair (1986)

Background

Kieras & Bovair were interested in how the model of cognitive skill acquisition proposed by Anderson could be examined. In particular they wanted to find out (a) how declarative knowledge as represented by the instructions for carrying out various procedures were converted into production rules; and (b) if a representation of procedural knowledge in terms of production rules allows one to predict the amount of transfer from one task to a related one.

Method

Participants had to learn a number of procedures for controlling a device (shown in Figure 4.3). There were two "normal" procedures and eight "malfunction" procedures. Examples are taken from Kieras and Bovair (1986, pp. 508–509).

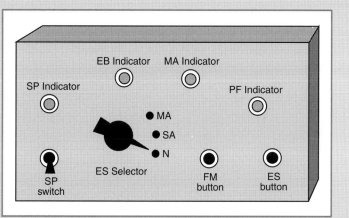

Figure 4.3.   Control panel device (adapted from Kieras & Bovair, 1986).

Example of a normal procedure:

If the command is to do the MA procedure, then do the following:

Step 1. Turn the SP switch to ON.
Step 2. Set the ES selector to MA.
Step 3. Press the FM button, and then release it.
Step 4. If the PF indicator flashes, then notice that the operation is successful.
Step 5. When the PF indicator stops flashing, set the ES selector to N.
Step 6. Turn the SP switch to OFF.
Step 7. If the procedure was successful, then type "S" for success.
Step 8. Procedure is finished.

Study Box 4.3 (continued)

Example of a malfunction procedure:

If the command is to do the MA procedure, then do the following:

Step 1.   Turn the SP switch to ON.
Step 2.   Set the ES selector to MA.
Step 3.   Press the FM button, and then release it.
Step 4.   If the PF indicator does not flash, then notice that there is a malfunction.
Step 5.   If the EB indicator is on, and the MA indicator is off, then notice that the malfunction might be compensated for.
Step 6.   Set the ES selector to SA.
Step 7.   Press the FS button, and then release it.
Step 8.   If the PF indicator does not flash, then notice that the malfunction cannot be compensated for.
Step 9.   Set the ES selector to N.
Step 10. Turn the SP switch to OFF.
Step 11. If the malfunction could not be compensated for, then type "N" for not compensated.
Step 12. Procedure is finished.

To take account of the possibility that there might be an order effect, there were three different training orders. Participants had to perform each procedure correctly three times in a row before moving on to the next procedure.

A program in LISP was written to simulate transfer effects on the basis of the production rules involved. To get a flavour of what a production system model of a task is like see Information Box 4.1. Kieras and Bovair's simulation program reported "the number of rules considered identical to existing rules, the number that could be generalized with existing rules, and the number of new rules added to the total" (1986, p. 513).

Results and discussion

There was a very great deal of overlap between the observed performance of the participants and the effects predicted by the simulation program. Furthermore the length of time required to learn a new procedure depends on the number of new production rules that have to be learned. For this particular training order the length of time to learn new procedures levels off, as later procedures require no or only one or two new procedures. (Other training orders reveal a different zig-zag pattern depending on the number of new productions that have to be learned.) As the simulation program is based on a production system representation of the rules for carrying out the procedures, and given the degree of agreement between the observed and predicted values, Kieras and Bovair argue that "a production rule representation can provide a very precise characterisation of the relative difficulty of learning a set of related procedures" (p. 507) and that "the amount of transfer is predicted very well from the similarities between the production system representations for the procedures" (p. 507).

Example of production rules from Kieras and Bovair (1986)

```
(MA-N-START
IF (AND (TEST-GOAL DO MA PROCEDURE)
    NOT (TEST-GOAL DO ??? STEP)))
THEN ((ADD-GOAL DO SP-ON STEP)))
(MA-N-SP-ON
IF (AND (TEST-GOAL DO MA PROCEDURE)
    (TEST-GOAL DO SP-ON STEP))
THEN ((OPERATE-CONTROL *SP ON)
    (WAIT-FOR-DEVICE)
    (DELETE-GOAL DO SP-ON STEP)
    (ADD-GOAL DO ES-SELECT STEP)))
(MA-N-ES-SELECT
IF (AND (TEST-GOAL DO MA PROCEDURE)
    (TEST-GOAL DO ES-SELECT STEP))
THEN ((OPERATE-CONTROL *ESS MA)
    (WAIT-FOR-DEVICE)
    (DELETE-GOAL DO ES-SELECT STEP)
    (ADD-GOAL DO FM-PUSH STEP)))
(MA-N-FM-PUSH
IF (AND (TEST-GOAL DO MA PROCEDURE)
    (TEST-GOAL DO FM-PUSH STEP))
THEN ((OPERATE-CONTROL *FM PUSH)
    (WAIT-FOR-DEVICE)
    (OPERATE-CONTROL *FM RELEASED)
    (DELETE-GOAL DO FM-PUSH STEP)
    (ADD-GOAL DO PFI-CHECK STEP)))
(MA-N-PFI-CHECK
IF (AND (TEST-GOAL DO MA PROCEDURE)
    (TEST-GOAL DO PFI-CHECK STEP)
    (LOOK *PFI FLASHING))
THEN ((ADD-NOTE OPERATION SUCCESSFUL)
    (DELETE-GOAL DO PFI-CHECK STEP)
    (ADD-GOAL DO ES-N STEP)))
(MA-N-ES-N
IF (AND (TEST-GOAL DO MA PROCEDURE)
    (TEST-GOAL DO ES-N STEP)
    (LOOK *PFI OFF))
THEN ((OPERATE-CONTROL *ESS N)
    (WAIT-FOR-DEVICE)
    (DELETE-GOAL DO ES-N STEP)
    (ADD-GOAL DO SP-OFF STEP)))
(MA-N-SP-OFF
IF (AND (TEST-GOAL DO MA PROCEDURE)
    (TEST-GOAL DO SP-OFF STEP))
THEN ((OPERATE-CONTROL *SP OFF)
    (WAIT-FOR-DEVICE)
    (DELETE-GOAL DO SP-OFF STEP)
    (ADD-GOAL DO TAP STEP)))
(MA-N-TAP
IF (AND (TEST-GOAL DO MA PROCEDURE)
    (TEST-GOAL DO TAP STEP)
    (TEST-NOTE OPERATION SUCCESSFUL))
THEN ((DELETE-NOTE OPERATION SUCCESSFUL)
    (ADD-NOTE TYPE S-FOR SUCCESS)
    (DELETE-GOAL DO TAP STEP)
    (ADD-GOAL DO FINISH STEP)))
```

Name of rule: MA-N-START
Condition: If the goal is to do the MA procedure AND you haven't started on any step yet
Action: THEN add the goal to do the SP-N step to WM

Name of rule: MA-N-SP-ON
Condition: If the goal is to do the MA procedure AND to do the SP-ON step
Action: THEN turn the SP switch to ON
wait for the device to respond
delete the goal to do the SP-ON step
and add the goal to do the ES-SELECT step

Name of rule: MA-N-ES-SELECT
Condition: If the goal is to do the MA procedure AND to do the ES-SELECT step
Action: THEN turn the ESS to MA
wait for the device to respond
delete the goal to do the ES-SELECT step
and add the goal to do the FM-PUSH step

There is evidence that an identical elements view of transfer is not the whole story. Payne, Squibb, and Howes (1990) gave subjects a set of a text-editing tasks and looked at transfer between two text editors. They found evidence for conceptual transfer. That is, subjects given one type of text editor (MacWrite) induced the concept of a string (strings of characters including blank spaces and punctuation) and were able to transfer this conceptual knowledge to a task involving another editor (IBM Personal Editor). This was despite the fact that the specific procedures for editing were different. "This aspect of transfer is not readily admitted in the common elements/productions model of transfer and is outside the scope of any model of user knowledge in which methods are the only encoding of expertise" (Payne et al., p. 442).

GENERAL TRANSFER

The discussion so far has looked at specific transfer from one problem to a similar problem of the same type where there is some overlap in the use of knowledge required. General transfer may include advice about how to choose operators, about looking at extreme conditions, changing representations, loosening constraints, focusing on different aspects of a problem, generating an analogy, and so on. Other domain-general skills such as essay writing, using information and communication technology, writing reports and the like, rely on learning sets of **schemas**. A schema is a knowledge structure composed of bits of semantic knowledge and the relations between them. Your knowledge about houses, for example, would include the fact that they have roofs, windows, walls, a door. It's hard to imagine a house without one of these features. These are the "fixed values" that would be incorporated into a house schema. You can also use your knowledge of houses to understand me if I tell you I have locked myself out. You can mentally represent my predicament because you know that houses have doors and doors have locks that need keys. These are "default" assumptions you can make. So if information is missing from an account you can fill in the missing bits from your general knowledge of houses—your house schema. Now it could be that I have locked myself out because I have forgotten one of these fancy push button locks and I forgot the number, but it's not what you would immediately assume.

Schemas have been proposed for a number of domains including problem solving. With experience of houses, or cinema-going, or "distance = rate x time" problems, you learn to recognise and classify them, and to have certain expectations about, for example, what goes on in a cinema or what you are likely to have to do to solve a particular type of problem.

Schemas are abstractions from our everyday experience and can be at different levels of abstraction. But what about transfer at a fairly abstract level? Are there aspects of some problems that can be transferred to other problems that are completely different?

Representational transfer

These questions have been explored by Laura Novick (Novick, 1990; Novick & Hmelo, 1994). Whereas analogical problem solving is normally thought of as looking back to an earlier problem to find a solution procedure that can be used in the current problem, representational transfer is where a useful way of representing a problem is transferred where there is no common solution procedure.

Novick and Hmelo (1994) examined four types of representation: networks, hierarchies, matrices, and part–whole representations (see Figure 4.4). They found that having access to appropriate representational schemas allowed solvers to transfer their learning of these schemas to new problems whose underlying structures lent themselves to a particular symbolic representation.

In Chapter 2, I mentioned that Wertheimer made a distinction between reproductive and productive thinking. Reproductive thinking involves "blindly" using previously learned knowledge to solve a problem or perform a task without necessarily taking into account the underlying structure of the problem. Productive thinking, on the other hand, needs an understanding of the deeper structure of a problem. Now it has been found that "good students" often engage in "self-explanations" (Chi et al., 1989; Chi & Bassok, 1989; Chi, de Leeuw, Chiu, & LaVancher, 1994) when learning new material, and that these explanations seem to allow those students to gain a more elaborate representation of the material they

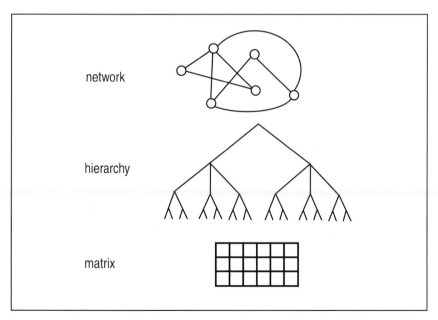

Figure 4.4. Three types of diagrammatic representations (adapted from Novick & Hmelo, 1994, p. 1299). Copyright © 1994 by the American Psychological Association. Adapted with permission.

are learning and hence a better understanding of a problem's structure. Further problem solving and transfer is thereby enhanced. On the other hand, when students attempt to learn something difficult for the first time, especially when the explanations given are relatively poor, then any transfer is likely to be limited to declarative knowledge, as few procedures have been learned (Robertson, 2000; Robertson & Kahney, 1996). Robertson (2000) found that transfer in such circumstances tended to be limited to those bits of declarative information that could be readily mapped across from one problem to another because they looked the same.

According to Pennington and Rehder (1996, p. 265) what the foregoing discussion suggests is that:

> learning by rote results in transfer to highly similar problems (i.e., procedural transfer) but learning by "understanding" results in transfer to less similar or novel problems as well [...] In the same way that information-processing concepts have allowed identical elements theories of transfer to progress from the early formulations, further investigation of the details of declarative elaboration and its translation into effective procedures may assist in bringing "understanding" as well into a theory of transfer.

Implicit transfer

Recent studies have shown that transfer need not involve the explicit mapping of one problem onto a source analogue. Schunn and Dunbar (1996), for example, found that knowledge of a concept in one domain could be spontaneously transferred to another domain despite large differences in the surface features of the problems in the two domains. One group of subjects was given a computer simulation of a problem in biochemistry designed to illustrate the role of inhibition. A control group was given a similar task not involving inhibition. Next day both groups were given a task in the domain of molecular genetics. The concept of inhibition was also relevant to this task. Schunn and Dunbar found that the experimental group who had been given the inhibition problem the previous day was more likely to find a solution than the control group. Concurrent verbal protocols and post-task questionnaires revealed that the subjects were unaware that they were using the relevant concept (inhibition) from the earlier domain. Schunn and Dunbar interpret these finding as evidence for conceptual priming. They point out, however, that only a single relation was involved rather than a system of relations. As analogical reasoning involves using a system of relations it is computationally expensive. Priming, on the other hand, "is computationally inexpensive and does not require a complex mental structure to occur" (p. 272).

WHAT KINDS OF KNOWLEDGE TRANSFER?

The discussion so far has shown that knowledge or skill can be transferred from one domain to another only under certain circumstances. Larkin (1989) has reframed the question of what transfers as: To what extent does domain-general knowledge transfer from one context to another, and to what extent can domain-specific knowledge transfer? The answer to the latter question would appear to depend on the overlap of the elements of a skill shared by two different tasks. As to the former, it depends on what kind of knowledge is being referred to. Domain- general knowledge is really knowledge about useful strategies—means–ends analysis, hill climbing, and so on. Singley and Anderson (1985) have pointed out that such knowledge is well known to most adults anyway. Improving such skills (in some general problem-solving course, say) may be difficult and would not lead to much of an improvement when someone has to learn a new domain. Furthermore, Larkin points out that the domain-specific knowledge that someone needs to solve problems far outweighs the domain-general knowledge that a person needs.

For example, domains such as calculus or experimental design involve a lot of domain-specific problem-solving skills and relatively few domain-general skills. If you spend time improving your domain-general skills then you are only going to make a small improvement to a small part of the skills used in the domain. On the other hand, if you had spent your time learning the domain-specific skills then you would probably have improved your grade even more.

A debate about whether—or even if—knowledge and skill can transfer from one domain or context to another has been going on in the pages of the journal *Educational Researcher*. Proponents of **situated learning** emphasise the degree to which learning is bound to a specific context, particularly a social context (Cobb & Bowers, 1999; Greeno, Moore, & Smith, 1993; Lave & Wenger, 1991). In one famous case Carraher, Carraher, and Schliemann (1985) showed that Brazilian street children were able to perform complex mathematical calculation in the street but not in a school context.

Anderson, Reder, and Simon (1996) reject a strong version of this claim that all knowledge, both specific and general, does not transfer. Learning to read in a classroom does not mean you can't read outside it. Learning arithmetic in school does not mean that you can't make calculations in a supermarket. Furthermore, as we have seen in this chapter, "there can be a large amounts of transfer, a modest amount, no transfer at all, or even negative transfer" (Anderson et al., 1996, p. 8).

Lave and Wenger (1991) regard learning as "legitimate peripheral participation". By this is meant that the acquisition of knowledge and skill involves engaging in the socio-cultural practices of the community of which a learner is a part. Thus you cannot and should not extract the learning from the social context in which it is embedded. Again, Anderson et al. beg to differ and see no problem in a tax accountant learning tax code separately from interacting with a client. Learning to use a calculator does not require a client, or anyone else for that matter, to be present.

As you may realise, this is far from being an academic debate. The effectiveness of and the prerequisites for transfer are fundamental to how we educate our children.

SUMMARY

1. Transfer is fundamental to the educational process. We assume that what is learned in a classroom can transfer to situations outside the classroom. However, there is a lot of debate about the extent to which this can happen.
2. Transfer comes in various flavours:

   - Positive transfer means that learning something in one context makes learning something new easier.
   - Negative transfer means that learning something in one context makes learning something new harder.
   - Both positive and negative transfer occur because of the same underlying learning processes (e.g., skill learning)—it may be that a particular situation is inappropriate for the skill leading to negative transfer.
   - Specific transfer is the most frequent type of transfer and occurs when there is an overlap of the specific knowledge used in two situations.
   - General transfer occurs when general strategies for problem solving or representational schemas are learned in one context and can be applied in a (superficially) completely different one.
   - Implicit transfer occurs when there is conceptual priming, i.e., a piece of declarative (conceptual) knowledge is carried over unconsciously from one domain to another when there is little delay between presentation of the two situations.

3. People find it difficult to transfer what they have learned in one context to another context unless:

   - a hint is provided to use the earlier problem;
   - the earlier problem is harder than the current one;
   - there is a clear goal–sub-goal structure that maps across from one problem to another;
   - solvers can represent the problems in a "useful" way;
   - the two problems share productions and the problems are seen as similar;
   - two different domains share the same knowledge (e.g., a knowledge of mathematics gained while learning physics would make learning chemistry easier; or, at a more abstract level, two different domains may share the same forms of argument or rationale—e.g., scientific method in the case of chemistry and physics);
   - one is aware of and can access general strategies for representing problem types.

4. The relative roles of domain-specific knowledge, domain-general knowledge, and the effects of context on learning are extremely important for educational practice.

CHAPTER FIVE

Problem similarity

Love is like the measles—all the worse when it comes late in life

Douglas Jerrold

Love is like quicksilver in the hand. Leave the fingers open and it stays. Close it and it darts away

Attributed to Dorothy Parker

Love is like war: easy to begin but very hard to stop

H.L. Mencken

In these examples love is being likened to something else. In each case the similarity between love and that other thing is explained. At one level, of course, love is nothing like the thing it is being compared with. Love is not a dense silver metal that is liquid at room temperature; it does not normally bring you out in a rash; it does not normally involve tanks, artillery, and death. The similarity therefore lies somewhere else: at a "deeper" level. In his discussion of metaphors Black (1993, p. 30) has stated: "Every metaphor is the tip of a submerged model". (I include similies such as the examples at the beginning of the chapter in my discussion of metaphor.)

Clearly, if we are to understand what is going on when analogies are noticed and used, we need some way to describe what is meant by "similarity". That is, we need some way to express precisely in what way two (or more) problems or ideas can be said to be similar and in what ways they can be said to differ. We will look first at the similarities between ideas or concepts, and then at the similarities between the relations linking concepts before looking at the similarities between problems that involve complex systems of relations.

are temporarily strengthened and others, weakened. It is thus hard for the system to take a detour, as it were, through a "weakened" link which may lead to a solution. In such cases it may be best to forget about the problem (or the name of that actress that is on the tip of your tongue) until the strengthened links have dropped back to their resting state. You may then find that the answer you have been looking for unexpectedly "pops" into your head. In problem solving this phenomenon is known as **incubation** (see Simon, 1966; Yaniv & Meyer, 1987, for different explanations of incubation). Spreading activation is a mechanism proposed by Ohlsson (1992) to explain how we might find solutions to insight problems (see Chapter 3).

In analogical problem solving objects that are seen as semantically similar are more likely to be mapped across. The mapping of related objects from one situation to another is illustrated in Table 5.3.

TABLE 5.3

Mapping similar objects

Source	⇨ (maps to)	Target
Identical objects		
car	⇨	car
Similar (semantically related) objects		
car	⇨	truck
laser beams	⇨	X-rays

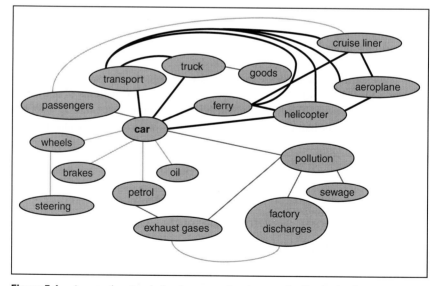

Figure 5.4.   A semantic network showing connections between "car" and other forms of transport (black lines). Other links have been inhibited (grey lines).

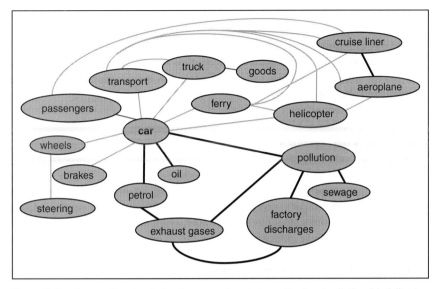

Figure 5.5.   A semantic network showing connections between "car" and pollution (black lines). Other links have been inhibited (grey lines).

If you are on a picnic and find you have a bottle of wine and no corkscrew, you may remember that you read once in a problem-solving book about a way to remove a cork with a piece of string and a pencil. However, having searched your pockets you can only come up with a biro and a thin piece of electric cable you just happen to have with you. It is very probable that you would realise that you can substitute the biro for the pencil and the electric cable for the string. When objects are strongly semantically related they often also share a number of features. Not only can objects be similar in the sense of belonging to the same category but they can also be similar because they share the same properties. Now you may have noticed that string and electric cable are not particularly close in terms of function or category membership. If you didn't notice, it is probably because they are very similar in terms of their shared properties or **attributes**. Both are relatively long, both are very thin, both are flexible. In problems that involve vehicles it is usually the functional aspects of vehicles that are important—vehicles are for carrying things from point A to point B. With the biro and pencil mapping it is not the fact that both belong to the same category or have the same sort of function that is important in solving the problem, but rather that both are fairly narrow and rigid.

Objects can be alike, then, because they share some important attributes and those attributes may (or may not) be useful in solving problems. Semantically related objects are likely to share several attributes in common. A tomato and a strawberry are similar in that both are red, edible, soft, sweet, and contain seeds. On the other hand, objects that are semantically unrelated can have attributes in which can be represented in natural language as "Joe opened the wine bottle", can also be represented by:

opened (Joe, wine_bottle).

In this example there are two slot fillers, and the term before the brackets is a relation rather than an attribute. The relations and attributes that are outside the brackets are collectively known as **predicates**. The things inside the brackets are **arguments**. A predicate can have many arguments. The verb "give", for example, involves a giver, a receiver, and an object that is given. "Charles gave Daphne a bunch of flowers" can be represented as:

gave (Charles, Daphne, bunch_of_flowers).

It is because we can understand the nature of relational similarity that we can make sense of analogies such as "Currency speculation is the AIDS of the world economy". In Table 5.1 "AIDS" was shown as mapping onto "currency speculation". However, this is a bit of a simplification. The point of making the analogy in the first place was because we expected to infer from the statement that currency speculation has a debilitating effect on the world economy and that there is nothing much that can be done about it. How are we able to make these inferences? In fact, there is something missing from the statement that we have to put back in. AIDS is not a disease that affects the world economy. It affects human beings. So another way of understanding the statement is to read it as "Currency speculation bears the same relation to the world economy as AIDS does to human beings". Before analysing the implications of this kind of analogy, I am going to take you on a brief diversion into proportional analogies.

Proportional analogies

Proportional analogies are the kinds of items often found in IQ tests. They often take the form:

2 : 4 :: 6 : ? ("2 is to 4 as 6 is to ?"—"what is the relation between 2 and 4, and what would you get if you applied it to 6")

You are then given four options:

a.   8
b.   7
c.   9
d.   12

The difference between 6 and whatever the answer is, is the same "proportion" as the difference between 2 and 4. The goal is to work out what the relation is between 2 and 4 and apply that relation to the 6. You have to infer a relation between the 2 and the 4 and generalise it to the 6. In fact several relations can be inferred from the first part of the analogy. The relation could be "increase by 2", or "double", or any "higher number". If you infer that the relation is "increase by 2" and you apply that to the 6 then the answer would be 8; if you infer that the relation is "double" then the answer is 12; and so on. Verbal analogies are of the same form, as in:

cat : kitten :: dog : ?

Proportional analogies of the form A : B :: C : D are known as 4-term analogies. The processes involved in solving proportional analogies are dealt with in more detail later. In the mean time we shall be looking at a simpler, if not simplistic, model for the purposes of illustrating relational mappings. Suppose you were asked to complete the 3-term analogy:

hot : cold :: dry : ?

First of all you would have to know what the words meant (Figure 5.6a). Based on the information you retrieve about the words, you can generate a hypothesis about the likely relation between "hot" and "cold" (Figure 5.6b). You would then attempt to apply this relation to "dry" (Figure 5.6c) and generate the answer "wet" (Figure 5.6d). By inferring or inducing a relation between "hot" and "cold" you create the structure:

opposite_of (hot, cold).

This inference process is known as *induction*. When you come to apply it to another item in the analogy you are generalising from that one instance. This gives rise to the structure:

opposite_of (A, B).

Applying a generalisation to a specific instance is known as *deduction*. Indeed, you can apply this structure to items other than "dry" to generate:

opposite_of (tall, *short*),
opposite_of (fat, *thin*), etc.

In these examples it is the relation that is being mapped across from the source to the target, and the items that are inside the brackets are largely irrelevant except to establish the relation in the first place and to provide the specific instance to which the relation should be applied.

We are now in a better position to understand Jacques Chirac's analogy: "Currency speculation is the AIDS of the world economy". Whereas establishing the higher-order relation "opposite_of" was a means to the end of establishing the missing term, in Jacques Chirac's analogy the end is to establish the higher-order relation itself. In other words, if you understand the effects of AIDS then you can understand the effects of currency speculation on the world economy (Figure 5.7).

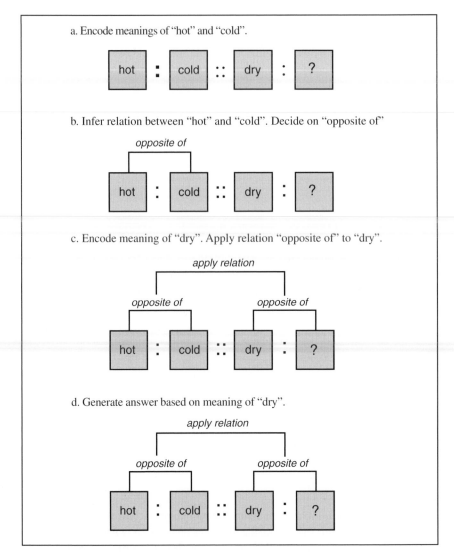

Figure 5.6.   A summary of processes needed to solve the analogy: hot : cold :: dry : ?

Relational similarity: Reproductive or productive?

Earlier I mentioned that the preliminary requirement to finding a relation between two concepts was a search through our semantic system. One of the features of the metaphors just discussed is that two ideas have been juxtaposed *that may never have been juxtaposed before*. Generating such analogies and, indeed, understanding them is a creative ability. Compare the following two analogies.

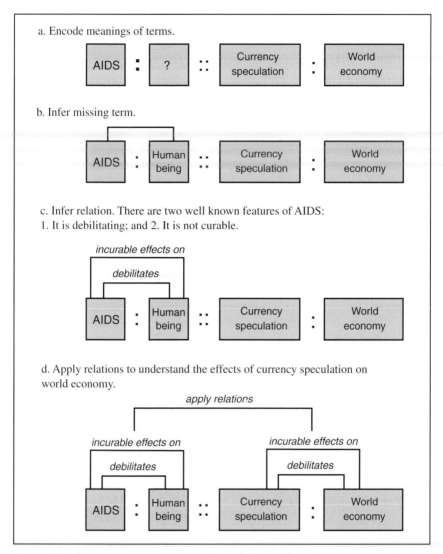

a. Encode meanings of terms.

b. Infer missing term.

c. Infer relation. There are two well known features of AIDS:
1. It is debilitating; and 2. It is not curable.

d. Apply relations to understand the effects of currency speculation on world economy.

Figure 5.7.   Relational mappings used to understand effects of those relations in a target domain.

1.   uncle : nephew :: aunt : ?
2.   alcohol : proof :: gold : ?

In the first case there is a well known set of relations between uncle and nephew. The latter is the offspring of the former's brother or sister. Both are male. The next item, "aunt", invites us to generate a parallel known relation for a female offspring. We are reconstructing known sets of relations when we complete this analogy.

> **Activity 5.2**
>
> Using Figure 5.7 as a model, how would you analyse the metaphor: "The Falklands thing was a fight between two bald men over a comb". (Answer on p. 236)

In the second case, as in the case of metaphors, the solver has possibly never juxtaposed these items before. Any solution the solver generates will therefore be constructed for the very first time. That is, the similarity between the relations (here the second item is a measure of the purity of the first item) is a novel one. Indeed if we couldn't invent new relations on the spur of the moment, then we wouldn't be able to understand what Jacques Chirac was going on about. For this reason, our ability to generate and understand a presumably infinite number of possible relations is seen as a productive ability (Bejar, Chaffin, & Embretson, 1991; Chaffin & Herrmann, 1988; Johnson-Laird, Herrmann, & Chaffin, 1984).

Relational elements theory

Bejar et al. (1991) argue that relations are of two types: those that the person generating the relation already knows, and those that have to be constructed on the spot. "The variety of relations suggests that people are capable of recognizing an indefinitely large number of distinct semantic relations. In this case, the explicit listing of all possible relations required in a network representation of relations will not be possible" (p. 18).

Bejar et al. argue that theories of concept formation and representation do not readily explain how relations can be generated. Johnson-Laird (1989) said something similar when he argued that finding relevant relations (category membership relations) was an algorithmic process. However, the "deep" analogies involved in complex problem solving or in understanding a new domain required further explanation.

Bejar and co-workers' (1991) theory covers A : B :: C : D analogies where A and B are given and the subject has to choose from alternative C : D pairs which ones are similar. They provide evidence that people can readily evaluate the similarity of relations fairly quickly (Bejar et al., 1991, p. 26).

> The fact that people evaluate the similarity of relations is important because it implies that relations are decomposable into more primitive elements. To judge that two things are similar it is necessary to identify ways in which they are the same and ways in which they are different (Tversky, 1977). The aphorism "You can't compare apples and oranges" expresses this point. Apples and oranges cannot be compared if they are considered to be unitary, unanalysable wholes. On the other hand, if they are decomposed into aspects in which they are the same—size, shape, nutritional value —and different—texture, taste, color—then the comparison can be made. The ability to readily compare relations means that relations are readily decomposable into more primitive elements.

Bejar et al. give the example of types of "inclusion relations". These include: *spatial inclusion* where something is *in* something else (MILK : BOTTLE);

part–whole inclusion where something is *part of* something else (ENGINE : CAR); and *class inclusion* where something is *an example of* something else (ROBIN : BIRD). These three inclusion relations vary in their complexity. Spatial inclusion is fairly simple and refers to something being in, on, under, etc., something. Part–whole inclusion not only requires that something be in, on, under, etc., something but also that the part is *connected* to the whole in some way. Bejar et al. go onto argue that class inclusion involves one object being in the set of some general (superordinate) category, being connected to that category, and further: having certain features that make the object *similar* to the general category. These inclusion relations can therefore be characterised by three **relational elements**: <inclusion>, <connection>, and <similarity>.

The inclusion relations can have one or more of these relational elements. If you want to compare relations this can only be done on the basis of *shared* relational elements. Bejar et al. give the following examples:

| part–whole | The wheel is part of the bike | <inclusion, connection> |
| spatial | The bike is in the garage | <inclusion> |

You can look upon these statements as premises and draw conclusions from them. However, the conclusions can only be based on the shared relational elements. In other words, we can readily infer that if the wheel is part of the bike and the bike is in the garage then the wheel must be in the garage, too. However, we would not readily conclude that the wheel is part of the garage. This is because only the relational element <inclusion> is common to both statements.

| spatial | The wheel is in the garage | <inclusion> |
| part–whole | The wheel is part of the garage | <inclusion, connection> |

By breaking down relations into "relational elements" Bejar et al. were able to divide a very large number of IQ test items into 10 categories which varied in difficulty. In fact, they argued that the processes involved in solving the analogy problems were different for different categories.

Most other models of proportional analogies downplay the role of semantics (e.g., Pellegrino & Glaser, 1982). However, Bejar et al. found that the semantic characteristics of the test items were important determinants of how easily the items were likely to be solved. Variations in the semantic features of the relations explain much of the individual differences between subjects on verbal analogy IQ tests.

Furthermore, Sternberg and Nigro (1983, p. 36) used proportional analogies as a means of investigating how metaphors in general are understood:

On the present theory, an interaction between tenor [target] and vehicle [source] occurs when the semantic subspace containing the tenor of a metaphor is mentally superimposed upon the semantic subspace containing the vehicle of a metaphor [...] in some cases this mapping results is a shift in one's perception of the respective natures of the tenor and vehicle.

STRUCTURAL SIMILARITY

So far we have seen that two things can be seen as similar if they are closely semantically related (e.g., trucks and vans); they can also be similar if they share the same attributes (yellow trucks and yellow books); and the relations between objects can also be regarded as similar. We have been climbing up a hierarchy of similarity, as it were. However, we can go even further and look at similarity between even more complex structures. The best example of how similar hierarchical structures can be mapped can be seen in the work of Dedre Gentner.

Gentner's structure-mapping theory

According to Dedre Gentner, an analogy is not simply saying that one thing is like another. "Puppies are like kittens" or "milk is like water" are not analogies. They are in Gentner's terms "literally similar" because they share the same attributes, such as "small" in the first case and "liquid" in the second, as well as the same relations. Gentner (e.g., Falkenhainer, Forbus, & Gentner, 1989; Gentner, 1989; Gentner & Toupin, 1986) and Vosniadou (1989) argue that "real" analogies involve a causal relation. In the analogy "puppies are to dogs as kittens are to cats", there is a relation between "puppies" and "dogs" which also applies between "kittens" and "cats", and this relation can readily be explained. An analogy properly so-called involves mapping an explanatory structure from a base (source) domain (puppies and dogs) to a target (kittens and cats).

Analogising, according to Gentner (1983), involves mapping a relational structure that holds in one domain onto another. This is known as the principle of **systematicity**, which states that people prefer to map hierarchical systems of relations in which the higher-order relations constrain the lower-order ones. In other words, it is only because we can infer that two bald men fighting over a comb is pointless that we can map the bald men to Britain and Argentina and the comb to the Falklands *and* generate the assumption that the fight was pointless.

The structure-mapping theory is implemented as the Structure Mapping Engine (Falkenhainer et al., 1989) and uses a **predicate calculus** of various orders to represent the structure of an analogy. At the lowest order, order 0, are the objects of the analogy (the salient surface features), such as "army", "fortress", "roads", "general". When an example is being used as an analogy, the objects in one domain are assumed to be "put in correspondence with" the objects in another to obtain the best match that fits the structure of the analogy.

At the next level the objects at level 0 can become arguments to a predicate. So "army" and "fortress" can be related using the predicate "attack" giving "attack(army, fortress)". This would have order 1.

A predicate has the order 1 plus the maximum of the order of its arguments. "Army" and "fortress" are order 0; "greater_than (X, Y)" would be order 1; but

"CAUSE[greater_than(X, Y), break(Y)]" would be order 2, because at least one of its arguments is already order 1.

CAUSE, IMPLIES, and DEPENDS ON are typical higher-order relations. "On this definition, the order of an item indicates the depth of structure below it. Arguments with many layers of justifications will give rise to representation structures of higher order" (Gentner, 1989, p. 208).

Mapping an explanatory structure allows one to make inferences in the new domain or problem, as the relations that apply in the source can be applied in the target. Notice that the inferences are based on purely structural grounds. A structure such as: CAUSE [STRIKE (ORANGE, TREE), FLATTEN (ORANGE)] can be used in a Tom and Jerry cartoon to decide what happens when Tom smashes into a tree—CAUSE [STRIKE (TOM, TREE), ?]— to generate the inference CAUSE [STRIKE (TOM, TREE), FLATTEN (TOM)]. The missing part concerning what happens when Tom strikes a tree can be filled in by referring to the structure expressing what happens when an orange hits the tree. The predicate FLATTEN (ORANGE) is inserted into the target with ORANGE mapped to TOM.

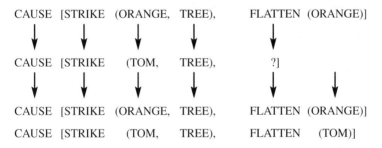

For Gentner, analogising involves a one-to-one systematic mapping of the structure of the base domain onto the target. The surface features—the object descriptions—are not mapped onto the target because they play no role in the relational structure of the analogy. For example, the colour of the orange or of Jerry is irrelevant because it plays no part in the structure. The problems dealt with by Gick and Holyoak (1980, 1983) are therefore analogous under this definition.

Some researchers are happy to give analogy a very broad definition (e.g., Anderson & Thompson, 1989). Holyoak (1985), for example, refers to analogies as ranging from the "mundane to the metaphorical". However, Gentner (e.g., 1989) is much stricter in her definition. She provides a taxonomy of similarities between problems in which analogy is distinct from other types of similarity (Falkenhainer et al., 1989; Gentner, 1989; Gentner et al., 1993). Figure 5.8 shows different types of similarity and where they might lie on a continuum (see also Gentner, 1989, p. 207).

Literal similarity.   Literal similarity is almost always found in within-domain comparisons. When two problems or situations are literally similar, both the

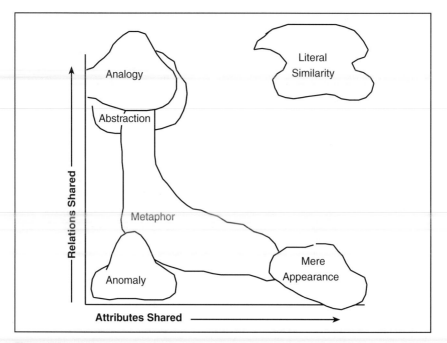

Figure 5.8.   Similarity space: Classes of similarity based on the kinds of predicates shared. (From Gentner, 1989, p. 207. Reproduced by permission of Cambridge University Press).

structure of the problem and the surface features (or attributes) are similar. You tend to find literal similarity in within-domain comparisons. In the example "milk is like water" many of the attributes of water can also be applied to milk. There is a fuzzy boundary between what is technically analogy, where just the relational structure is shared between problems, and literal similarity which also includes object descriptions.

Mere appearance match.   With mere appearance match only the lower-order predicates match. The relational structure is ignored. Gentner gives the example "the glass tabletop gleamed like water" in which only the physical description is shared between the source and target. She claims that novices are prone to mere appearance matches (see Chapter 9).

Abstraction mapping.   Abstraction mapping involves mapping variables or abstract principles to a target such as "heat is a through variable". Abstraction mapping assumes prior knowledge on the part of the reader because, as in the example just given, the abstraction can be used to categorise a problem or instantiate a procedure or rule. Abstraction mapping also forms a continuum with analogy.

Mapping one structure on to another

Gentner and her co-workers have produced a great deal of evidence to back up her claim that analogising comes about by mapping entire relational structures. Study Box 5.1 gives one example by Gentner and Toupin (1986). In Gentner and Toupin's study, where the children understood the story's underlying rationale, they were able to adapt their characters to fit the story's structure. The rest of the time they simply imitated the sequence of actions taken by the semantically similar counterparts in the earlier story. The younger children may not have had an adequate understanding of the earlier story to be able to apply the rationale behind it.

These results do not confine themselves to children. Gentner and Schumacher (1987; Schumacher & Gentner, 1988) found the same results with adults. Their subjects had to learn a procedure for operating a computer-simulated device and then use it to learn a new device. Once again the systematicity and transparency were manipulated. The systematicity was varied by providing either a causal model of the device or simply a set of operating procedures. The transparency referred to the type of device components. The results showed that systematicity constrained learning and transfer to the target device. Transparency also had strong effects on transfer. The speed of learning the new device was greater when corresponding pairs of components were similar than when they were dissimilar.

PRAGMATIC CONSTRAINTS

So far we have looked at similarity in terms of the objects, attributes, relations, and structure. Each if these can be said to act as *constraints* on analogising. There is one further constraint on which analogy depends, and that is the purpose of the analogy (Holyoak, 1985). The main constraints are therefore:

- *semantic:* referring to the degree of similarity between the objects, the features or attributes of the objects, and the relations between objects;
- *syntactic:* referring to the structure of the analogy along the lines of Gentner's systematicity principle;
- *pragmatic:* referring to the analogiser's goals in making an analogy.

Holyoak argues that the context and the goals of the thinker are important constraints on thinking. Pragmatic constraints, like syntactic constraints, reduce the amount of information about a problem or situation that we need to attend to. If your goal was to make children laugh at cartoons by having a cat named Tom chasing a mouse and crashing into a tree, then you might not want the result to be too horrible. So you would limit your analogy to the flattening of Tom's face, say, just as an orange would flatten if hurled against a tree. If, on the other hand, you were a cartoonist for "The Simpsons" and were making fun of the nasty things that happen to Tom in "Tom and Jerry" cartoons, then SPURT_FROM(JUICE,

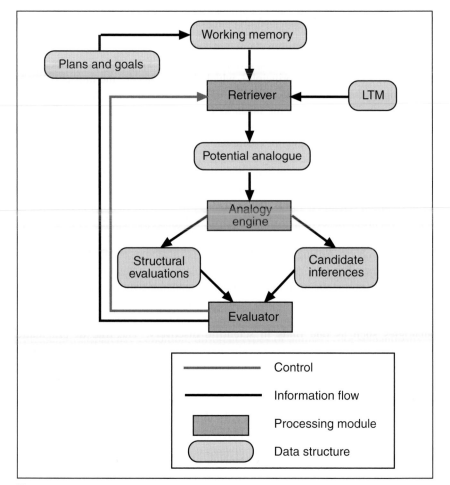

Figure 5.9. An architecture for analogical processing (adapted from Gentner, 1989, p. 216. Reproduced by permission of Cambridge University Press).

a causal relation with the underlying feature of "ripeness". This knowledge can come about either from experience with tomatoes or from an analogy with the relation between redness and ripeness in apples. If novices are presented with an example in which the same surface features occur, then they might reasonably infer that the example will involve the same underlying relation and that this relation can be applied in the current problem. By the same token, when there are no obvious featural similarities between problems, there is no particular reason why the features of the target problem will allow you to access a relevant source.

The relation between surface and structure is also pertinent in concept formation. Medin and Ortony (1989) argue that similarity judgements are based on our *representations* of objects (and of problems) not on actual entities themselves. The descriptive properties of objects, or their surface features, are usually related to deeper, less accessible properties. It therefore makes sense to attend to the surface properties of objects because they are a good heuristic for accessing the underlying structure.

It is not only novices that use surface features as a useful heuristic in accessing possibly relevant source problems or in categorising problems. Hinsley, Hayes, and Simon (1977) found that their expert subjects could categorise problems after hearing only a few phrases. Blessing and Ross (1996, p. 806) argue that there is a correlation between problem types and their contents (surface features) and that experienced solvers use these correlations to make hypotheses about the problem type:

> Quick access on the basis of surface content, even if it is not guaranteed to be correct, may be an attractive initial hypothesis given the longer time required for determining the deep structure … experts would be able to begin formulating the problem for solution while still reading it, thus saving time in solving the problem

It is a consistent finding in problem-solving research and in everyday life that people are strongly influenced by the surface features of problems or situations. We tend to remember, and hence are influenced by the information that stands out. We may remember a US presidential candidate falling off a podium and base our judgement of his adequacy as a president on that. If one reads about genetically modified foods, one may recall the phrase "Frankenstein foods" applied to them, and, although it is meaningless, the phrase may influence our view of such foods.

Gentner et al. (1993) have posed the question: "How can the human mind, at times so elegant and rigorous, be limited to this primitive retrieval mechanism?" (p. 567). They suggest that accessing information based on surface features is an older mechanism in evolutionary terms than reasoning. Indeed, there are strong arguments suggesting that accessing information on the basis of surface features is an extremely fast and efficient way of "thinking" even if it does occasionally lead to error. After all "if something looks like a tiger, it probably is a tiger" (1993, p. 567). Gentner et al. refer to this as the *kind world hypothesis*. In the environment, salient surface features are strongly correlated with structural features. Gigerenzer and Todd (1999) have argued that we have adapted to such an environment, and the fast and efficient ways we have developed to deal with it make us smart. Although relying on surface features can lead to errors, most of the time it allows quick and effort-free decisions. You gain more on the swings than you lose on the roundabout.

SUMMARY

1. Analogical problem solving requires the solver to see some kind of similarity between a current problem (the target) and an earlier problem in memory (a source). The degree of similarity depends on how the problems are represented.

of transfer in relatively well-defined problems discussed in Chapter 4, the main difficulty in APS are first of all accessing a relevant analogue, and second adapting and using it to solve a new problem or understand a new concept or situation. The second part of the chapter looks at teaching and explaining using analogies.

THE IMPORTANCE OF ANALOGISING

Mithen (1996) argues that the evolutionary development of the human mind involves the development of special-purpose "intelligences". Alongside a general-purpose intelligence there arose: a Natural History intelligence, a Social intelligence, a Technical intelligence, and language growing out of Social intelligence. Furthermore, consciousness developed out of the need to have a theory of mind to deal with complex social relationships; this idea is based on those of Nicholas Humphrey (1984, 1992). These special-purpose intelligences were originally "**informationally encapsulated**"—that is they were each "sealed off" from the others and so there was no cross talk between the different intelligences. In modern humans, however, there was a breakdown of the barriers between the intelligences. Blending combinations of intelligences led to art, religion, and science. Indeed, the ability to see similarities and draw analogies between disparate domains has caused the explosion of thought that has led to human civilisation.

Mithen uses three main analogies: a Swiss army knife represents multiple intelligences, in that the early hominid brain had a separate intellectual tool for different kinds of thought; a cathedral represents the mind, in that there are different chapels for different types of thought, each built more or less separately over time and whose walls in modern humans have been pierced to provide free access between them; and a play represents our prehistory, with different Acts standing for different stages in our evolution. To provide further examples of the importance that has been ascribed to analogical thought, I can do no better than quote Mithen himself (1996, pp. 153–154):

> ...Jerry Fodor (1985, p. 4) finds the passion for the analogical to be a central feature of the distinctly non-modular central processes of the mind and [...] Howard Gardner (Gardner, 1983, p. 279) believes that in the modern mind multiple intelligences function 'together smoothly, even seamlessly in order to execute complex human activities'. [...] Paul Rozin (1976, p. 262) concluded that the 'hall mark for the evolution of intelligence ... is that a capacity first appears in a narrow context and later becomes extended into other domains' and Dan Sperber (1994, p. 61) had reached a similar idea with his notion of a metarepresentational module, the evolution of which would create no less than a 'cultural explosion'. [Annette Karmiloff-Smith (1994, p. 706) argued that] the human mind 're-represents knowledge', so that 'knowledge thereby becomes applicable beyond the special-purpose goals for which it is normally used and representational links across different domains can be forged', which is so similar to the notion of 'mapping across different knowledge systems' as proposed by Susan Carey and Elizabeth Spelke (1994, p. 184), and the ideas of Margaret Boden (1994, p. 522) regarding how creativity arises from the 'transformation of conceptual spaces'.

STUDIES OF ANALOGICAL PROBLEM SOLVING

"The essence of analogical thinking is the transfer of knowledge from one situation to another by a process of mapping—finding a set of one-to-one correspondences (often incomplete) between aspects of one body of information and aspects of another" (Gick & Holyoak, 1983, p. 2). Ah, but you have to find the right analogue first…

In Chapter 5 you were presented with the Fortress problem, and I mentioned that you had encountered the solution before in Chapter 3. Most people are unlikely to have noticed the similarity between the Fortress problem and the Radiation problem in an earlier chapter. This is a difficulty facing students reading mathematics or science textbooks. They are often presented with exercise problems at the end of chapters, and there is often an implicit assumption by textbook writers that the poor student can remember and understand everything that has been presented and explained in earlier chapters. Textbooks contain examples and exercise problems within the same domain (and these will be dealt with in the next chapter). Much research, however, has been into the effects of analogising between different domains.

Gick and Holyoak (1980, 1983) were interested in the effect of previous experience with an analogous problem on solving Duncker's Radiation problem. They used various manipulations. Some subjects were given different solutions to the Fortress problem to find out what effect that would have on the solutions they gave for the Radiation problem. For example, when subjects were given a solution to the Fortress problem whereby the general attacked down an "open supply route" (an unmined road) they tended to suggest a solution to the Radiation problem involving sending rays down the oesophagus. If the general dug a tunnel, then more subjects suggested operating on the patient with the tumour. The solution involving dividing the army into groups and converging simultaneously on the fortress is known as the "divide and converge" solution (or the "convergence" solution). Thus the type of solution presented in the early problem influenced the types of solution suggested for the later one.

Another important point about Gick and Holyoak's studies was that their subjects were often very poor at noticing an analogy and would only use one when they were given a hint to do so. Only about 10% of those in a control group who did not receive an analogy managed to solve the problem using the "divide and converge" solution. Of those who were given an analogy, only 30% used the Fortress problem analogue without being given a hint to do so; and between 75% and 80% used the analogy when given a hint. So, if you subtract the 10% who manage to solve the problem spontaneously, this means that only about 20% noticed that the two problems were similar. This is in line with the findings by Simon and Hayes (1976) and Reed et al. (1974) who found that their subjects were very poor at noticing that the well-defined problems with which they were presented were analogous. Although the Fortress and Radiation problems are not well-defined, they be found for tyrant, army, and villages and for converging the groups simultaneously onto the fortress. However, look at 4, 5, 6, and 7 in Table 6.2. In 6 and 7 in particular, it is not obvious how one might go about dividing a ray machine or rays, or dispersing whatever results from the dividing around the tumour.

Another point that Table 6.2 brings out is that to adapt a solution one often has to find the most appropriate level of abstraction.

ACCESSING A SOURCE TO SOLVE A TARGET

Figure 6.1 presents an "ideal" model of analogical problem solving. In the Figure there is a source problem (A) that is assumed to be in long-term memory. The memory also includes information about how to solve the problem—represented in the Figure by the line linking the A box to the B box. C in the figure is the current problem you have to solve. If problem A is to be of any use, then the solver has to know that A and C are the same type of problem.

Accessing a relevant source problem means that there is some perceived similarity between the two problems; that is, A and C in the figure must be seen as being similar in some way. Once a relevant source is accessed, the solution procedure in the source problem (P) can then be applied to the new problem. As the solution procedure is applied, the objects in A are mapped onto the objects in C that appear to perform the same role (Chapter 5 dealt with this in more detail). The procedure in the source is adapted where necessary to fit the new problem, resulting in a slightly modified version of the original solution procedure (P'). For example, in Table 6.2, where objects and relations between objects are missing, new ones have to be inferred, such as reducing the intensity of the rays

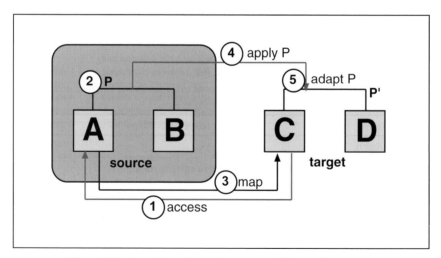

Figure 6.1.   Accessing and adapting a source problem to solve a target.

and either finding several ray machines or constructing some complicated system of mirrors.

The reason Figure 6.1 represents an idealised process of analogical reasoning is because actual human behaviour may differ from this. For example, Heller (1979) found that people trying to solve proportional analogies of the type A : B :: C : D (A is to B as C is to D—see Chapter 5) made a variety of mappings, only a few of which could be called relevant. A solver might engage in a number of possible comparison processes between the A and B terms, the A and C terms, the B and D terms, the C and D terms, and so on. Some of Heller's subjects also made comparisons that violated the structure of these problems. For example, they made irrelevant inferences and comparisons between the A and D terms, the B and C terms, the A-B-C terms, and so on (see Kahney, 1993, for a fuller discussion of Heller's model).

Similarly, in looking at subjects' problem-solving performance using instructional texts, Kahney (1982) and Conway and Kahney (1987) found that the subjects would often look back to the solutions of previous problems, ignore the relation between the example problem statement and its solution, and instead try to map the exercise problem statement onto the example solution (the C term onto the B term).

GENERATING YOUR OWN ANALOGIES

Blanchette and Dunbar (2000) have tried to elucidate the paradox of why people tend to find it hard to retrieve a relevant source when presented with a target based on the source's structural features. They argue that most laboratory experiments use a "reception paradigm" where subjects are given a source and a target by the experimenter. Using a "production paradigm" they got subjects to generate their own source analogues to a target. They found that subjects chose source analogues whose structural features matched those of the target (arguments about the desirability or otherwise of the Canadian government's budget deficit). On the other hand, when they were put back into a reception paradigm and presented with the sources that were both superficially similar or structurally similar, then a source analogue tended to be chosen based on superficial characteristics.

Blanchette and Dunbar (2000, p. 109) argue that "the reception paradigm may constrain the search for structural relations and provide a picture of analogical reasoning that underestimates the subjects' abilities to use deep structural features in the retrieval of source analogues. In real world contexts people generate their own analogies." They also argue that one explanation for retrieval based on superficial features (despite being asked which of the source texts "might make a good analogy to this one") might be that the original sources were encoded on the basis of superficial features (subjects were asked to evaluate the pleasantness of the text).

Nevertheless, the study does not encompass situations where the target is a problem that subjects are not readily able to solve despite the fact that an analogy may have been presented earlier.

Principle cueing

Ross (1984, 1987, 1989b) discusses two possible scenarios in APS: the **principle-cueing** view and the **example-analogy** view. In the principle-cueing view, learners may be reminded of an earlier example by some feature or combination of features of the current one. This reminding triggers or cues the abstract information or principle involved in the earlier problem which is relevant to the current one. In the case of Gick and Holyoak's work, the principle here would be the divide and converge solution schema; in algebra problems it might be an equation such as distance = rate × time. The principle thus accessed can then be used to make sense of a new situation or solve a new problem with the same structure. The role of the surface features of problems is to cue or access a possible relevant source problem.

Holland, Holyoak, Nisbett, and Thagard (1986) refer to analogues as having an "implicit" schema which is reconstructed during the solution process. In Figure 6.2, A represents a problem statement and B the solution. The relation or set of relations between A and B is represented by the line linking them. If the problem is an instance of a category of problems then the solution procedure used to get from A to B can be applied to other problems of the same type. There is therefore a schema implicit in the solution that can be applied to a range of problems of the same type. This is shown as the S box in Figure 6.2. When a source problem is accessed (A and B in Figure 6.3) then the principle underlying the solution to the source is accessed (the S on the line linking A and B) and applied to the target (C) to generate the solution (D).

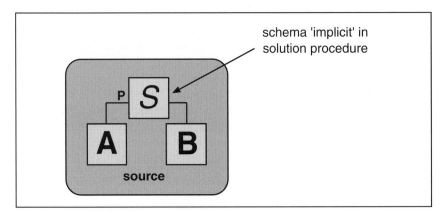

Figure 6.2.   The relation between a problem and its solution involving an implicit schema.

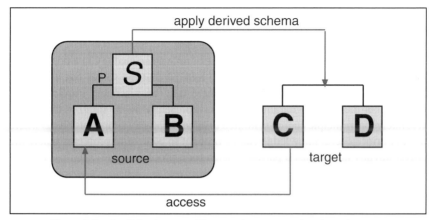

Figure 6.3.   Implicit schema cued by accessing source and used to solve target.

In the principle-cueing view, when people are reminded of an analogy the remindings serve to categorise the current problem. When presented with a problem involving two boats on a river going at different speeds one might be reminded of an earlier problem (or problems) of the same type and hence categorise the current problem as a riverboat problem, or a rate times time problem, or whatever. The studies by Gick and Holyoak have shown that only one presentation of a problem type is required for the solver to abstract out the underlying schema. This is probably true only when the underlying schema is relatively straightforward and easily understood. More complex concepts such as recursion, say (see Chapter 2 and Figure 4.1), would presumably require several examples before a schema would emerge that would help solve new examples. Whether the source problem be simple or complex, the abstract principle that the source exemplified has to be already understood by the learner, and the surface details in the source problem are no longer required to solve the target. The original source problem was nevertheless important in that it allowed the learner to understand the principle in question and how it is used.

The principle-cueing view implies that solving another problem from an example involves abstracting out the principle or procedure from the example and applying it to the target. This smacks of *abstraction mapping* where an abstract principle such as an equation is mapped on to the target problem rather than the specific elements in the example (see page 124). In the present case, the abstraction is "hidden" or implicit within the example and has to be extracted before it is applied. Much of the literature on expert–novice differences has concentrated on how the correct perception of a problem can cue access to the "problem schema" (Chi, Glaser, & Rees, 1982; Larkin, 1978). This problem schema in turn suggests a straightforward, stereotypical solution method. Novices, however, are often unable to identify the problem schema or categorise problems accordingly. Furthermore, principle cueing by definition presupposes that the analogiser understands the

EXPOSITORY ANALOGIES

Instructing with analogies refers to "the presentation of analogical information that can be used in the form of analogical reasoning in learning" (Simons, 1984, p. 513). Another aim of using analogies in texts is to make the prose more interesting. Now, it may be that these two aims are sometimes in conflict. Not only that, but there is always a point at which analogies break down. As a result writers have to be very careful about the analogies they use.

In expository texts writers make much use of analogies to explain new concepts, and they are often quite effective in helping students understand them. The flow of water, for instance, is traditionally used to explain the flow of current in electricity. Indeed, "flow" and "current" applied to electricity derive from that analogy. Rutherford made the structure of the atom more comprehensible by drawing an analogy to the structure of the solar system. When analogies are used in a pedagogical context, their aim is often to allow the student to abstract out the shared underlying structure between the analogy and the new concept or procedure the student has to learn. Writers hope that it can thereafter be used to solve new problems or understand new concepts involving that shared structure.

The kind of analogy people develop or are told can have a strong influence on their subsequent thinking. If you think that some countries in the Far East stand like a row of dominoes, then when one falls under Communist control the rest will fall inevitably one after the other—that's what happens to rows of dominoes. If you think that Saddam Hussein is like Hitler and that the invasion of Kuwait was like the invasion of Poland in the Second World War, then this will influence your response to the invasion and to your dealings with Iraq. If your theory of psychosexual energy (Freud) or of animal behaviour (Tindbergen) takes hydraulics as an analogy, then you will naturally see aspects of human behaviour as the results of pressure building up in one place and finding release in another.

Flowing waters or teeming crowds:
Mental models of electricity

Our understanding of physical systems is often built on analogy. There are, for example, two useful analogies of electricity: one that involves the flow of water and one that involves the movement of people. These analogies can either help or hinder one's understanding of the flow of electricity.

Gentner and Gentner (1983) used these two analogies to examine their effects on how the flow of electricity is understood. The analogy with a plumbing system can be quite useful in understanding electricity. Several aspects of plumbing systems map onto electrical systems (see Figures 6.4 and 6.5 and Table 6.4). Gentner and Gentner found that subjects who were given an analogy with flowing water were more likely to make inferences about the effects of the flow of current in batteries that were in series and in parallel than those subjects who were given a

TABLE 6.4

Mappings between the source domains of water and crowds and
the target domain of electricity

Target		Source: flowing water	Source: teeming crowds
resistor	⇨	narrow section of pipe	turnstile
current	⇨	rate of flow of water	movement of people
voltage	⇨	pressure	number of people
battery	⇨	reservoir	?

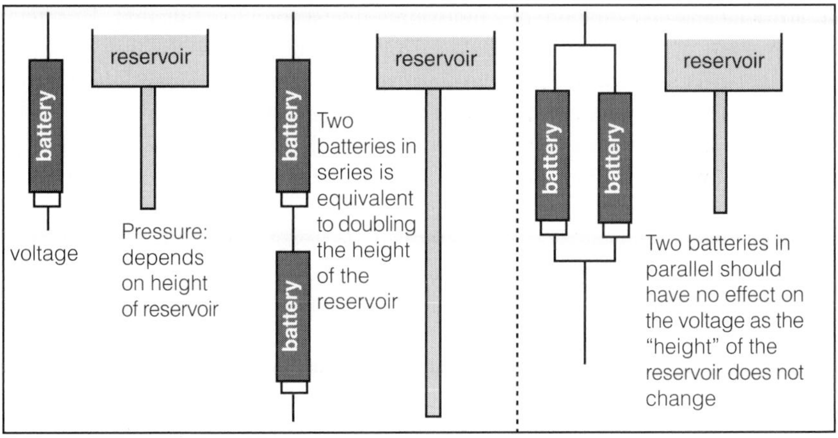

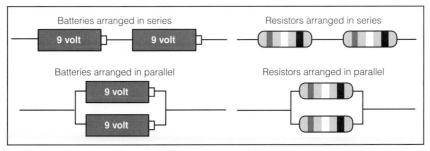

Figure 6.4. Effects of the analogy between batteries and water reservoirs.

Figure 6.5. Batteries and resistors arranged in series and in parallel.

moving-people analogy. However, when the problem concerned resistors more
subjects who had been given the moving-people analogy were able to infer the
effects of the resistors than those who had been given the flowing-water analogy.
Those who were reasoning from a flowing-water analogy believed the flow would
be restricted no matter how the resistors were arranged. People using the analogy
with people moving through turnstiles had a better mental model of the flow of
electricity through the resistors.

Issing, Hannemann, and Haack (1989) performed an experiment in which they examined the effects of different types of representation on transfer. The representations were pictorial analogies of the functioning of a transistor. They presented subjects with an expository text alone, the text plus a sluice analogy, the text plus a human analogy, and finally the text plus an electronics diagram of the transistor. Issing et al. found that the sluice analogy (involving the flow of water) led to better understanding of the function of the transistor. The human analogy was less effective and the diagram and text alone were the least effective.

Issing et al. argue that analogies depicting human-like situations are regarded as artificial and take on more of a motivating than a cognitive function. This, they say, explains why the human analogy fails to be as effective as the flow of water. This is, perhaps, a strange conclusion given that they are taking into account Gentner's view of structure-mapping (see Chapter 5). A more likely reason is that the water analogy shares more higher-order relations with the operation of transistors than the human analogy, and this would account for the stronger effect of the sluice analogy.

Donnelly and McDaniel (1993) performed a series of experiments on the effects of analogies on learning scientific concepts. Subjects were given either a literal version of the scientific concept, an analogy version, or a familiar-domain version (their Experiment 4). Three examples are given in Table 6.5.

The study showed several important features of the effectiveness of analogies in teaching. First, the analogies helped subjects answer inference questions but did not help with the recall of facts in the target domain. One can understand this in terms of the goals of learning: providing an analogy obliges the learner to look at how the structure of the analogy can help their understanding of the new concept. Providing just a literal version obliges the learner to concentrate more on the surface features. To put it yet another way, people will tend to concentrate on the surface features of new concepts (or situations or problems) unless given a way of re-analysing the concept (or situation or problem).

TABLE 6.5

Different ways new concepts were presented in Donnelly and McDaniel (1993)

Literal version

Collapsing Stars. Collapsing stars spin faster and faster as they fold in on themselves and their size decreases. This phenomenon of spinning faster as the star's size shrinks occurs because of a principle called "conservation of angular momentum".

Analogy version

Collapsing Stars. Collapsing stars spin faster and faster as their size shrinks. Stars are thus like ice skaters, who pirouette faster as they pull in their arms. Both stars and skaters operate by a principle called "conservation of angular momentum".

Familiar-domain version

Imagine how an ice skater pirouettes faster as he or she pulls in his or her arms. This ice skater is operating by a principle called "conservation of angular movement" (p. 987)

Second, the analogies helped novices but not advanced learners. If the concept being tested is in a domain that is already known, then the analogy performs no useful purpose. One can therefore solve problems using one's pre-existing domain-relevant knowledge (see also Novick & Holyoak, 1991). Analogies work for novices because they provide an anchor, or advance organiser (Ausubel, 1968). That is, novices can use a domain they know to make inferences about a domain they do not know.

Third, Donnelly and McDaniel suggest that subjects were able to argue (make inferences) from the analogy *prior to* the induction of a schema (that is, before a schema has been formed from experience of individual instances). In other words, there was no integration of the source analogy with the target. This emphasises that schema induction is a by-product of analogising and that schemas are built up gradually (depending on the complexity of the domain).

Giora's study

Giora (1993) has argued that analogies in expository texts are superfluous and tend to impede understanding and recall of texts. In a series of experiments she gave subjects a number of passages and asked them at the end "What is this passage about?" Some of the passages contained analogies (see Table 6.6). Giora found that the inclusion of an analogy impaired both recall of facts and understanding of the passage. In fact, the longer the analogy the worse the subjects' performance became.

These results appear to go against other studies that seem to demonstrate the power of analogies in influencing thinking. Giora argues that "Analogy, an example from a distant domain, is a digression from relevance and will therefore require more processing" (p. 597). She also argues that "a well-formed informative text is easy to understand since it contains enough redundancy to be easily assigned meaning and its ordering [the structure of the argument] is indicative of 'importance,' which I would rather term informativeness" (p. 596). In other words, a well-written text does not need analogies.

TABLE 6.6

Examples of texts with and without an analogy (from Giora, 1993)

Literal version

It has often occurred in the history of science that an important discovery was come upon by chance. A scientist looking into one matter, unexpectedly came upon another which was far more important than the one he was looking into. Penicillin is a result of such a discovery.

Analogy version

It has often occurred in the history of science that an important discovery was come upon by chance. A scientist looking into one matter, unexpectedly came upon another which was far more important than the one he was looking into. *Such scientists resemble Saul, who, while looking for donkeys, found a kingdom.* Penicillin is a result of such a discovery (Giora, 1993, p. 592).

If one compares the texts in the Donnelly and McDaniel study with the texts used in Giora's study then we might begin to see why there are differences in interpreting the role of analogies. The stories and analogies Giora used were rather simple. A concept such as the fact that many discoveries in the history of science have been accidental is simpler than concepts such as "conservation of angular momentum". The subjects in Giora's experiments did not *need* to use the analogies to understand the texts. They were indeed digressions. "Conservation of angular momentum", on the other hand, is not a simple concept to understand when it is encountered for the first time and so an analogy would be useful in helping people understand it.

The influence of far and near analogies

The studies so far have shown that distant analogies can have an influence on the way we reason about a new concept. Presumably, then, close analogies would have an even greater effect on understanding because there would be more shared surface features between the concept to be learned and the analogue as well as shared underlying structural features. This assumption was tested by Halpern, Hanson, and Riefer (1990). They gave subjects booklets to study containing passages on the lymphatic system, electricity, and enzymes. The booklets contained combinations of near, far, and no analogies. For example, the far-domain analogy with the lymph system involved the movement of water through a sponge; the near domain was a comparison with blood through the veins. Halpern et al. found that the far-domain analogies produced greater recall both immediately and after a week of the target texts, and subjects were able to answer more inference questions than in the near-domain and no-analogy conditions (see also Iding, 1993, 1997).

Halpern et al. argued that the far-domain analogies led to the subjects putting more effort into mapping the structure of the analogy onto the target domain. It was this "effort after meaning" (Bartlett, 1932), or the encoding of the information in the source and target at a "deeper" level, that produced the strong results from the far analogies. Generally speaking, when far domains are used in teaching texts they are more likely to enhance understanding than near domains, because the far domains tend to be ones that the learner already knows and understands. Textbook writers choose them for that very reason. If the domain is a new one and the material is difficult then a near-domain analogy is also likely to be difficult and hence is of little use to analogise from. This is summed up in Figure 6.6.

Influencing thought

It is obvious from the preceding discussion that analogies can play an important role in influencing thinking. One way that analogies can operate is by activating a schema that in turn influences the way we think about a current situation. Even relatively simple metaphors such as a "flood" of asylum seekers may bring to mind something uncontrollable and damaging. It is certainly more emotive than simply

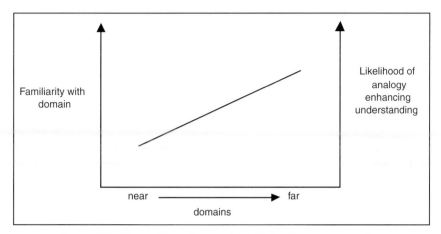

Figure 6.6.   Near and far analogies and their likely effect on understanding.

saying "a large number" of asylum seekers. Genetically modified (GM) food was labelled "Frankenstein food" by one British newspaper. The phrase probably helped influence the direction in which the debate about GM food in Britain was going at the time. Similarly, Keane (1997) points out that using a war analogy when discussing drug pushing is likely to bring to mind "solutions that are based on police action and penal legislation rather than solutions that involve the funding of treatment centres or better education (an illness-of-society analogy might have the opposite effect)" (p. 946).

We have to be extremely careful about the nature of the analogies we present when demonstrating something, as they can have a profound effect on thinking about the current situation. Before we go on to look at possible problems with using analogies to teach with, here is one last example about how analogies can be used to affect people's thinking (Halpern, 1996, pp. 84–85):

> We frequently use analogies to persuade someone that X is analogous to Y, therefore what is true for X is also true for Y. A good example of this sort of "reasoning by analogy" was presented by Bransford, Arbitman-Smith, Stein, & Vye (1985). They told about a legal trial that was described in the book, *Till death us do part* (Bugliosi, 1978). Much of the evidence presented at the trial was circumstantial. The attorney for the defense argued that the evidence was like a chain, and like a chain, it was only as strong as its weakest link. He went on to argue that there were several weak links in the evidence: therefore, the jurors should not convict the accused. The prosecutor also used an analogy to make his point. He argued that the evidence was like a rope made of many independent strands. Several strands can be weak and break, and you will still have a strong rope. Similarly, even though some of the evidence was weak, there was still enough strong evidence to convict the accused. (The prosecutor won.)

"AESTHETIC" ANALOGIES

A second way in which analogies are used in texts is as aesthetic devices to make the prose more interesting. However, often the boundaries between the two uses are a little unclear. Here are some examples from developmental psychology, evolution and cosmology:

> ...emotion is a Cinderella of cognitive development. I won't pretend to be her fairy godmother, but I can bring together some of the recent work which might be put together into the magic coach that will take her to the ball (Meadows, 1993, pp. 356–357).

> My 'river' is a river of DNA, flowing and branching through geological time, and the metaphor of steep banks confining each species' genetic games turns out to be a surprisingly powerful and helpful explanatory device (Dawkins, 1995, p. xii).

Concepts such as the fact that time ceases to exist when we go back to the beginning of the universe are hard to grasp. "Before" and "after" seem so natural that we can't readily imagine what it means that there was no "before" the Big Bang. It is a consequence of Einstein's theory of relativity that matter and time are intimately bound up and that both were created together. How might one therefore make such concepts easier to grasp? Stephen Hawking has tried by presenting an analogy with the earth (Figure 6.7).

Nevertheless, there is always a point at which analogies break down. Structure-mapping theory argues that lower-order relations are ignored when making an analogy. For example, Rutherford made the analogy between the structure of the atom and the structure of the solar system. In Gentner's structure-mapping theory the size of the sun and the fact that it is very hot are irrelevant to the analogy and play no part in it. However, sometimes there are higher-order relations that are

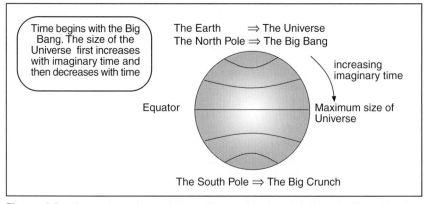

Figure 6.7. Hawking's analogy of the universe with the earth (adapted from Hawking, 1988, p. 138).

ignored when making an analogy. Compare Hawking's analogy in Figure 6.7 with these comments by Darling (1996, p. 49):

> One of the most specious analogies that cosmologists have come up with is between the origin of the Universe and the North Pole. Just as there is nothing north of the North Pole, so there is nothing before the Big Bang. Voilà! We are supposed to be convinced by that, especially since it was Stephen Hawking who dreamt it up. But it will not do. The Earth did not grow from its North Pole. There was not ever a disembodied point from which the material of the planet sprang. The North Pole only exists because the Earth exists—not the other way round

The moral of the story is: you can only take an analogy so far. There is always a point at which an analogy breaks down. In the next chapter we will look at what makes problems or situations similar, and just what aspects can and cannot reasonably be mapped.

SUMMARY

1. Analogising has been regarded as a fundamental property of human thinking.
2. Studies of analogical problem solving (APS) have shown that retrieving a relevant analogy is not often a spontaneous process. The context or domain in which a situation is embedded can profoundly affect the likelihood that it will be retrieved in a different context later.
3. Holyoak has listed in various places the processes assumed to be involved in APS (see Information Box 6.1).

Information Box 6.1

The processes involved in analogical problem solving

Holyoak has listed several steps involved in analogical problem solving*. Each step depends on the previous ones although there is likely to be some iteration (i.e., the analogiser may have to go through some stages more than once) particularly in stages 3 and 4. They are:

Forming a representation of the source problem and the target problem.

Accessing "a plausibly relevant analogue in memory" (Holyoak & Thagard, 1989b). This depends on the form of representation the solver has of the problems. If solvers are to access a previously encountered problem from memory, then the representation they form of the target must match that of the source. This point begs the question of what constitutes problem similarity.

Mapping across corresponding elements in the source and target. Correspondences are features that appear to play the same role in the source and target. Narrow sections of pipe restricting the flow of water have to be seen as corresponding to resistors in an

Information Box 6.1 (continued)

electric circuit before an analogy between the flow of water and the flow of electricity in complex systems can be understood.

Adapting the mapping, constrained by the shared underlying structure of the problems, to generate a solution in the target. This step is also known as analogical inference or transfer. Knowing what happens to water when it passes through two narrow sections of pipe one after the other should allow students to infer what will happen when electricity has to pass through two resistors arranged in series.

Learning. This takes the form of schema abstraction from comparing examples (either implicitly or explicitly). With experience in solving a type of problem, students abstract out the underlying structure and can thereafter apply it to new versions of the problem type without having to refer to a previous solution.

Mapping and adapting are not regarded as being strictly sequential. Mapping "can be conducted in a hierarchical manner, the process may be iterated at different levels of abstraction" (Holyoak, 1985). Analogical problem solving assumes that the solver has a representation of the source in LTM, and that the underlying structure of the problem is understood well enough so that the solver can map it across and generate inferences in the target.

Holyoak lists different steps at different times. The five presented here are derived from different sources (Catrambone & Holyoak, 1989; Holyoak, 1984, 1985; Holyoak & Thagard, 1989a, b).

4. Schunn and Dunbar have argued that the reason people seem to be poor at analogising is due to the nature of the experiment. When asked to generate their own analogies, subjects produced structurally appropriate ones.
5. The end result of the comparison of analogous problems is learning that takes the form of schema induction. Learning from examples is considered in more depth in Chapter 8.
6. Expository analogies are ones that are used to help learners understand new material. They provide an anchor or bridge between what the novice already knows and the new material that has to be understood. The nature of whatever analogy is used in teaching is important as it is likely to influence the way the new material is understood; and, indeed, the way it is likely to be misunderstood.
7. Analogies in texts have an effect when the material to be learned is difficult. When the material is already easily understood, analogies have little impact. Analogies can also have a purely aesthetic effect in this context—they liven up the text rather than add to it.

CHAPTER SEVEN

Textbook problem solving

I once attempted to learn the rudiments of the programming language Prolog from textbooks. At one point I found myself reading a section on recursion. The section attempted to explain the concept of recursion and presented about half a dozen examples. As I read the section I felt that the concept was quite well explained and that the examples were readily understandable. At the end of the section there were some exercise problems and so I got a sheet of paper and had a go at the first one. I quickly discovered that I hadn't a clue where to begin to solve the problem.

Now a couple of reasons might be adduced for this state of affairs. My first, fortunately fleeting, thought was that I just couldn't "do" Prolog; I wasn't cut out to be a computer programmer. (This thought could lead to what Bransford and Stein, 1993, called a "mental escape": when presented with a problem from a particular domain the solver exclaims "Oh no, I can't do algebra" or "geometry" or "statistics" or whatever. The solver gives up before even reading the problem because of a kind of learned helplessness.)

My second thought was that I had simply missed something when I had read the section. So I went back over the worked examples looking for one that looked similar to the exercise problem I was trying to solve. I couldn't find one. I still had no idea how to solve the very first exercise problem, so I did what most people probably do in such circumstances—I looked up the answer at the back of the book.

This was revealing—not only because it told me the answer, but also because it showed me that the section I had just read had not, in fact, told me how to solve this particular exercise problem. If I had gained a deep understanding of the concept of recursion from reading the

Activity 7.1
Have you ever had to do exercise problems in textbooks?
Have you ever been stuck on one?
Who did you "blame"?

section then perhaps I could have solved it, and presumably the author believed that he had provided enough of an explanation to produce just such a deep understanding. Nevertheless I would venture to suggest that students reading textbooks in domains they are unfamiliar with do not always understand things particularly well on a first reading.

It is hard to imagine a modern culture where most of its teaching is not done through textbooks or an electronic equivalent. It is equally hard to imagine anyone not getting stuck on exercise problems, or getting them wrong, at least some of the time. In Activity 7.1, I would hazard a guess that your answer to question 3 was you yourself. It is a reasonable bet that most people would tend to "blame" themselves (if they thought about it) for failing to solve a textbook problem. We tend to take it on faith that the textbook writer has provided all the information we need to solve exercise problems. This may well not be the case for a number of reasons, some of which we will look at in the next section.

One way of examining the difficulties facing students engaged in textbook problem solving is by looking at the processes involved in using examples to solve problems. There is an important distinction between the kinds of analogical problem solving discussed in the last two chapters and the use of an example as an analogy in a textbook. So far, we have concentrated on analogy as the transfer or mapping of knowledge from a *familiar* domain onto a less familiar one. In the case of metaphors, the transfer is often from one familiar domain to another familiar one. In textbook examples, on the other hand, the student is trying to use an example from an *unfamiliar* domain to solve a problem in the same unfamiliar domain.

Analogical reasoning works when you can reason from a domain that you understand well to solve a present problem that is puzzling. In textbook problem solving the student is presented with examples to use as analogies to solve exercise problems. The big difference here is that the example and the exercise problem are both in the same domain, and the student (who is presumably a novice) *does not yet understand the domain*, otherwise the student would not be a novice. This, in a nutshell, is what makes problem solving from textbook examples difficult.

DIFFICULTIES FACING TEXTBOOK WRITERS

Textbook writers face a number of difficulties when writing textbooks. To make the task a little easier they have to make some assumptions about the reader.

Assumed prior knowledge

If a textbook is aimed at a readership that has presumably reached a certain level of competence in a specific domain (for example, by passing exams in that domain), then the writer has a good idea of the prior knowledge of the readers. If the textbook is aimed at a more general readership, then there are likely to be parts that are better understood by some readers than by others and conversely some parts that are likely to be well-known to some and completely new to others.

The Lisp textbook by Winston and Horn (1989), for example, presents an example of a recursive function in LISP that computes the Fibonacci series (p. 73). If you already know what the Fibonacci series is, then you may have little problem understanding what the function is trying to do. If you don't, then fortunately the textbook spends half a page explaining what it is. Having to explain what the problem statement means before explaining what the solution is can present an added level of difficulty for the reader.

Assumed recall of already presented information

The writer has to make assumptions about how much the reader remembers from previous chapters. When a problem is presented in chapter 5, say, it would probably be foolish to suppose that everything presented in chapters 1 to 4 will be readily recalled. In a study into novice programmers, one of Anderson, Farrell, and Sauers' (1984) subjects had to be reminded of an earlier example from a previous chapter (problem 2-5 in chapter 2 of the Winston and Horn textbook) before she could go on and solve the problem she was working on (problem 3-1 in chapter 3).

Assumed understanding

Another assumption that it would be unwise to make is that all the material from earlier chapters or the current one has been understood. Several studies have shown that learners do not always have a clear idea of how much they understand from a textbook (Chi et al., 1989, 1994; Ferguson-Hessler & de Jong, 1990; VanLehn, Jones, & Chi, 1992). In analysing the study processes of students studying physics texts, Ferguson-Hessler and de Jong, for example, found that "poor" students said "everything is clear" three times more often than good students, whereas their performance showed that this was not the case. They also found that poor performers processed declarative knowledge more than good performers, who concentrated more on situational and procedural information.

The finding that poorer students felt that everything was clear more often than "better" students can be explained in terms of Hiebert and Lefèvre's (1986) distinction between **primary understanding** and **reflective understanding**. Primary understanding occurs when the student understands a new domain at a surface level; that is, at the same level of abstractness as, or at a less abstract level than, the information being presented. This type of understanding is highly context-specific. The specific examples presented seem to be clear but the student is unlikely to see how the examples can be adapted or applied to another problem. Reflective understanding is at a more abstract level when students recognise the deeper structural features of problems and can relate them to previous knowledge.

Assumed schematic knowledge of the structure of teaching texts

Writers need to ensure that they do not violate the student's schema for what the layout of a scientific textbook should look like. Students are likely to have expectations about how textbooks are laid out in formal domains such as mathematics, science, and computer programming because they tend to have a particular stereotypical layout (Beck & McKeown, 1989; Kieras, 1985; Robertson & Kahney, 1996; Sweller & Cooper, 1985). With experience of such textbooks, students come to develop a schema for that type of text. Such a schema includes the default assumptions that solutions follow statements of the problem rather than vice versa, and that a particular section of a textbook will give them enough information to solve exercise problems at the end of that section. However, it may be the case that textbooks are not structured that way (see Britton, Van Dusen, Gulgoz, & Glynn, 1989).

Assumptions about generalisation

Another difficulty facing writers is whether to present close variants of the problem type or a range of variants (see Figure 7.1). Principles, concepts, how to generate an equation, etc., can be understood better by presenting a concrete example (such as Example 1 in Figure 7.1). This concrete example often acts as an exemplar or *paradigm* representing the problem type. Table 7.1 shows some concrete examples.

However, it may be hard for the reader to recognise whether a concept, principle, or solution procedure is relevant or applicable based on one example alone. Often, therefore, a range of examples is presented. If this range of examples is composed mainly of close variants of the exemplar, then the reader might be better able to abstract out the commonalities between them and hence be better able to understand the concept, principle, or solution procedure, and to automate the procedure for

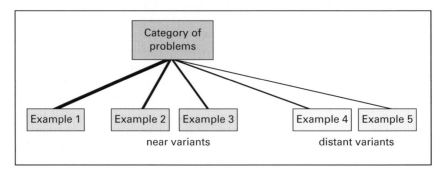

Figure 7.1.   Is a category of problems best explained by presenting a number of close variants or a range of examples including distant variants?

TABLE 7.1

Close and distant variants of different problem types

Domain	Problem category	Paradigm	Close variant	Distant variant

Prolog	Recursion	has_flu(bill).
		has_flu(X):-
		  kisses(X,Y),
		  has_flu(Y).
			on_top(floor).
			on_top(A):-
			  above(A,B),
			  on_top(B).
				member(X[X|Tail]).
				member(X[Head|Tail]):-
				member(X,Tail).

French grammar	Agreement of past principle with preceding direct object	*Je l'ai achetée hier.*	*Je les ai achetés la semaine dernière.*	*C'est bien la voiture que j'ai vue.*
Algebra	Rate1 × Time1 = Rate2 × Time2	A car travelling at a speed of 30 mph left a certain point at 10.00 a.m. At 11.30 a.m., another car departed at the same place at 40 mph and travelled the same route. In how many hours will the second car overtake the first?	A car travels south at the rate of 30 mph. Two hours later, a second car leaves to overtake the first car, using the same route and going 45 mph. In how many hours will the second car overtake the first car?	A pick-up truck leaves 3 hours after a large delivery truck but overtakes it by travelling 15 mph faster. If it takes the pick-up truck 7 hours to reach the delivery truck, find the rate of each vehicle.

solving a subset of such problems. This, however, would be at the expense of demonstrating the range of applicability of the concept, etc. (Cooper & Sweller, 1987).

If students are expected to solve distant variants of a problem, writers have to provide explicit information about the relationship between source examples and other problems of the same type (Conway & Kahney, 1987; Reed et al., 1974). As examples provide information about a category of problems, the more information about the features of that category that is given to the reader the better.

THE ROLE OF EXAMPLES IN TEXTBOOKS

Why bother with examples at all? Isn't a textual explanation sufficient? If people are asked to perform a complex procedure, then the best method of teaching it is by demonstration. Once people have read the text in a subject such as physics, mathematics, or computer programming, they tend not to re-read it if they can help it. Instead they concentrate on worked-out examples if they are trying to solve exercise problems at the end of a section. Ross (1989a) has referred to examples as "potent teachers" and there is a lot of evidence suggesting that they are more important for problem solving than the rest of the text. This phenomenon has been commented on in a number of studies (LeFèvre, 1987). For example, Pirolli (1991) states: "When a learner is faced with novel goals, the preferred method of problem solving involves the use of example solutions as analogies for the target solution" (p. 209). VanLehn (1990) also argues that concrete examples of problem solving are more important than the textual explanations that accompany them. Study Box 7.1 contains some more specific examples.

VanLehn (1986) has referred to a "folk model" of how students learn from textbook examples and explanations. The explanations are seen as the important aspect of instruction and are assumed to be adequate for students to learn procedures for solving problems. In contrast he argues that explanations serve as guides to help students make more accurate inductions from examples.

So why are examples so important for learning? According to Ross (1989b) being reminded of an earlier example can have four possible effects which amount to different roles played by worked-out examples. First, it may allow the learner to remember the details of a solution procedure rather than an abstract principle or rule (such as an equation). "The memory for what was done last time is highly interconnected and redundant, allowing the learner to piece it together without remembering separately each part and its position in the sequence" (Ross, 1989b, p. 439).

Second, even if the learner can remember the rule or principle that is supposed to be applied to a problem, the learner may not know how to apply it. Activity 7.2 gives some indication of what this means. For novices in algebra, being told the principle (the relevant equation) underlying the problem may be of no use because they do not necessarily know how to instantiate the variables. The novices still have to make a number of inferences based on domain knowledge before they can solve the problem.

Study Box 7.1

LeFevre and Dixon (1986) found that students learning a procedural task prefer to use examples as a source of information and that written instructions tend to be ignored.

VanLehn (1986, 1990) has built a theory of children's errors on the evidence he has gleaned that people prefer to use examples rather than written explanations. VanLehn (1986) has estimated that some 85% of children's systematic errors are due to misunderstanding textbook explanations of problems.

Pirolli (1991; Pirolli & Anderson, 1985) found that novice programmers relied heavily on examples rather than instructions to help solve LISP recursion problems.

Carroll, Smith-Kerker, Ford, and Mazur-Rimetz (1987–1988) redesigned computer training manuals partly to take account of the fact that learners are put off by the "verbiage" in traditional training manuals.

Activity 7.2

Car A leaves a certain place at 10 a.m. travelling at 40 mph, and car B leaves at 11.30 a.m. travelling at 55 mph. How long does it take car B to overtake car A?

The equation to use is:

$$Rate_{CarA} \times Time_{CarA} = Rate_{CarB} \times Time_{CarB}$$

What figures would you use to replace the variables in the equation?

Third, novices may not understand the concepts embodied in the rule or principle, or may have misinterpreted them. For example, the equation in Activity 7.2 is based on the more general equation *Distance = Rate × Time*. As both cars travel the same distance then Distance$_{CarA}$ = Distance$_{CarB}$; and as the distances are equal the *Rate × Time* for both cars must be equal too: hence the form of the equation. Now if you know something about algebra or mathematics in general, then that explanation might make sense and you can understand where the equation comes from. If you have little knowledge of mathematics, then the origin of the equation may be rather obscure. That is, you may not understand the concepts involved in the equation.

Fourth, trying to solve a current problem may force novices to extract more information from an earlier problem than they did at the time. If you saw how to solve the Fortress problem based on the Radiation problem, you may have been able to abstract out information from the Radiation problem that was more relevant to "divide and converge" problems.

Reimann and Schult (1996) point to three problems that the use of examples helps to overcome. These are the "interpretation problem", the "control problem", and the "generalisation problem".

The interpretation problem. Examples show how theoretical principles can be interpreted and instantiated in a problem (the second of Ross's four roles). They show the relationship between a problem description and the concepts or principles they embody.

The control problem. At any one time in the middle of an algebra problem there may be a number of possible operators that you can apply (related to the first of Ross's roles). Examples show what specific operators apply and therefore demonstrate the specific solution procedure.

The generalisation problem. It is always difficult for novices to know what the salient aspects of a problem (or a textbook for that matter) are. That is, they are poor at distinguishing between those surface features that are related to the structural ones and those that are irrelevant (see the discussion of Gentner's structure-mapping theory in Chapter 5). Only the superficial features can be generalised over.

THE PROCESSES INVOLVED IN TEXTBOOK
PROBLEM SOLVING

Various representations can be derived from a textual presentation of a problem. The first thing a student finds when confronted with a word problem to solve in a textbook is a piece of text. The first thing the student has to do, therefore, is to make sense of the text itself. This in turn requires several layers of representation.

First of all there are the individual words that compose the text. Understanding these comes through our semantic knowledge of the items in our **mental lexicon** —our mental dictionary. From the individual words and the context of the sentence, our overall understanding of the text of a problem is constructed, and so on. Kintsch (e.g., 1986, 1998; Nathan et al., 1992; Van Dijk & Kintsch, 1983) has argued that word problems require the solver to generate a number of different representations. The initial representation of the text is a propositional representation called the **textbase**. However, knowing what the text of a question means does not therefore entail an understanding of the problem. Kintsch (1986, p. 89) gives the example of trying to understand a computer manual:

> all too often we seem to "understand" the manual all right but remain at a loss about what to do; more attention to the text as such would be of little help. The problem is not with the words and phrases, nor even with the overall structure of the text; indeed, we could memorize the text and still not know which button to press. The problem is with understanding the situation described by the text. Clearly understanding the text as such is not a sufficient condition for understanding what to do.

From the textbase students have to develop a representation of the situation described in the text. This is a mental model which Van Dijk and Kinstch (1983) termed a **situation model**. For problem solving to be successful, the solver has to generate all the necessary inferences in order to build a representation of the problem that is useful enough to solve it. This, in turn, means that novices have to have enough domain-relevant knowledge to do so.

In a later formulation of the theory, Nathan, Kintsch, & Young (1992) divided the situation model into two. They explicitly distinguished between the situation model and the **problem model.** The situation model includes elaborated inferences generated from an understanding of the text. Such inferences might include the fact that if two cars leave from the same point at different times and the second car overtakes the first then both cars will have travelled the same distance at that point. The fact that both cars travelled the same distance may not be explicitly mentioned in the text. Nathan et al. (1992, p. 335) also add that:

> because of the added demands of inference making, readers will make inferences only when they seem necessary. Poor problem solvers will tend to omit them from their representations, and so they will *omit* the associated equations (supporting relations) from their solutions to story problems. Problem solvers who reason situationally will tend to include these inference-based equations

The other representational form proposed by Nathan et al. is the *problem model* which includes formal knowledge about the arithmetic structure derived from the text, for example, or the operating procedure constructed from information in the text. The ability to make inferences from texts in order to derive a useful problem model depends on the relevant prior domain knowledge of the learner.

Kinstch (1986) argues that the text determines what situation model is constructed and how it is constructed. The situation model is important for learning and the textbase is important for remembering text (bear in mind that the situation model and problem model are conflated here). In a study of problem solving and retrieval of earlier problems, he found that recall of word problems that had already been solved was determined both by the properties of the textbase and the model constructed to solve a problem. It was the situation model that provided recall of earlier problems and not a reproduction of the textbase. Learning, according to Kintsch, depended on the problem model constructed from examples, and remembering depended on the coherence of the text. For example, common terms repeated in succeeding sentences lead to greater coherence and greater recall (Kintsch & Van Dijk, 1978). He argued that it was easier (at least for children) to form an appropriate situation model if there is a concrete, familiar structure. However, other studies (e.g., Chen & Daehler, 1989; Novick, 1990) have shown that this is not the whole story. Problem-solving transfer by adults and children from *abstract* representations can also take place (see Chapter 4).

The distinction between a propositional (textbase) representation of a text and the elaborated situation model was examined by Tardieu, Ehrlich, and Gyselinck (1992). They argued that novices and experts in a particular domain would not differ in the propositional representation they derived from a text, but that there would be differences between the two groups in the situation model (here again the situation model and the problem model are synonymous). Tardieu et al. found that there was no difference between experts and novices on their ability to paraphrase a text (i.e. they both generated much the same *textbase*) but experts performed better on inference questions than novices (they had derived different situation models from the textbase).

These hierarchical forms of representation have two implications for how novices understand textbook explanations and examples. First, as they are unfamiliar with the domain, they tend to have only a propositional representation of the surface features of the examples. Using examples to solve further problems means matching propositions and is unlikely to be guided by an understanding of the deeper relational structure. Second, novices may not know enough to make necessary **elaborative inferences** to generate a complete situation or problem model.

The next section presents an example of a study where the students were unable to generate a complete situation or problem model.

LABORATORY STUDIES OF WITHIN-DOMAIN AND TEXTBOOK PROBLEM SOLVING

Figure 7.2 represents a hierarchy of "Rate" problems. The lower down the hierarcy, the more specific or concrete the problem becomes. The distance between any two nodes in the hierarchy represents a crude measure of the amount of transfer that would be involved between them. Generally speaking solving problems using examples in textbooks usually involves problems that would be adjacent in the hierarchy.

Reed, Dempster, and Ettinger (1985) describe four experiments in which one example problem and solution is presented and the student is thereafter expected to solve a transfer problem, or a problem whose solution procedure was unrelated to the practice problem. In the terminology of Reed et al., the transfer problems were called "equivalent" or "similar". We will look at the experiments in general and at some of the algebra word problems in particular with a view to discovering just what the solution explanations that were provided *failed* to explain.

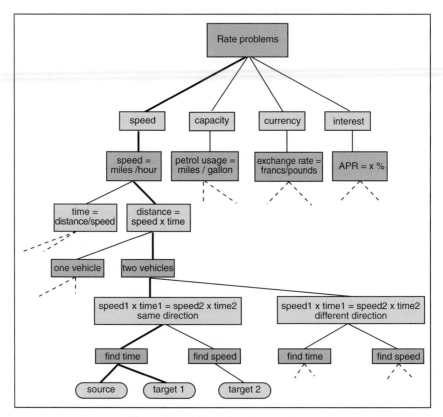

Figure 7.2.   A hierarchy of Rate problems.

Study Box 7.2

Reed et al. (1985)

Rationale

Reed et al. were interested in establishing how transfer could be produced in within-domain problem solving. They used the kinds of problems one finds in mathematics textbooks and gave explanations of how to solve them (which were generally better than the explanations one normally finds in such textbooks). Using one example problem and associated explanation they looked for transfer to close and distant variants of the example problem.

Methodology

Subjects were given six minutes to solve the following problem and then given the solution. In the discussion that follows this is referred to as the source problem.

A car travelling at a speed of 30 miles per hour (mph) left a certain place at 10.00 a.m. At 11.30 a.m. another car departed from the same place at 40 mph and travelled the same route. In how many hours will the second car overtake the first car?

The problem is a distance-rate-time problem in which

$$\text{Distance} = \text{Rate} \times \text{Time}$$

We begin by constructing a table to represent the distance, rate, and time for each of the two cars. We want to find how long the second car travels before it overtakes the first car. We let t represent the number that we want to find and enter it into the table. The first car then travels $t + \frac{1}{2}$ hr because it left $1\frac{1}{2}$ hrs earlier. The rates are 30 mph for the first car and 40 mph for the second car. Notice that the first car must travel at a slower rate if the second car overtakes it. We can now represent the distance each car travels by multiplying the rate and the time for each car. These values are shown in the following table.

Car	Distance (miles)	Rate (mph)	Time (hours)
First	$30(t + \frac{1}{2})$	30	$t + \frac{1}{2}$
Second	$40 \times t$	40	t

Because both cars have travelled the same distance when the second car overtakes the first, we set the two distances equal to each other:

$$30(t + \frac{1}{2}) = 40t$$

Solving for t yields the following:

$$30t + 45 = 40t;$$
$$45t \quad = 10t;$$
$$t \quad = 4.5 \text{ hours}$$

Problem adaptation takes a variety of forms, each of which presents a particular kind of difficulty for the solver. Novick and Holyoak list three of them:

1. *Substitute numbers from the test problem into the source operators.* Elements of one problem have to correspond to elements in the other. An example would be substituting 30 mph in one problem for 40 mph in another in distance-speed-time problems. Failure to map the correct numbers led to what Reed et al. called a "quantity error", and using a number in a source problem without changing it in the target led to a "matching error". This form of adaptation is not a major source of difficulty when the problems to be solved are very close variants.
2. *Postulate new test-problem elements not described in that problem.* This occurs when the target is a distant variant of the source problem. If the source contains "time taken" but the target does not, or if the target gives "rates of travel" but none is given in the source, then the subject will have to generate new test-problem elements. This was the difficulty faced by the subjects of Reed et al.
3. *Generalise source procedure in ways that preserve the essential structure of the procedure.* If the procedure involves generating an equation in an example, then the equation has to have the same form in any test problem. Failure to preserve the problem structure would lead to what Reed et al. call a "frame error", where the form of the equation is wrong.

How difficult a problem is depends on the level of the student's understanding of the domain and of the nature of the problem. Generating a situation model from the textbase and thence a problem model depends on the student's prior knowledge, both factual and conceptual. So what does it mean to "understand" a problem in an unfamiliar domain?

UNDERSTANDING PROBLEMS REVISITED

"Understanding is arguably the most important component of problem solving (e.g., Duncker, 1945; Greeno, 1977), and representations indicate how solvers understand problems … *One cannot solve a problem one does not understand (except by chance)*" (Novick, 1990 , p. 129, italics added). On the other hand, you can solve problems you don't understand if they involve very little adaptation and all you are doing is copying the example (Robertson, 2000).

There are several reasons why novices may fail to make elaborative inferences from a reading of a problem. First, their representations of the text are often fragmentary and incomplete, as they may not know what aspects of the text are important or relevant to the solution. Second, they require practice at solving problems before they develop the necessary inference rules. In other words, their declarative knowledge of the domain (or conceptual knowledge) is not in a form that can support inferences.

Many models of learning such as ACT-R, SOAR, Sierra, PI, etc. (see Chapter 8), emphasise the deriving of knowledge from experience. That is, procedures are created from experience of instances of problem solving. During this phase learners might show procedural skill but not necessarily much conceptual understanding. An example would be learning to write recursive functions in LISP from a purely "syntactic" point of view (Hasemer & Domingue, 1989)—one can learn to write recursive functions successfully without at first a full understanding of how recursion works. Even when concepts are not fully understood they can nevertheless be useful tools for thought. Procedures in mathematics still allow problems to be solved even though the problem or procedure is not fully understood. VanLehn (1990), among others, has shown that having a procedure that successfully solves a problem involving a concept does not mean that the student has a proper understanding of the concept (Brown & Burton, 1978; Brown & VanLehn, 1980; VanLehn, 1986, 1990; Young & O'Shea, 1981).

Of course, it is also possible to understand a concept without knowing how it can be used; that is, without knowing how it can be instantiated. One can understand concepts at an abstract level such as recursion or "the past participle agrees with the preceding direct object" and yet rarely apply them. Even though a concept is understood by a student, this does not mean that the student has acquired the necessary procedures to implement that concept (Ohlsson & Rees, 1991).

Byrnes (1992) proposed a "dynamic-interaction" model to account for the interface between conceptual and procedural understanding. His model assumes that concepts and procedures are stored in separate memory systems. The interface between the two types of knowledge involves the activation of procedures that are indexed to concepts. The procedures, however, do not define concepts. Silver (1979, 1986), in contrast, believes that the two are more fundamentally interrelated and that there is little point in distinguishing between them. Just as there is a conceptual basis for procedures, there is also a procedural basis for concepts. For example, the concept "equilateral triangle" may include procedures for distinguishing between examples and non-examples of such triangles. Concepts can therefore be defined by the operations that apply to them (see also Ross, 1996).

Conceptual knowledge has been referred to as "knowledge rich in relationships" (Hiebert & Lefèvre, 1986). When concepts are learned, they are by definition learned with meaning. Procedures, on the other hand, may or may not be learned with meaning. This leads to a paradox. If conceptual (declarative) understanding comes first, then procedures are surely also learned with meaning, as those procedures make reference to known concepts. If, however, procedures are acquired first, then conceptual understanding comes *after* the procedures have been learned. In other words, it is possible for procedural knowledge to *precede* certain types of declarative knowledge. Some of these issues are dealt with further in the next chapter.

THE ROLE OF DIAGRAMS AND PICTURES IN AIDING UNDERSTANDING

Many concepts in a new domain do not lie within people's previous experience. For this reason it is often useful to provide some *intermediate* means of relating the new concepts to something that the learner does know. People understand new concepts better if they are "anchored" to existing knowledge schemas. If the text succeeds in providing this anchor then readers will more readily understand and remember new material. One way to explain concepts in textbooks is therefore to try to relate them to the assumed prior knowledge of the reader. This general point has already been discussed in previous chapters. Here we will discuss one form of aiding conceptual understanding using illustrations.

Bridging analogies and intermediate representations

Graphs, figures, and tables are ways of representing information pictorially. In many cases they therefore serve the role of making textual information easier to understand. They can also serve to re-represent a question statement or a solution procedure. In this role they are "intermediate representations".

One example is what is known as an "intermediate bridging analogy" (Brown & Clement, 1989). The role of such analogies is the same as any other intermediate representation. For example, people often find it hard to understand that a surface such as a table top is deformed by, and has to push up with, a force exactly equal to the force of gravity exerted by an object—even a sheet of paper—sitting on the surface. To help understand the concept, imagine a heavy block resting on a sheet of rubber; the deformation of the rubber sheet should be obvious. Now imagine the block on a sheet of hardboard; the deformation should be less but still noticeable. Finally imagine the heavy block on a table top. The previous imagined situations should allow you to see that the table top is likewise deformed by the weight but that the deformation is not noticeable to the human eye (Figure 7.4).

Diagrams, graphs, and tables are often used in textbooks to provide an intermediate representation of the material presented there. Where learners find it difficult to understand the structure of novel abstract concepts, or relate such concepts to the concrete examples in texts, they may find it easier to understand the relation if an intermediate representation is used. In Figure 7.5, R represents the relation between a concept (A) and a concrete example (B); R1 represents the relation between the concept and some intermediate representation (B'); and R2 represents the relation between the intermediate representation and the concrete example. These intermediate representations are an important part of the explanation of new abstract material in textbooks and act as a form of "scaffolding" to help bridge the gap between the learners' prior knowledge (represented as B' in Figure 7.5) and the new concept (A in the Figure along with the relation between it and a specific concrete example represented by B).

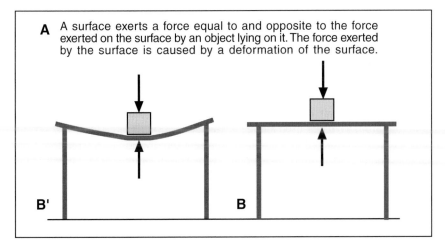

A A surface exerts a force equal to and opposite to the force exerted on the surface by an object lying on it. The force exerted by the surface is caused by a deformation of the surface.

Figure 7.4.   Intermediate bridging representations

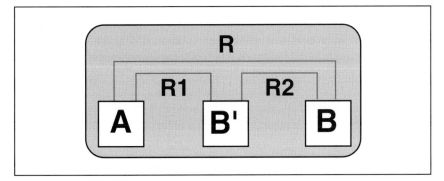

Figure 7.5.   A bridging analogy or intermediate representation (B′) helps the analogiser to make the leap from a concept (A) to a concrete example (B).

According to Resnick (1989) by providing a different representation of the textual material, writers can "bootstrap" learners' constructions of novel concepts. "Objectifying theoretical constructs", that is, making the abstract more concrete, can be done in texts by presenting the learner with some form of physical display. In that way the theoretical construct can be "seen".

There have been a number of experiments to test the effects of intermediate representations as an aid in problem solving. Such representations may involve some kind of visual representation (Beveridge & Parkins, 1987; Gick, 1985, 1988; Lewis, 1989), or an analogy whose purpose is to clarify a concept (Brown & Clement, 1989), or some other way of representing problems such as tables (Reed & Ettinger, 1987).

Both Gick (1985) and Beveridge and Parkins (1987) examined the effects of visual analogues on problem solving and found that visual representations can act as effective retrieval cues. Beveridge and Parkins used both diagrams and coloured strips as cues, and the results suggested that the coloured strips of different intensities, representing summative effects analogous to the concepts in the problems presented, were the most effective retrieval cue. Presenting a problem along with a visual representation seems to facilitate recall of a solution. Similarly Gick used a large arrow representing a large force and several smaller arrows arranged in a circle to represent the division of a large force and its convergence on a target (see Figure 5.1). The diagram was presented along with an explanation of the solution to the Fortress problem. When the diagram was reproduced in the target problem, it facilitated spontaneous transfer. The same was true for subjects who were presented with diagrams alone before solving the transfer problem.

Robinson and Kiewra (1995) found that students learned more and could apply that learning more if they had been presented with text that included graphic organisers, compared with students given text outlines.

Writers still have to be very careful that the textual representation of a new construct and the intermediate representation they provide are structurally equivalent. The inferences that readers can make in the known source domain should also be made in the target. If this is not the case then learners will have difficulty transferring the induced structure to novel problems of the same type.

The reasons why pictorial or diagrammatic representations are so effective are discussed by Larkin and Simon (1987). Texts present information in a linear sequence. Understanding this **sentential representation** incurs a great deal of computational cost in terms of search. The larger the data-structure contained within the sentential representation, the greater the search time. It is as if you had to search through a lot of "mental text" to retrieve relevant information or make a useful inference. In a **diagrammatic representation** the information is indexed by its 2-D location—diagrams can make relations *perceptually* explicit, which is not the case in sentential representations. According to Larkin and Simon, diagrams:

- allow a large number of automatic perceptual inferences;
- avoid the need to match symbolic labels (matching a variable in one part of a sentential representation to a related variable elsewhere);
- obviate the need to search for problem-solving inferences.

While graphical representations can help us understand concepts or systems, they also have a number of other functions. Levin (1988) classifies the functions of "pictures-in-text" into five categories:

1. *decoration*, where pictures are designed to make a text more attractive but are not related to the content;

2. *representation*, where pictures make the text more concrete, as in children's books;
3. *organisation*, where pictures enhance the structure of a text;
4. *interpretation*, where pictures are supposed to make a text more comprehensible;
5. *transformation*, where pictures are presented to make a text more memorable.

Levin relates these functions to different prose-learning outcomes by appealing to the notion of **transfer-appropriate processing** (Morris, Bransford, & Franks, 1977). Learners have to take account of the goals of the learning context and adapt their learning strategies accordingly. In the context of using pictures in text, Levin argues that writers should use different pictorial representations depending on whether they want to encourage the learner to *understand* the material, *remember* the material, or to *apply* the material. For example, in the studies by Beveridge and Parkins (1987) and Gick (1985) the function of the intermediate representation was principally to aid retrieval.

PROVIDING A SCHEMA IN TEXTS

Another method of providing the reader with help in understanding new concepts is by using an explanatory schema. Figure 7.1 showed that examples can represent a category of problems. It is possible to provide a general schema for solving a range of problems of the same type. The difficulty here is presenting the schema at the appropriate level of abstraction (see Chapter 9). If it is too abstract, then it might be hard to see how it applies in a specific example. If it is too specific, then it might be hard to see how it can be transferred to another more distant variant of the problem type.

Chen and Daehler (1989) examined the relation between the type of story representation (specific or abstract schema) and positive and negative analogical transfer in children. Where an abstract schema was provided, the children were able to transfer analogous solutions spontaneously even when the source and target problems shared few surface similarities. Indeed the abstract representation of the source analogue was a strong determinant of positive transfer. When the target problem involved a solution principle different from the source, negative transfer resulted. However, although schema training had a strong effect on positive transfer, another important aspect was the ability to determine when it should be applied.

Some of the benefits of providing an explanatory schema have been listed by Smith and Goodman (1984). They apply equally well to the benefits of diagrams and other pictorial representations such as graphs and tables and can be related to the information-processing model of Larkin and Simon (1987). These are compared in Table 7.3.

Learning to solve problems in an unfamiliar domain can be a difficult and taxing business. The writer can make the learner's task a little easier in three main ways:

TABLE 7.3

The benefits of an explanatory schema and of diagrams

Schemas Smith and Goodman (1984)	Diagrams Larkin and Simon (1987)
Schemas provide an explanatory framework or "scaffolding". They improve understanding, as the pre-existing connections between the framework slots can be mapped to the new domain directly.	In Larkin and Simon's terms the diagram and text should be "informationally equivalent" so that information in one representation is also inferable in the other.
Schemas contain information that can be added to fill in gaps in knowledge and help form connections between gaps.	In diagrams this includes the ability to generate perceptual inferences.
Schema-based instructions reduce the time required to understand the relation between steps.	In diagrams there is less need for search.
Schemas boost memory for specific information.	According to Larkin and Simon, diagrams allow the reader to focus on perceptual cues and so retrieve problem-relevant inference operators from memory.
Schemas boost performance where they depend on understanding the relations between steps.	Similarly, diagrams have computational benefits, as the information in them is better indexed and is supported by perceptual inferences.
Schemas should lead to a hierarchical organisation of material which should, in turn, lead to "chunking" and hence improve recall (Eylon & Reif, 1984)	The information in diagrams is perceptually grouped—related bits of information are adjacent to each other.

1. By not making too many assumptions about what the learner understands. Unfortunately, what constitutes "too many" is an empirical question.
2. New concepts and information can be made easier to grasp by including *intermediate representations* such as analogies and illustrations that relate the new material to what the reader already knows, or that make the material visually clearer.
3. Presenting both concrete examples and an explanation at a moderately abstract level (a schema) might help the learner see how the examples might be adapted to different situations.

SUMMARY

1. Analogical problem solving involves reasoning from a familiar domain to solve problems in an unfamiliar one. Textbook problem solving, on the other hand, tends to involve mapping an unfamiliar example onto an even less familiar exercise problem.

2. Textbook writers have to make some assumptions about the readership. These include assumptions about:

   • The readers' prior knowledge.
   • How much the readers are likely to remember from previous chapters.
   • How much they understand from previous chapters.
   • Their schema knowledge of how such texts are constructed.
   • How much the readers can generalise from the examples and explanations given.

3. Examples in textbooks are the salient aspects of instruction. They are the parts of the text that readers pay most attention to and use when solving later problems. They show:

   • How abstract principles can be made concrete.
   • What operators to choose at any given point.
   • What features can readily be generalised over.

4. Different forms of representation are necessary to understand word problems. These include knowledge of the lexicon, understanding of the text including local coherence (the textbase), the mental model of the situation described in the text including inferences derived from it (the situation model), and the relation between the latter and the solver's knowledge of the domain (e.g., mathematical knowledge) that allows the generation of the problem model.

5. When solvers attempt to use an example as a source to solve a target problem they are likely to be successful if the two are close variants. If they are distant variants then the textual explanation needs to include an explanation of how to generalise over the different variants (i.e., a problem schema needs to be provided).

6. Diagrams and analogies provide a means of forming a bridge between a familiar situation and the novel unfamiliar situation. Although pictures, graphs, and illustrations can have a variety of functions in texts, they share the same pedagogical function as analogies and schemas in texts.

PART FOUR

Learning and the development of expertise

example would be "if it rains then take an umbrella". You might see the "if" part and the "then" part referred to in various ways, such as the left side of a rule and the right side of a rule, or goal and sub-goal, or condition–action. The condition part of a rule specifies the circumstances ("it is raining") under which the action part ("take an umbrella") is triggered. If a set of circumstances matches the condition part of a rule then the action part is said to "fire". A production memory can be likened to a *procedural memory*, which is our memory for how to do things, and can be contrasted with a *declarative memory*, which is our memory for facts and episodes. A production system is therefore a set of condition–action rules, and a production system architecture has some form of production memory with other parts bolted on, such as a working memory or a declarative memory, along with connections between them and the outside world.

In Anderson's (1983, 1993) ACT architecture, there are three memory systems: a production memory that is the system's long-term procedural memory, a declarative memory that is the system's memory for facts (the facts are not isolated but interrelated in a "tangled hierarchy"), and a working memory. Information entering working memory from the outside world or retrieved from declarative memory is matched with the condition parts of rules in production memory and the action part of the production is then executed. The executed part of the production rule is now in working memory and may in turn lead to the firing of other rules. For example, information entering the senses from the world ("it is raining") may enter working memory. This information may match with the condition of a production rule ("if *it is raining* then take an umbrella") in which case the action part of the rule fires ("take an umbrella"). This in turn enters working memory ("you have an umbrella") and may in turn trigger a further production ("if *you have an umbrella* and it is raining then open the umbrella"), and so on.

Declarative knowledge, however, can be expressed as productions. In the SOAR architecture (Laird et al., 1987; Laird & Rosenbloom, 1996) there is no separate declarative memory store. Both models of human cognitive architecture claim to model a wide variety of human thinking. Because of their explanatory power, both claim to be unified theories of cognition with Alan Newell championing SOAR (Newell, 1990) and John R. Anderson claiming the prize for ACT-R (Anderson, 1993). Anderson, for example, has made the strong assertion that "cognitive skills are realised by production rules" (1993, p. 1).

Another model of how we induce both categories and rules from experience is that of Holland and co-workers' (1986). They have produced a general cognitive architecture that lays emphasis on induction as a basic learning mechanism. An important aspect of Holland and co-workers' model is the emphasis placed on rules representing categorisations derived from experience. Rules that lead to successful attainment of a goal are strengthened and are more likely to fire in future. Information Box 8.2 presents some of the main features of the model.

Processes of Induction (PI)

Holland et al. (1986) present a model of induction based on different types of rules. **Synchronic rules** represent the general features of an object or its category membership. **Diachronic rules** represent changes over time. There are two kinds of synchronic rule: categorical and associative (Holland et al., 1986, p. 42).

Categorical rules include rules such as:

> *If an object is a dog, then it is an animal.*
> *If an object is a large slender dog with very long white and gold hair, then it is a collie.*
> *If an object is a dog, then it can bark.*

Note that these rules encompass both a hierarchy (dogs are examples of animals) and the properties of individual members (dogs belong to the set of animals that bark) in contradistinction to the conceptual hierarchy of Collins and Quillian (1969) where properties are attached to examples at each level of a hierarchy.

Associative rules include:

> *If an object is a dog then activate the "cat" concept.*
> *If an object is a dog then activate the "bone" concept.*

Associative rules therefore represent the effects of spreading activation or priming.

Diachronic rules are also of two kinds: "predictor" and "effector".

Predictor rules permit expectations of what is likely to occur in the world. Examples of predictor rules are:

> *If a person annoys a dog then the dog will growl.*
> *If a person whistles to a dog then the dog will come to the person.*

Effector rules tell the system how to act in a given situation. They include rules such as:

> *If a dog chases you then run away.*
> *If a dog approaches you with its tail wagging then pet it.*

Our mental representation of the world tends to simplify the real world by categorising aspects of it. To make sense of the world and not overload the cognitive system, a categorisation function "maps sets of world states into a smaller number of model states". The model of the world produced by such a "many-to-one" mapping is known as a **homomorphism**.

Now sometimes generalisations (categorisations) can lead to errors. If you say "Boo" to a bird it will fly away. However, no amount of booing will cause a penguin to fly away despite the penguin being a bird. To cope with penguins another more specific rule is required. You end up with a hierarchy from superordinate (more general) categories to subordinate (more specific) categories and instances. Higher-level categories provide default

Information Box 8.2 (continued)

expectations (birds fly away when you say "Boo!"). An exception (penguins waddle swiftly away when you say "Boo!") evokes a lower level of the hierarchy. A hierarchical model that includes a set of changes of state brought about by a set of transition functions (one for each level) is known as a *quasi-homomorphism* or *q-morphism* for short.

Figure 8.4 represents a mental model based on a state of affairs in the world (a sequence of operators applied to a sequence of problem states). The top half represents the world including transitions between states, and the bottom half is a mental model of that world.

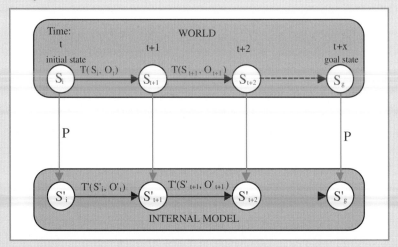

Figure 8.4.   A problem model as a homomorphism. T is a transition function, S_i is the initial problem state, S_g is the goal state, O is a category of operators, and P is a categorisation function. The prime (T', S', O') represents the mental representations of those operators, states and functions (adapted from Holland et al., 1986, p. 40).

A problem model is valid only if (1) given a model state S'_i, and (2) given a model state S'_g that corresponds to a goal state S_g in the environment, then (3) any sequence of actions (operator categories) in the model, {O' (1), O' (2), ... O' (n)}, which transforms S'_i into S'_g in the model, describes a sequence of effector actions that will attain the goal S_g in the environment. An ideal problem model thus is one that describes all those elements in the world necessary and sufficient for the concrete realization of a successful solution plan. The process of induction is directed by the goal of generating mental models that increasingly approximate this ideal.

(Holland et al., 1986, p. 40)

In the homomorphism represented in Figure 8.4, P is a categorisation function that serves to map elements in the world to elements in the model.

Analogical problem solving can be modelled in this system by assuming a "second order morphism". A source model as in Figure 8.4 can be used to generate a model of the target.

Generalisation

Similar conditions producing the same action can trigger condition-simplifying generalisation. Suppose there are learned rules such as "If X has wings and X is brown then X can fly" and "If X has wings and X is black then X can fly". A simplifying generalisation would remove the "X is brown" and "X is black" conditions since they do not seem to be relevant to flying.

People have beliefs about the degrees to which instances of objects that form categories tend to vary. That is, the generalisations that we form depend on the nature of the categories and our beliefs about the variability of features of instances of the category. Induction therefore ranges from liberal to conservative. The Processes of Induction (PI) system takes this variability into account in inducing instance-based generalisation.

Specialisation

It is in the nature of our world that there are exceptions to rules. Once we have learned a rule that says that if an animal has wings then it can fly, and we encounter a penguin, our prediction is going to be wrong. PI can generate an exception rule (the q-morphism is redefined) that seems to cover the case of penguins. The unusual properties of penguins can be built into the condition part of the rule.

Expertise

The acquisition of expertise can be modelled by assuming that the sequence of rules that led to a successful solution are strengthened by a "bucket brigade" algorithm. This algorithm allows strength increments to be passed back along a sequence of linked rules. The final rule in the chain is the one that gets the most strength increments. As PI is a model designed to show how we learn from experience of instances, and as it includes algorithms for both generalisation and specialisation, it is a general model that explains the development of expertise.

SKILL LEARNING IN ACT-R

Anderson has produced a series of models that attempt to approximate as closely as possible to a general theory of cognition. Anderson's model, known as Adaptive Control of Thought (ACT), has evolved over the past two decades and has gone through a number of manifestations. The most recent is known as ACT-R where the "R" stands for Rational. Unfortunately, over the years there has been a kind of "genetic drift" in the meaning of the term "rational". The earliest sense was "logically correct reasoning". Another sense refers to the fact that organisms attempt to act in their own best interests. Chapter 2 referred to Newell and Simon's idea of "intendedly rational behaviour" or "limited rationality". Laird and Rosenbloom (1996, p.2) refer to the principle of rationality ascribed to Newell that governs the behaviour of an intelligent "agent" whereby "the actions it intends are those that its knowledge indicates will achieve its goals". Anderson's term is based on the sense used by economists. In this sense "human behavior is optimal in achieving human goals" (Anderson, 1990, p. 28). Anderson's "General Principle of Rationality" states that "The cognitive system operates at all times to optimize the adaptation of the behavior of the organism" (1990, p. 28). Anderson (1993, p. 47) later wrote:

> Certain aspects of cognition seemed to be designed to optimize the information processing of the system … optimization means maximizing the probability of achieving [one's] goals while minimizing the cost of doing so or, to put it more precisely, maximizing the expected utility, where this is defined as expected gain minus expected cost.

In a sense, where Anderson's definition emphasises the evolutionary process that shapes our thinking, Laird and Rosenbloom's emphasises the results of that process. Our cognitive system has evolved to allow us to adapt as best we can to the exigencies of the environment in which we find ourselves, and in line with our goals. This entails a balance between the costs involved in, say, a memory search, and the gains one might get from such a search (the usefulness of the retrieved memory). As a result of taking this view of rationality, the cognitive mechanisms built into ACT-R are based on Bayesian probabilities (see Information Box 8.3). For example, the world we inhabit has a certain structure. Features of objects in the world tend to co-vary. If we see an animal with wings and covered in feathers, there is a high likelihood that the animal can fly. It would be useful for a cognitive system to be constructed to make that kind of assumption relatively easily. It's wrong; but it's only wrong in a very small percentage of cases. The gains of having a system that can make fast inductions of this kind outweigh the costs of being wrong on the rare occasion. Assume that you are an experienced driver and you are waiting at a junction. A car is coming from the left signalling a right turn into your road. There is a very high probability that the car will, indeed, turn right. In this case, however, the costs of being wrong are rather high, so you might wait for other features to show themselves, such as the car slowing down before you decide to pull out.

The general structure of ACT-R is shown in Figure 8.4. There are two types of long-term memory in ACT-R: a declarative memory and a production (procedural) memory. Declarative knowledge (factual and episodic knowledge) can be verbalised, described, or reported. Procedural memory can be observed and is expressed in a person's performance. People can get better at using procedural skills but forget the declarative base.

Anderson has consistently argued that all knowledge enters the system in a declarative form. Using that knowledge in context generates procedural knowledge which is represented as a set of productions in production memory. Bear in mind that there is an argument that says that some forms of conceptual knowledge might come about as a result of procedural knowledge, as explained in Chapter 7. For example, as a result of becoming reasonably proficient at solving the Tower of Hanoi puzzle one may notice that the smallest ring is moved on every second move;

Information Box 8.3

Bayes' Theorem

Almost all events or features in the world are based on probabilities rather than certainties. The movement of billiard balls on a table becomes rapidly unpredictable the more the cue ball strikes the other balls; uncertainties govern the movement and position of fundamental particles; if someone has long hair then that person is probably a woman; most (but not all) fruits are sweet, and so on. Fortunately, some events or co-variations of features are more likely than others, otherwise the world would be even more unpredictable than it already is. Our beliefs reflect the fact that some things are more likely to occur than others. Aeschylus probably did not weigh up the benefits of going out in a boat against the potential costs of being killed by a falling tortoise.

Bayes' Theorem allows us to combine our prior beliefs, or the prior likelihood of something being the case, with changes in the environment. When new evidence comes to light, or if a particular behaviour proves to be useful in achieving our goals, then our beliefs (or our behaviour) can be updated based on this new evidence. The theorem can be expressed as:

$$Odds(A\ given\ B) = LR \times Odds(A)$$

where A refers to one's beliefs, a theory, a genetic mutation being useful, or whatever; B refers to the observed evidence or some other type of event. Odds(A given B) could reflect the odds of an illness (A) given a symptom (B), for example. In the equation, Odds(A) refers to what is known as the "prior odds"—a measure of the plausibility of a belief or the likelihood of an event. For example, a suspicion that someone is suffering from malaria might be quite high if that person has just returned from Africa. The LR is the Likelihood Ratio and is given by the formula:

$$LR = \frac{P(B\ given\ A\ is\ true)}{P(B\ given\ A\ is\ false)}$$

where P is the probability, B is an event (or evidence), and A is the aforementioned belief, theory, or other event. The Likelihood Ratio therefore takes into account both the probability of an event (B) happening in conjunction with another event (A) (a symptom accompanying an illness) and in the absence of A (the probability of a symptom being displayed for any other reason).

Anderson has used Bayesian probabilities in his "rational analysis" of behaviour and cognition. For example, in the domain of memory, the probability that an item will be retrieved depends on the how recently the item was used, the number of times it has been used in the past, and the likelihood it will be retrieved in a given context. In problem solving there is an increased likelihood that the inductive inferences produced by using an example problem with a similar goal will be relevant in subsequent similar situations.

Production memory in ACT-R

The production is the basic unit of knowledge in procedural memory. Examples of productions have already been encountered in Chapter 4 along with aspects of their role in the transfer of procedural skill. Declarative knowledge is the basis for procedural knowledge. ACT-R requires declarative structures to be active to support procedural learning in the early stages of learning a new skill. Productions in ACT-R are modular. That is, deleting a production rule will not cause the system to crash. There will, however, be an effect on the behaviour of the system. If you had a complete model of two-column subtraction and deleted one of the production rules that represented the subtraction problem, then you would generate an error in the subtraction. This is one way you can model the kinds of errors that children make when they learn subtraction for the first time (Young & O'Shea, 1981).

Procedural memory in ACT-R can respond to identical stimulus conditions in entirely different ways depending on the goals of the system.

Learning in ACT-R

The development of cognitive skill involves somehow transforming declarative knowledge (such as the instructions for driving a car) into procedural knowledge (skilled driving). As a result of this process, knowledge is **compiled**. This is an analogy with computers where "high-level" languages have to be interpreted by the computer's built-in machine code before the program can run. That is, the program has to be *compiled,* and the result of converting it to machine code means it is no longer directly accessible in its original form. Anderson's views on how this comes about have evolved over the years.

When we encounter a novel problem for the first time we hit an impasse—we don't immediately know what to do. We might therefore attempt to recall a similar problem we have encountered in the past and try to use that to solve the current one. According to Anderson, this process involves interpretive problem solving. This means that our problem solving is based on a declarative account of a problem-solving episode. This would include, for example, using textbook examples or information a teacher might write on a board. Anderson argues that even if we have only instructions rather than a specific example to hand, then we interpret those instructions by means of an imagined example and attempt to solve the current problem by interpreting this example. As a result the information is compiled. "The only way a new production can be created in ACT-R is by compiling the analogy process. Following instructions creates an example from which a procedure can be learned by later analogy" (Anderson, 1993, p. 89).

In short Anderson is arguing that learning a new production—and, by extension, all skill learning—occurs through analogical problem solving. In this sense the model is similar to Holland and co-workers' (1986) PI model.

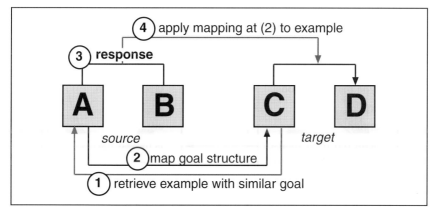

Figure 8.6.   The analogy mechanism in ACT-R.

Figure 8.6 shows the analogy mechanism in ACT-R in terms of the problem representation used throughout this book. In this model, the A and C terms represent goals (the problem statement including the problem's goal). The B term is the goal state, and the line linking the A and B terms is the "response": the procedure to be followed to achieve the goal state. As in other models of analogy, mapping (2 in Figure 8.6) involves finding correspondences between the example and the current problem.

Before looking in a little more detail at ACT-R's analogy mechanism try Activity 8.1. The mapping of the elements in the example onto elements in the current problem is shown in more detail in Figure 8.7. The structure in the example shows you that the problem involves a Lisp operation, that the operation involves multiplication, that there are two "arguments": arg1 and arg2, and that there is a method for doing it shown by response1. These elements can be mapped onto the elements of the current problem. The problem type is different, nevertheless both are arithmetic operations. They are similar because

---

Activity 8.1

Imagine you are given the problem of writing a Lisp function that will add 712 and 91. You have been given an example that shows you how to write a Lisp function that will multiply two numbers together:

   Defun multiply-them(2 3)

   *2 3

You know that "*defun*" defines a function and that "*multiply-them*" is a name invented for that function and that * is the multiplication symbol.

How would you write a function in Lisp that will *add* 712 and 91? (See p. 237 for answer.)

TABLE 8.2

Information presented in evaluation and generation tasks in
McKendree and Anderson (1987)

Type of information	Evaluation	Generation
V1	(A B C)	(A B C)
Function call	(CAR V1)	?
Result	?	A

Adapted from Müller (1999).

P1:   If the goal is to evaluate (CAR V1)
      And A is the first element of V1
      Then produce A.
P2:   If the goal is to generate a function call
      And ANSWER is the first element of V1
      Then produce (CAR V1)

As the condition sides of these two productions do not match, the transfer between them would be limited, bearing in mind that the knowledge they represent is compiled. A similar finding was made by Anderson and Fincham (1994) who got participants to practise transformations of dates for various activities such as: "Hockey was played on Saturday at 3 o'clock. Now it is Monday at 1 o'clock." Transforming one day and time into another involves adding or subtracting 1 or 2 from Day 1 (e.g., Saturday + 2) and Hour 1 (1–2). Practising on one transformation did not transfer to the reverse transformation.

Müller (1999), however, challenged the idea of use-specificity of compiled knowledge. One effect of such use-specificity is that skilled performance should become rather inflexible; yet expertise, if it is of any use, means that knowledge can be used flexibly (this aspect of expertise is discussed in the next chapter). Müller also used LISP concepts such as LIST, INSERT, APPEND, DELETE, MEMBER, and LEFT. He also got his participants to learn either a generation task or an evaluation task using those concepts in both. His study was designed to distinguish between the results that would be obtained if the use of knowledge was context-bound and those that follow on from his own hypothesis of **conceptual integration**. According to this hypothesis concepts mediate between a problem's givens and the requested answers. Concepts have a number of features that aggregate to form an integrated conceptual unit. The basic assumptions of the hypothesis (Müller, 1999, p. 194) are:

(a) conceptual knowledge is internally represented by integrative units; (b) access to the internal representation of conceptual knowledge depends on the degree of match between presented information and conceptual features; (c) conceptual units serve to monitor the production of adequate answers to a problem; and (d) the integration of a particular feature into the internal representation depends on its salience during instruction, its relevance during practice, or both.

Whereas ACT-R predicts that transfer between different uses of knowledge would *decrease* with practice, the hypothesis of conceptual integration predicts that transfer between tasks involving the same concepts would *increase* with practice. Müller found typical learning curves in his experiments, but did not find that this pre-sumably compiled knowledge was use-specific. There was a relatively high transfer rate between evaluation and generation tasks. Thus the overlap and relevance of conceptual features was important in predicting transfer and allowed flexibility in skilled performance. Going back to our example of the crossword puzzler, it seems reasonable to suppose that a skilled puzzle solver can transfer his or her knowledge of how to solve crossword puzzle clues to the task of generating them. Müller's hypothesis can account for this type of transfer whereas use-specificity of productions should make such transfer unlikely. Others have criticised production systems as representations of cognitive skill.

As Copeland (1993, p. 101) puts it:

> When I turn out an omelette to perfection, is this because my brain has come to acquire an appropriate set of if–then rules, which I am unconsciously following, or is my mastery of whisk and pan grounded in some entirely different sort of mechanism? It is certainly true that my actions can be described by means of if–then sentences: if the mixture sticks then I flick the pan, and so on. But it doesn't follow from this that my actions are produced by some device in my brain scanning through lists of if–then rules of this sort (whereas that is how some computer expert systems work).

Copeland is arguing here that regarding knowledge as production rules may simply be a useful fiction. In a similar vein, Clancey (1997) argues that it is a mistake to equate knowledge with knowledge representation. The latter is an artefact. Architectures such as ACT-R and SOAR are descriptive and language-based, whereas human knowledge is built from activities: "Ways of interacting and viewing the world, ways of structuring time and space, pre-date human language and descriptive theories" (Clancey, 1997, p. 270). Furthermore he argues that too much is missed out of production-system architectures, such as the cultural and social context in which experts operate.

Johnson-Laird (1988a, b) has suggested that production-system archi-tectures can explain a great deal of the evidence that has accrued about human cognition. However, their very generality makes them more like a programming language than a theory and hence difficult to refute experimentally. He also argues (Johnson-Laird, 1988b) that condition–action rules are bound to content (the "condition" part of the production) and so are poor at explaining human abstract reasoning. Furthermore, he has argued (1988b) that regarding expertise as compiled procedures suggests a rigidity of performance that experts do not exhibit (this aspect is discussed further in the next chapter).

ARE EXPERTS SMARTER? ARE THERE DIFFERENCES IN ABILITIES?

Is knowledge the only or main factor that leads to expertise, or are there other factors (such as "ability") to be taken into account? For over a century there have been many diverging explanations for exceptional performance in a particular domain. They have generally tended to take a stance somewhere along two dimensions: innate versus acquired ability, and domain-specific versus domain-general ability (Ericsson & Smith, 1991). Some explanations have included the role played by personality, motivation, and thinking styles.

One specific ability that has long been assumed to play a part in exceptional performance is "intelligence" (the quotation marks are meant to represent the slipperiness of this concept). In other words one could ask the question: Do you need to be intelligent to be an expert? This question is essentially asking if there is a domain-general ability that leads to expertise in a chosen field. Some studies have suggested that expert chess players also performed well in other fields such as chess journalism and languages (DeGroot, 1965; Elo, 1978). However, there seems to be remarkably little correlation between intelligence and other measures such as subsequent occupation, social status, money earned, and so on, despite a high correlation with success in school tests (Ceci, 1996; Sternberg, 1997a). Schneider, Körkel, and Weinert (1989) found that children who were highly knowledgeable about football, but who were low on measured IQ scores, could nevertheless outperform other children with high IQ scores in reading comprehension, inferencing, and memory tasks if those tasks were in the domain of football. Ceci and Likert (1986) compared two groups of racetrack goers, one of which was expert at predicting what the odds would be on a horse at post time. The expert group, unlike the other non-expert group, used a complex set of seven interacting variables when computing the odds. Each bit of information (one variable) they were given about a real horse or a hypothetical one would change the way they considered the other bits of information (the other six variables). Despite the "cognitive complexity" of the task, the correlation between the experts' success at the racetrack and their IQ scores was −.07—no correlation at all, in fact.

Swanson, O'Connor, and Carter (1991) divided a group of schoolchildren into two sub-groups based on their verbal protocols while engaged in a number of problem-solving tasks. One sub-group was designated as having "gifted intelligence" because of the sophistication of the heuristics and strategies they employed. The sub-groups were then compared with each other on measures of IQ, scholastic achievement, creativity, and attribution (what people ascribe success or failure to). No substantial differences were found between the two groups. Swanson et al. concluded that IQ, among other measures, is not directly related to intelligence defined in terms of expert/novice representations. If a person shows "gifted intelligence" on a task, this does not mean that that person will have a high IQ.

Does becoming an expert in a domain help you in understanding or developing expertise in another? In a review of the literature, Frensch and Buchner (1999) have pointed out that there is little evidence for expertise in one domain "spreading" to another. Ericsson and Charness (1997) have also stated (although with specific reference to memory) that "Experts acquire skill in memory to meet *specific* demands of encoding and accessibility in *specific* activities in a *given* domain. For this reason their skill is unlikely to transfer from one domain to another" (Ericsson & Charness, 1997, p. 16, emphases added).

On the other hand, there can be skills developed in one domain which can be transferred to another where the skills required overlap to some extent. Schunn and Anderson (1999) tested the distinction between domain-expertise and task-expertise. Experts in the domain of the cognitive psychology of memory (with a mean of 68 publications), social science experts (mean of 58 publications—task experts), and psychology undergraduates were given the task of testing two theories of memory concerning the effects of massed versus distributed practice. As they designed the experiment they were asked to think aloud. All the experts mentioned the theories as they designed the experiment, whereas a minority of students referred to them—nor did the students refer often to the theories when trying to interpret the results. Domain experts designed relatively complicated experiments manipulating several variables, whereas task experts designed simple ones keeping the variables under control. The complexity of the experiments designed by the students was somewhere in between. Schunn and Anderson claim that, at least in this domain, there are shared general transferable skills that can be learned more or less independently of context.

Nevertheless, we need some way of explaining why one person can be outstanding in a field whereas someone else with the same length of experience is not. Factors that have been used to explain exceptional performance are personality and thinking styles. People vary. Some are better at doing some things than others. Gardner (1983) has argued that there are multiple intelligences that can explain exceptional performance by individuals in different domains. In this view, exceptional performance or expertise comes about when an individual's particular intelligence profile suits the demands of that particular domain.

Furthermore, people differ in their thinking styles. While some prefer to look at the overall picture in a task or domain, others are happier examining the details. While some are very good at carrying out procedures, others prefer to think up these procedures in the first place (Sternberg, 1997b).

Because people vary in their experience, predispositions, and thinking styles, it is possible to devise tests in which person *A* will perform well and person *B* will perform poorly and vice versa (Sternberg, 1998). *A* might do well in a test of gardening and poorly in an IQ test; *B* may perform well in the IQ test but poorly in the test of gardening. In this scenario measures of intelligence such as IQ tests are really measures of *achievement*. Sternberg has therefore argued that intelligence unpredictable as "they arise from a complex interaction between 'bounded rationality' and incomplete or inaccurate mental models ... No matter how expert people are at coping with familiar problems, their performance will begin to approximate that of novices once their repertoire of rules has been exhausted by the demands of a novel situation" (1990, p. 58).

There are therefore circumstances when novices may do better or at least no worse than experts. As novices and experts differ in the way they represent information, Adelson (1984) hypothesised that expert programmers would represent programs in a more abstract form than novices. Novices, she argued, would represent programs in a more concrete form than experts, who would represent them in terms of what the program does. An entailment of this theory is that novices and experts would differ in how they dealt with questions based on a concrete or an abstract representation of a program. In one experiment Adelson represented a program as a flowchart (an abstract representation) or described how it functioned (a concrete representation). She then asked questions about either what the program did (abstract) or how it did it (concrete). She found that she could induce experts to make more errors than novices if they were asked a concrete question when presented with an abstract representation. Likewise novices made more errors in the abstract condition.

Flexibility in thinking

There would appear to be something wrong with this conception of expertise where learned procedures, automatisation, compiled knowledge, schematisation—call it what you will—lead to degraded performance. Experts wouldn't be experts unless they could solve problems flexibly.

Hatano and Inagaki (1986) have distinguished between **routine expertise**, which refers to the schema-based knowledge experts use to solve standard familiar problems efficiently, and **adaptive expertise** that permits experts to use their knowledge flexibly by allowing them to find *ad hoc* solutions to non-standard unfamiliar problems.

According to Lesgold et al. (1988), expert radiologists flexibly change their representations when new problem features manifest themselves. For example, Feltovich et al. (1984) gave expert and novice clinicians clinical cases to diagnose that had a "garden path" structure. That is, the pattern of symptoms indicated a "classical" (but wrong) disease. It was the novices who misdiagnosed the disease rather than the experts with their supposed abstracted out schema for patterns of disease. Experts were more likely to reach a correct diagnosis after consultation with the patient. Feltovich, Spiro, and Coulson (1997) argue that the very fact that experts have a large well-organised and highly differentiated set of schemas means that they are more sensitive to things that don't fit. When that happens the expert is more likely to engage in more extensive search than the novice.

Table 9.1 shows a protocol from an expert examining an X-ray of a patient who had had a portion of a lung removed a decade earlier. As a result the slide seemed to show a chronic collapsed lung. An effect of the removed portion was that the internal organs had moved around. The protocol in the Table shows the expert testing the "collapsed lung" schema and finding that there are indications that there are other features which don't quite fit in with that schema. He switches to a lobectomy schema which, in the final part of the protocol, he also checks.

From their work, Lesgold et al. (1988, p. 317) have suggested that the behaviour of the expert radiologist conforms to the following general pattern:

> First, during the initial phase of building a mental representation, every schema that guides radiological diagnosis seems to have a set of prerequisites or tests that must be satisfied before it can control the viewing and diagnosis. Second, the expert works efficiently to reach the stage where an appropriate general schema is in control. Finally, each schema contains a set of processes that allows the viewer to reach a diagnosis and confirm it.

According to Voss, Greene, Post, and Penner (1983) experts' knowledge is flexible because information can be interpreted in terms of the knowledge structures the experts have developed and new information can be assimilated into appropriate structures. Similarly, Chi, Glaser, and Rees (1982) have stated that experts have both more schemas and more specialised ones than novices, and this allows them to find a better fit to the task in hand. Experts' extensive knowledge and categorising ability may lead to expert intuition. As intuition is by definition not accessible to consciousness it can best be modelled in a connectionist system rather than a rule-based one (Partridge, 1987).

TABLE 9.1

Protocol excerpts from an expert, showing early schema invocation, tuning, and flexibility

---

Something is wrong, and it's chronic: "We may be dealing with a chronic process here…"

Trying to get a schema: "I'm trying to work out why the mediastinum and the heart is displaced into the right chest. There is not enough rotation to account for this. I don't see a displacement of fissures [lung lobe boundaries]."

Experiments with collapse schema: "There may be a collapse of the right lower lobe but the diaphragm on the right side is well visualized and that's a feature against it…"

Does some testing; schema doesn't fit without a lot of tuning: "I come back to the right chest. The ribs are crowded together… The crowding of the ribcage can, on some occasions, be due to previous surgery. In fact, … The third and fourth ribs are narrow and irregular so he's probably had previous surgery…"

Cracks the case: "He's probably had one of his lobes resected. It wouldn't be the middle lobe. It may be the upper lobe. It may not necessarily be a lobectomy. It could be a small segment of the lung with pleural thickening at the back."

Checks to be sure: "I don't see the right hilum… [this] may, in fact, be due to the postsurgery state I'm postulating… Loss of visualization of the right hilum is… seen with collapse …"

Source: Lesgold et al. (1988).

could recall more lines of code than novices and had larger chunk sizes for encoding information.

The role of perception in skilled performance

According to DeGroot, and Chase and Simon, perception is the key to chess skill (Cooke, 1992). However, this may be putting the cart before the horse to some extent. The ability to recognise perceptual patterns and to categorise problems or situations appropriately is the *result* of expertise. You can't teach people to categorise problems unless they already have the requisite knowledge of principles —the conceptual knowledge. You can't chunk stuff perceptually without the experience and concepts with which to do so.

Egan and Schwartz (1979) repeated the "traditional" expert–novice memory task for meaningful and meaningless displays. The domain this time was electronic circuit drawings. In one condition experts tried to recall drawings of randomly placed electronic circuit symbols in terms of functionally related units, and were faster than the novices on the task. Egan and Schwartz argued that there was more of a top-down process taking place than a perceptual chunking hypothesis could account for. It was not so much perceptual chunking that was taking place, but conceptual chunking. That is, higher-level concepts were being used to govern perceptual chunking of the display.

Conceptual chunking can also be seen in a study by Cooke, Atlas, Lane, and Berger (1991, cited in Cooke, 1992). Meaningful board configurations were presented to chess players. A verbal description of the configurations either preceded or followed the visual presentation of the chess board. Where a verbal description preceded the visual presentation, the performance of the experts was enhanced. This suggests that higher-level (conceptual) information prepared them for the pattern-recognition (perceptual) task. Johnson and Mervis (1997) performed a categorisation study with experts on songbirds. They also found that conceptual knowledge interacted with perception.

Experts' categories can be less distinct than those of novices. Murphy and Wright (1984) asked experts and novices to list attributes of three childhood disorders. Experts listed more features for each disorder than novices and agreed with each other more, but there were fuzzier boundaries between the categories of disorder than those produced by novices. An explanation for the difference is that novices learn about prototypical cases during training, but experts have had experience of exceptions to the prototype and hence have developed a broader view of the category.

Norman, Brooks, and Allen (1989) also argue that experts' processing of information is "effortful" unlike the findings from more "visual" areas of expertise such as patterns in chess. Nevertheless, some forms of expertise rely on making very fast decisions based on perceptual cues. In many sports the ability to make accurate predictions from subtle cues improves a sportsperson's chances of hitting a ball. In baseball, for example, an experienced player can predict the pitch within the first 80 milliseconds (Paull & Glencross, 1997).

Expert categorisation of problems, and indeed of things such as dogs, fish, or trees, is often based on the goal of the categorisation rather than just a concern with simple taxonomy (Ross, 1996). Ross cites a number of studies where the experts' judgements were based on goal-defined categories that come about as a result of repeated interaction with the category members. The experts' classification of items in Chi and co-workers' study is not the goal so much as a means to an end (solving the relevant problem). The development of expertise is therefore a question of shifting from a classification based on surface features to one based on the solution method, which can only come about through solving such problems in the first place.

The role of memory in expert performance

Chase and Simon's original studies assumed a short-term working memory capacity of around seven chunks, as did most of the studies of expert memory in the 1970s and 1980s. More recently, however, a number of studies and papers have caused a re-assessment of those early findings. For example, Gobet and Simon (1996) found that expert chess players could recall the positions of more pieces than the original theory predicted. In one experiment, a Master chess player was able to increase the number of chess boards he could reproduce to nine with 70% accuracy and around 160 pieces correctly positioned. Gobet and Simon suggest that experts in a particular domain can use long-term memory templates to encode and store information.

Ericsson and Kintsch (1995) provide an explanation for how experts and skilled performers can manage a ten-fold increase in performance tests of short-term memory. They cite a number of studies in the memory and expertise literature that do not seem to fit well with the notion of a limited-capacity working memory limited to around only seven items.

Ericsson and Polson (1988) describe a well-known case of a waiter (JC) who could memorise long and complex dinner orders. He used a mnemonic strategy that allowed him to retrieve relevant information later. Furthermore his strategy could transfer to categories other than food orders, so the strategy was not domain-specific.

Medical diagnosis also presents a problem for a limited-capacity short-term working memory. Many symptoms and facts have to be maintained in memory in a form that can be retrieved readily until a diagnosis is made.

Ericsson and Kintsch therefore propose a long-term working memory associated with skilled memory performance and expertise. Experts are able to store information in long-term memory rather than maintaining it in short-term memory. In order to be able to do this and to do it quickly, three criteria have to be met:

the writing process using mainly protocol analysis as their method for finding evidence (Figure 9.4). The model owes a lot to Newell and Simon's (1972) model of human problem solving.

In the model the assignment topic is embedded in the task environment which "includes everything outside the writer's skin that influences the performance of the task" (Hayes & Flower, 1980, p. 12). There are three main writing processes: **planning**, **translating**, and **reviewing**.

Planning. This involves three sub-processes of generating, organising, and goal-setting. The *generating* process uses cues in the task environment including motivational and situational cues to retrieve relevant information from long-term

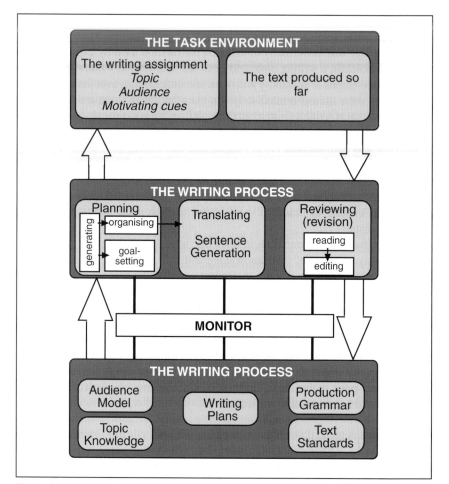

Figure 9.4. The Hayes–Flower model of composition (based on Hayes, 1989b; Hayes & Flower, 1980).

memory. The *organising* process selects from information retrieved material that seems most useful and organises that material into a writing plan. *Goal-setting* refers to the fact that some of the information retrieved may not necessarily be content information but criteria relevant to the intended audience. Plans are like artists' preliminary sketches. They give useful information about the general outline and content but can readily be modified. "Good plans are rich enough to work from and argue about but cheap enough to throw away" (Flower & Hayes, 1980, p. 43).

Translating. The information retrieved from long-term memory is presumed to be in the form of propositions. These propositions need to be translated into written prose.

Reviewing. This process is subdivided into reading and editing. The process detects violations of written expression. It also involves making some kind of evaluation of the text to see whether it fits in with the writer's goals.

The Hayes–Flower model is a model of *competent* writing. As such it tends to lay most emphasis on ideal writing processes. However, there is scope in the model for individual differences, particularly in terms of the goals of writers at different levels and in the constraints under which they operate. A novice writer may be operating under a set of constraints such as: time, availability of textbooks, lack of subject knowledge, avoidance of plagiarism, length, style, structure, and appropriate **genre** language (language appropriate to the type of text being written —a report, a formal essay, a thank-you letter to granny). Expert writers may be operating under a different set of constraints: originality, desire to be interesting, coherence, audience design, and so on. "Writing is like trying to work within government regulations from various agencies" (Flower & Hayes, 1980, p. 34). One of the effects of trying to juggle a large number of constraints is "cognitive overload".

The major constraint imposed on writers is the **rhetorical problem**: "whatever writers choose to say must ultimately conform to the structures posed by their *purpose* in writing, their sense of *audience* and their *projected selves* or imagined roles" (Flower & Hayes, 1980, p. 40). The other constraints of domain knowledge and written language production are subsumed and directed by the rhetorical problem—how to achieve the writer's goals in writing. In order to make the writing task manageable and avoid cognitive overload there are several strategies we can adopt:

Drop constraints: "I won't bother taking the reader's point of view"; "I won't worry about punctuation or spelling".

Partition the problem: "I'll divide the task into sub-problems and deal with each one at a time".

Satisficing: "I'll go with the first solution that meets my criteria".

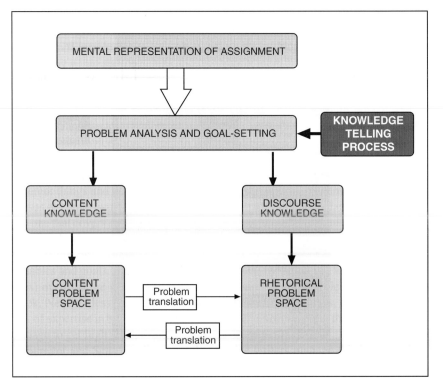

Figure 9.6.   Structure of the knowledge-transforming model (adapted from Bereiter and Scardamalia, 1987).

Experts are fast: They are faster than novices at performing the skills of their domain, and they quickly solve problems with little error.

Experts have superior short-term and long-term memory: How this might manifest itself in writing expertise is unclear.

Experts see and represent a problem in their domain at a deeper (more principled) level than novices; novices tend to represent a problem at a superficial level: This reflects the difference between novice and expert writers in various aspects of the writing process, notably planning and revision. Overall, knowledge telling is a relatively superficial strategy compared with knowledge transforming, which requires a "deeper" representation of how one's goals can be achieved in composition.

Experts spend a great deal of time analysing a problem qualitatively: This is generally true of expert writers. It manifests itself in representing the writing problem and in planning.

Experts have strong self-monitoring skills: This is also generally true of expert writers. It manifests itself most obviously in revision.

SUMMARY

1. Theories of both expertise and exceptional performance have been around for centuries. The earliest concentrated on innate differences in personality, intelligence, and aptitudes. However, recent studies have shown little correlation between expertise and IQ. Nevertheless differences in thinking styles or intelligence profiles can lead to different people becoming expert in different domains.

2. Experts tend to be experts in one domain. Expertise does not seep into another domain unless the two domains share a set of skills. Thus there can be "content" knowledge specific to a domain and "task" knowledge that can be shared with closely related domains.

3. There are several stage models of expertise development. On the way to expertise there is evidence of an "intermediate effect" in which people with some knowledge of a domain perform worse than others with a little knowledge of the domain. Raufaste et al. (1999) argue that the intermediate effect is a side-effect of confusing "basic experts" and "super experts" in these studies.

4. Zeitz (1997) argues that experts' knowledge is best understood as involving representations at an intermediate level of abstraction. Moderately abstract conceptual representations (MACRs) provide a level of representation between the concrete and specific and the abstract and content-free.

5. Automatisation ought to make expert performance "rigid" because routine well-practised procedures are no longer accessible to consciousness. Although automaticity can indeed lead to errors in certain circumstances, experts would not be experts if they could not use knowledge flexibly. The paradox can be overcome if one assumes routine expertise for dealing with typical problems and adaptive expertise for dealing with novel problems. Experts have schemas and strategies that cover exceptions as well as typical cases.

6. Consequences of expertise in many domains include:

   • Fast categorisation processes: experts categorise problems differently from novices.
   • Perceptual chunking: experts can "chunk" larger configurations of elements than novices.
   • Long-term working memory: experts have developed strategies within their domain of expertise for using long-term memory for tasks that novices would rely on limited-capacity short-term memory to deal with.

7. Ericsson and Charness (1994) have argued that it is more profitable to examine what it is in a domain that experts do well. Expertise involves effortful adaptation to the demands of a domain.

constraints or switching to a different problem space may permit a new way of representing the problem.

Operators

In order to solve problems you need to know what to do. That is, you have to be able to retrieve the relevant operators from memory. It goes without saying that, if you don't have them in the first place then you can't retrieve them. This is even more difficult when the domain is unfamiliar. Another barrier to successful problem solving is if you have the relevant operators but retrieve the wrong ones. You might add instead of subtract. In insight problems you might know what to do, but don't know that you know. The more you know about a domain, the more you are likely to be able to retrieve the relevant operators when necessary and hence the more likely you are to solve the problem. Domain knowledge is more important than analogical reasoning ability (Novick & Holyoak, 1991). Creative solutions to problems often involve finding a new metaphor or analogy that opens up a new set of potential operators. Schön (1993) gives the example of a product-development team working for a paintbrush manufacturer. They were at first unable to get synthetic bristles to work as well as natural bristles. Eventually someone came up with the idea that a paintbrush was actually a kind of pump. This metaphor gave rise to a whole new research endeavour. There was suddenly a new set of things they could do.

Another way of ensuring that you apply the correct operators in a new domain is to use an example. Indeed to ensure that you use the correct operators it is best if you actually copy the example as much as possible. In a study by Robertson (2000) children were given an example where two cars left a location at different times and the second vehicle overtook the first. If the example gave a one-and-a-half-hour difference as $\frac{3}{2}$, some of the children would change the two-hour difference in the exercise problem into $\frac{1}{2}$ even though that was completely unnecessary. They converted it because that's what happened in the example. The moral of the story is that when you are unsure what you are doing it's best to keep your inductions conservative.

Goals

Problems vary in the nature of their goals. In some the answer is given and the solver has to find out how to get there. In others the goal may be only vaguely stated but you would recognise it when you see it. Thus in an algebra problem where the goal is to find the value of "x", as soon as you end up with "$x =$ something" you have got an answer. Similarly, if you are trying to find a catchy name for a new product, you will know if you've got one when you've got one. Of course there's going to be some kind of test against explicit or implicit criteria that will tell whether the goal is adequately satisfied. Other goals are even vaguer still.

You might have no idea what you are going to end up with until you have finished. Writing is one example, and artistic creation is another.

PROBLEM REPRESENTATION

The way you go about trying to solve a problem or making a decision, or even just what to pay attention to, depends on the salience of elements in the environment. Salience is therefore one of the factors that influence the way we represent the world, including the problems we face. A housebuyer, an architect, and a burglar looking at a house are going to find different aspects salient. People are therefore going to generate different representations of problems and situations depending on their past experience. A result of this is that it is possible to manipulate the likelihood of a solution by manipulating the instructions (Hayes & Simon, 1974; Simon & Hayes, 1976). Spin doctors manipulate information in an attempt to get us to represent it in certain ways.

Features of the environment that stand out in some way are likely to be relevant or important. Although paying attention to what appear to be the salient features of the environment is an extremely useful heuristic most of the time, there are times when it can lead you up the garden path. Our perceptual systems have evolved over millions of years to allow fast recognition of objects and faces. Our perceptual systems are also prey to visual illusions for the same reason. The way we read sentences can lead to initial misunderstandings as in "the old man the boats". Similarly, the kinds of trick questions you get in puzzle books rely on the fact that certain features stand out and influence how you respond. Activity Box 10.1 gives some typical, though frivolous, examples (see p. 237 for answers).

What people find salient influences their behaviour in more serious circumstances for good or for ill. Solving insight problems or generating a creative solution to a problem often involves making some hitherto irrelevant feature salient. In Schön's example of the new paintbrush, the spaces between the bristles suddenly became important rather than the bristles themselves (that's where the paint gets pumped out of). Experience (learning) causes changes in the features that are salient. Variability in the way different features of things stand out for different people is due to the fact that people vary in their

---

Activity 10.1

1. A farmer had 17 sheep. All but 9 died. How many did he have left?
2. If joke is spelt **J O K E** and folk is spelt **F O L K**, how is the white of an egg spelt?
3. There are 6 apples in a basket in a room and 6 girls in the room. Each girl takes an apple. One apple remains in the basket. How come?
4. Two Romanians get on a bus. One Romanian is the father of the other Romanian's son. How come?

schemas have to be general enough to apply to a range of situations and detailed or concrete enough to be used to solve a specific example. $e = mc^2$ doesn't really tell you how to solve a given problem. Equations and general principles are often too abstract to help the learner. Schema representations formed from experience have to be at a moderately abstract level.

Having induced a problem schema from a number of examples, we should be able to apply that schema to new instances. There are various models of how we generalise from experience and Chapter 8 has dealt with only some of them. Although generalisation is a very important mechanism, specialisation is also important. We need to learn the exceptions to the rules as well as the rules themselves: *i* comes before *e* except after *c* and except after a few other letters that don't conform to the rule. The development of expertise includes the learning of schemas that cover exceptions as well as the generality of cases. For this reason experts' representations can be flexible and they can get over the effects of automaticity—at least to some extent.

Although this book has concentrated mostly on the general cognitive processes involved in problem solving and learning, there are many other variables that affect whether an individual successfully solves a problem, achieves his or her goal, learns a new domain, becomes well-versed in it, or manages to achieve a level that could be called exceptional performance. As the last chapter pointed out, there are many factors that affect how we solve problems and eventually develop expertise. Charness, Krampe, and Mayr (1996) have described a taxonomy of factors that are important in skill acquisition and the development of exceptional performance. External social factors (e.g., parental, cultural, financial support), internal factors (e.g., motivation, competitiveness) and external "informational" factors (the nature of the domain and the sources of information about it) all affect the amount and quality of the practice a person puts in. That, in turn, interacts with the cognitive system which includes "software" (knowledge base and problem-solving processes) and "hardware" (e.g., working-memory capacity, processing speed). For some domains different factors are likely to be emphasised more than others. For example, skilled chess performance may rely more on the cognitive system than on the external factors, although the latter are not negligible.

Figure 10.1 includes certain areas that have *not* been covered in this book. Individual performance on any task is influenced by a whole host of cultural, social, and contextual factors interacting with usually stable motivational, personality, and physical factors. These interact with inherent differences in knowledge that change over time, and differences in cognitive processes that remain relatively stable over time (within limits). A specific problem is embedded in some immediate context which may have certain demand characteristics. Solvers may ask themselves "Why am I being asked to do this experiment. Is this perhaps a memory task?" Alternatively the problem may be something like a car breaking down in the middle of nowhere during a thunderstorm, where physical factors such as the temperature may affect the nature of the problem solving that can take place.

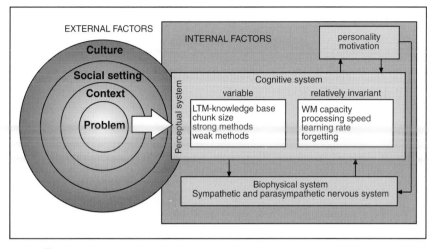

Figure 10.1.   External and internal factors affecting problem solving and learning.

The social setting can be very important. The very presence of other people can affect processing speed, for example (Zajonc, 1965, 1980). The cultural setting can affect how one regards a problem or even whether a situation is a problem at all. One culture may spend time over the problem of how many angels can dance on the end of a pin or whether women have souls. Another culture may not regard these as problems worth considering in the first place. Context, social setting, an individual's nervous system, and personality factors can together influence performance. During an exam, performance on an essay question can be entirely different from performance on the same question while sitting at home by the fire.

This book, however, has concentrated on the interaction between a problem in its context and the cognitive system, and tried to show how human beings in general (and occasionally some other forms of information-processing system) attempt to solve problems. Other areas outlined in Figure 10.1 would need to be addressed if we want to fully understand how any given individual confronts a particular type of problem. They also need to be taken into account if we are to understand individual differences in how people faced with a problem that they are at first unable to solve, become (or fail to become) a world-class expert.

Answers to questions

CHAPTER 2

State-action spaces: finding your way in a building

The building is organised thus:

301–304	Stair	305–308	Stair	309–312
321–324	Lift	317–320	Lift	313–316

CHAPTER 3
The solution to the Nine Dots problem.

CHAPTER 4

Activity 4.3
(A) A simple hypothesis.

(B) A complex hypothesis.

The sequence of three shapes changes such that circle–square–triangle becomes square–triangle–circle which becomes triangle–circle–square, and so on. At the same time the colour of the shapes changes: one white–one black, two white–two black, three white–three black.

CHAPTER 5

Activity 5.2

Analyse the metaphor: "The Falklands thing was a fight between two bald men over a comb"

a. Encode meanings of terms.

b. Infer missing term.

c. Infer relation. Bald men don't need a comb. Nevertheless, they are fighting over it.

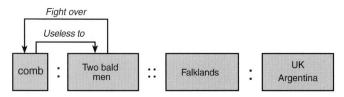

d. Apply relations to understand the relationship between the countries and the Falklands.

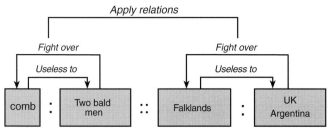

CHAPTER 8

Activity 8-1

    Defun multiply-them(2 3)

                *2 3

would turn into

    Defun add-them(712 91)

            +2 3

The name changes from "multiply-them" to "add-them" (although the function would still work even if you didn't change its name). The numbers change from 2 to 712 and from 3 to 91. Finally the arithmetic operator changes from a * to a +.

CHAPTER 10

Activity 10.1

1. 9
2. WHITE
3. One of the girls takes the basket with the apple in it.
4. One's his mother.

e.g., from solving crossword puzzles to generating them.

Condition-simplifying generalisation: a generalisation that is produced when features of two or more instances of a concept are deemed to be irrelevant. Such features can then be dropped from the representation of the concept. For example, the colour of a cat's fur has little to do with whether or not the cat can miaow.

Connectionism: cognitive architecture that consists of neuron-like nodes connected by links that have different connection strengths. Learning or representation consists of the pattern of weights between nodes.

Conservative induction: people tend to be careful about the inductive generalisations they make and therefore these generalisations may contain a lot of specific detail that may not be relevant.

Constraints: aspects of a problem that serve to limit what actions are available or appropriate.

Context-dependent information: information about a concept that tends to be restricted to certain contexts.

Context-independent information: features of a category or concept that tend to be invariant across contexts

Cover story: the "story" or situation described in the problem statement.

Declarative knowledge: "knowing that"—explicit episodic and general semantic knowledge that one has about the world. This knowledge is either right or wrong and is not use-dependent (see *procedural knowledge*).

Declarative memory: (see *declarative knowledge*).

Deduction: generalising from one or a few examples to a whole range of new examples.

Diachronic rules: rules that represent changes over time. Diachronic rules are of two kinds: Predictor rules permit expectations of what is likely to occur in the world, e.g., "If a person annoys a dog then the dog will growl"; Effector rules tell the system how to act in a given situation, e.g., "If a dog chases you then run away".

Diagrammatic representation: representation of a task, concept, or situation in the form of a diagram.

Difference reduction: general-purpose problem-solving heuristics that involve estimating the distance between where you are now and the goal, and trying to find an *operator* that will reduce that distance.

Discourse knowledge: knowledge in the form of schemas about the structure of certain types of written text (see also *genre*).

Distant variant: a problem that is different in some aspects of its structure from another problem of the same general type. Using one to solve the other would require a lot of adapting.

Domain: a field of knowledge, skill, or endeavour.

Domain-general: knowledge, strategies, procedures that apply to any or a range of domains.

Domain-specific: knowledge, strategies, procedures that are specific to a single domain.

Einstellung: a type of mental set (see *set effects*) where a habitual problem method is selected when a more straightforward one is possible.

Elaborative inferences: inferences made on the basis of an understanding of a text. For example, a problem about one car overtaking another that left earlier from the same place may include the elaborative inference that both cars have travelled the same distance.

Episodic knowledge: a type of *declarative knowledge*. Knowledge of personally experienced events.

Example-analogy: a view of *analogical problem solving* whereby the details of a *source* example are used to help solve a current *target* problem.

Experiential stage: second stage in the development of expertise. An understanding of the causal relations that underpin a system of knowledge emerges along with the abstraction of instances from experience.

Expert stage: third stage in the development of expertise. The learner can make abstractions across various system representations. The knowledge gained is therefore transferable.

External memory: any object in the environment that can be used to store information and that takes the load off working memory or aids long-term memory. Examples would be an address book or diary.

Factual knowledge: a type of *declarative knowledge*. General knowledge of facts.

Full insight: the solution to a problem becomes immediately available (see *partial insight*).

Functional fixedness: a type of set effect where the typical or most recent function of an object blinds one to seeing an alternative function for the object.

Functional fixity: (see *functional fixedness*).

General transfer: transfer of domain-general skills (also known as "transferable skills").

Genre: language appropriate to the type of text being written—a report, a formal essay, a thank-you letter belong to different genres.

Givens of a problem: the situation described in the problem statement.

Goal stack: the assumption that human behaviour is goal-directed. Goals are arranged hierarchically (stacked) so that if an overall goal involves attaining a sub-goal then that sub-goal goes to the top of the stack and is dealt with first.

Goal state: where you are when you have attained your problem-solving goal.

Heuristics: rules of thumb that help constrain a problem (and hence often speed up problem solving) but are not guaranteed to work.

Hill climbing: systematic search strategy that involves moving from a current state to one that seems closer to the goal. Used when the goal–sub-goal structure of a problem is not all that clear.

Homomorphic problems: problems that are similar in structure but not identical (for example there may be extra *constraints*— see *isomorphic problems*)

Homomorphism: a model of the world produced by a "many-to-one" mapping where a large number of states of affairs in the world are mapped onto a smaller

number of states in a mental model of the world.

Identical elements theory: transfer can take place between two situations or tasks only when there are similar surface elements.

Ill-defined problem: a problem where the means of solving it are not immediately apparent, either because relevant *operators* or a clear description of the goal are not explicitly stated.

Impasse: point in problem solving where one gets stuck. Usually one has to take a "detour" by creating a sub-goal to remove the impasse before problem solving can continue.

Incubation: presumed unconscious process where an answer to a problem seems to pop into one's head despite the fact that one is no longer consciously thinking about it.

Induction: the process of abstracting out general rules from specific examples.

Information processing: manipulating (processing) mental representations (information) about the world.

Information-processing system (IPS): a system that processes *symbols* and *symbol structures* that mentally represent the external world. Human beings have certain processing limitations.

Informationally encapsulated: systems, such as vision or hearing, that are cut off from other systems.

Initial state: the starting state of a problem (e.g., an essay question and a blank sheet of paper).

Insight: a phenomenon whereby a solution is arrived at without any apparent conscious working-out. The solution appears to pop into consciousness.

Instance-based generalisation: there is variability in the likelihood of generalising from one or more instances of a concept depending on one's beliefs about the variability of the features of instances. The PI system (Holland et al., 1986) can allow generalisation from a single instance or from experience of many instances.

Instantiation: a concrete form or example (an instance) of a general concept or variable.

Intermediate effect: in some domains, a stage learners go through on the way to becoming experts where there is a dip in performance on certain kinds of tasks, such that novices outperform the intermediates despite the greater experience of the latter.

Isomorphic problems: problems that have an identical underlying solution structure.

Isomorphs: (see *isomorphic problems*).

Knowledge state: the particular stage you are in during problem solving, specifically the mental state you have reached at that point.

Knowledge-lean: problems that require very little knowledge to solve them.

Knowledge-rich: problems that require prior *domain* knowledge to solve them.

Knowledge-telling strategy: a writing strategy that reduces the problem faced by the writer to one of telling what one knows about the topic.

Knowledge-transforming strategy: an expert writing strategy in which the writer tries to deal with the problem of presenting his or her knowledge and beliefs, and the problem of achieving the goals of the composition.

Lateral thinking: solving *ill-defined problems* or *insight* problems by searching for an alternative problem space rather than searching within a problem space.

Liberal induction: sweeping generalisations based on very little evidence—often only one example.

Long-term memory (LTM): memory for events, general knowledge, procedures, strategies, etc., that are stored for longer than a few minutes. There are no known limits to the duration or capacity of information in LTM.

Means–ends analysis: general-purpose problem-solving heuristic that involves breaking a problem down into manageable sub-goals. Problem solving then proceeds by analysing the difference between the current problem state and the sub-goal and choosing a method that will reduce that difference.

Mental lexicon: our mental store of words; their spellings, pronunciations, and meanings.

Mental model: generally image-based representation of how something works or how a situation can be imagined.

Mental representation: how knowledge about objects, problems, states of affairs, layouts, etc., is stored in the mind. Representations can be manipulated mentally in ways analogous to the ways states of affairs can be manipulated in the real world.

Metacognition: knowing how cognitive processes such as memory work so that one can come to control them.

Moderately abstract conceptual representation: a level of abstraction intermediate between abstractions, such as general principles or equations and concrete examples.

Negative transfer: learning to solve a problem in one situation prevents or impedes the solution of what looks like a similar problem in another situation (see *positive transfer*).

Nodes: points at which the *state–action diagram* branches; neuron-like elements in a connectionist system.

Operator: an action that can be taken to change the state of a problem, e.g., "move a ring", multiply, "take the bus".

Operator restrictions: *constraints* imposed by a problem, often stating what you are not allowed to do.

Partial insight: an insight into a problem that indicates how one might proceed in order to reach a solution (see *full insight*).

Planning: one of the processes involved in writing. It includes the sub-processes of generating information from *long-term memory* using information in the *task environment*.

Positive transfer: learning to solve a problem in one situation increases the speed and/or accuracy with which you solve a similar problem in another situation (see *negative transfer*).

Power Law of Learning: a law that seems to govern learning: the more we practise something the easier it gets, but the harder it gets to improve (improvement is a power function of practice).

Predicate calculus: system of representing knowledge based on *predicates* and their *arguments*.

Predicate: a relationship that exists between one or more objects can be represented as a predicate. "Gave" is the predicate in the example "gave(Bill, Mary, flowers)" (see also *arguments*).

Pretheoretical stage: first stage in the development of expertise where specific instances are retrieved from memory based on superficial features of the current situation and the instances stored in memory.

Primary understanding: occurs when students understand information at a surface level; usually at the same or a less abstract level than the information being presented.

Principle of rationality: in various guises the principle refers to the fact that people choose actions that they believe will attain their goals. The choice of actions is dependent on knowledge and the capacity limits of the processing system.

Principle-cueing: view of *analogical problem solving* whereby accessing a *source* problem cues the underlying principle which is used in turn to solve the *target* problem.

Problem model: a type of *situation model* that includes knowledge of how the situation described in a text of a problem can be converted into a *solution procedure*. For example, it may include formal knowledge about the arithmetic structure derived from the *textbase*.

Problem schema: problem structure abstracted from experience that allows us to identify new problems of a particular type and to access potentially useful solution strategies.

Problem space: a mental representation of a problem built up from information present in a problem statement, the context, and past experience. The representation includes the states that can be reached through applying problem-solving operators.

Problem understanding: the process of constructing an initial mental representation of a problem based on information in the problem statement (about the goal, the initial state, restrictions, and operators to apply where given) and personal past experience.

Problem variants: different problems of the same general type. Variants can be *close*—for instance, an exercise problem can be similar to an example problem—or *distant*—for instance, where an example problem needs to be adapted a lot to solve a current exercise problem.

Procedural knowledge: "knowing how"— knowledge of how to do something (riding a bike, swimming, baking a cake). Can be more or less useful in attaining one's goals.

Procedural memory: (see *procedural knowledge*).

Production systems: models of thinking and problem solving where behaviour is regarded as sequential and rule-governed in nature. Rules (productions) are generally of the form "if…then" (condition–action rules).

Productive thinking: generating a solution to a problem due to an understanding of the problem's "deep structure".

Proportional analogies: analogies of the form A : B :: C : D (A is to B as C is to D) where the relation between A and B is "proportional" to the relation between C and D.

Propositions: a unit of knowledge that represents a statement or assertion, usually in the form of a *predicate* with *arguments*.

Propositional representation: representation that captures underlying meanings in terms of sets of *propositions*.

Rationality: this can have two meanings: (a) logically correct thinking; (b) thinking that operates to advance our goals. Most often it is the second of these two meanings that is referred to in the text (see *principle of rationality*).

Recursion: a solution procedure that involves applying the same *algorithm* within itself until some halting condition is reached. For example, to find out if someone has flu, then check to see if they have kissed someone who has flu. To check whether that person in turn has flu, then check to see if he has kissed someone else who has flu; and so on.

Reflective understanding: occurs when students recognise the deeper *structural* *features* of problems and can relate them to previous knowledge.

Relational elements: a set of elements that constitute a relation between one concept and another. According to Bejar et al. (1991), "The wheel is part of the bike" involves the relational elements "inclusion" and "connection".

Reproductive thinking: using a previously learned solution method to solve a problem. Such a method is triggered by the problem type and not by a "deep" understanding of the problem (see *productive thinking*).

Restructuring: Gestalt term for the necessity in some problems to find an appropriate problem representation when a current representation is not working.

Reviewing: one of the processes involved in writing, subdivided into reading and editing. The process detects violations of written expression. It also involves making some kind of evaluation of the text to see whether it fits in with the writer's goals.

Rhetorical problem: the problem of writing prose in conformity with the writer's goals and that is directed at the intended audience.

Routine expertise: refers to the schema-based knowledge experts use to solve standard familiar problems efficiently (see also *adaptive expertise*).

Rule induction: (see *induction*).

Schema: a knowledge structure composed of bits of semantic knowledge and the relations between them (see *problem schema*).

Search: engaging in problem solving involves a search through a *problem space*. The solver seeks a sequence of *operators* that will solve the problem.

Search graph: (search tree) similar to a *state–action diagram*. Diagrammatic depiction of a *problem space*.

Semantic associations: (see *semantics*).

Semantic network: network of semantically related concepts (see also *semantics*; *spreading activation*).

Semantic space: (see *semantics*).

Semantically lean problems: problems where the solver has little prior knowledge to call upon. The problem has few *semantic associations* for the solver.

Semantics: the study of meanings. The more knowledge one has of a word or concept (the more associations and relations a word has) the bigger is its semantic space.

Sentential representation: representation of a task, concept, or situation that is generally linear in nature; that is, in the form of a textual description.

Set effect: applying a learned rule or procedure for doing something when there is a simpler way of doing it.

Short-term memory (STM): limited-capacity storage of information usually in focal attention. The information is unlikely to have undergone much processing or interpretation.

Situated learning: learning theory that emphasises the importance of the learning context (especially the social context) on learning for transfer.

Situation model: a mental model of the situation described in a text, derived from the *textbase*.

Slot: element in a *schema* representation (including a *propositional representation*). Slots can be filled with specific values.

Solution development: working towards a solution—failed attempts at solving a problem sometimes help refine what the problem is and hence direct the solver to a more fruitful solution path

Solution procedure: a method, usually involving a sequence of actions, used to solve a problem.

Source problem: (also known as *base problem*) earlier problem, usually in *long-term memory*, that can be used as an analogy for solving a current *target problem*.

Specific transfer: transfer of *domain-specific* skills—usually from one problem to another that is very similar

Spreading activation: memory traces in a semantic network related to the current context are activated, some more strongly than others. Activating a memory trace leads to many related memories also being activated above some threshold level.

State space: the space of all the problem states that can be reached and the paths between them (the *problem space*). A solver can go from one state to another along a path by applying an operator. The state space can be represented visually as a *state–action diagram* or *search graph*

State–action diagram: (see *state space*).

State–action space: (see *state space*).

Strong methods: known problem-solving methods that can reliably solve a problem type.

Structural features: those features of a problem that are relevant to its solution, and can be used to categorise the problem type.

Structurally blind: "reproductive" problem solving that does not take account of the problem's underlying structure (see *reproductive thinking*).

Structurally similar problems: problems with the same underlying solution structure (see also *structural features*).

Sub-goaling: (see *means–ends analysis*).

Subordinate category: certain categories can be organised hierarchically. "Spaniel" is a subordinate category of the *superordinate* "dog".

Superordinate category: certain categories can be organised hierarchically. "Spaniel" is a *subordinate* category of the superordinate "dog".

Surface features: those features of a problem that are irrelevant to the solution.

Surface similarities: two problems may be similar because they are about the same sorts of things (e.g., computers) although the underlying structure of the problems may be different (see also *surface features* and *structural features*).

Symbol structures: structures formed by collections of symbols.

Symbol tokens: a symbol token stands for a symbol. A specific occurrence of a word, object, event, etc. (a symbol token) refers the information processor to the symbol itself.

Symbols: a representation of something in the world such as words in sentences, objects in pictures, numbers, arithmetic operators, and so on.

Synchronic rules: rules that represent general features of an object or its category membership. There are two kinds of synchronic rule: categorical and associative. Categorical rules are of the type: "If an object is a dog then it is an animal". Associative rules are of the type: "If an object is a dog then activate the 'bone' concept".

Systematicity principle: according to Gentner's theory of analogy, people prefer to map hierarchical systems of relations in which the higher-order relations constrain the lower-order ones. Systematicity governs how well an analogy works.

Target problem: current problem that requires to be solved (currently in *working memory*). A *source problem* is sought (usually from *long-term memory*) to use as an analogy.

Task environment: a problem in its context. The task environment may contain specific problem-related information or cues that may help retrieve problem-relevant information from memory.

Terminal nodes: points at which the *state–action diagram* terminates (the solver can go no further). A terminal node can be either a goal state or a dead end.

Textbase: an initial *propositional representation* of a text. From the textbase, we can (hopefully) generate a *situation model*—a mental model of the situation described in the text that includes *elaborated inferences*.

Transfer-appropriate processing: in processing information, learners have to take account of the goals of the learning context and adapt their learning strategies accordingly. For example, if the goal is to do a rhyming task then it would be best to encode information in terms of the sound of the words.

Transition function: a function that produces a change of state in the world or in a model of the world. Applying an *operator* to elements in a particular state produces a transition to another state.

Translating: one of the processes involved in writing. Information retrieved from *long-term memory* is presumed to be in the form

Anderson, J.R., & Thompson, R. (1989). Use of an analogy in a production system architecture. In S. Vosniadou & A. Ortony (Eds.), *Similarity and analogical reasoning* (pp. 267–297). London: Cambridge University Press.

Ashcraft, M.H. (1994). *Human memory and cognition* (2nd ed.). New York: HarperCollins.

Atkinson, R.C., & Shiffrin, R.M. (1968). Human memory: A proposed system and its control processes. In K.W. Spence & I.T. Spence (Eds.), *The psychology of learning and motivation* (Vol. 2). London: Academic Press.

Ausubel, D.P. (1968). *Educational psychology: A cognitive view*. New York: Holt, Rinehart & Winston.

Baddeley, A. (1997). *Human memory: Theory and practice* (rev. ed.). Hove, UK: Psychology Press.

Baddeley, A.D. (1981). The concept of working memory: A view of its current state and probable future development. *Cognition, 10*, 17–23.

Ballstaedt, S.-P., & Mandle, H. (1984). Elaborations: Assessment and analysis. In H. Mandl, N.L. Stein, & T. Trabasso (Eds.), *Learning and comprehension of text* (pp. 331–353). Hillsdale, NJ: Lawrence Erlbaum Associates Inc.

Barsalou, L.W. (1989). Intraconcept similarity and its implications for interconcept similarity. In S. Vosniadou & A. Ortony (Eds.), *Similarity and analogical reasoning*. London: Cambridge University Press.

Bartlett, F.C. (1932). *Remembering: A study in experimental and social psychology*. Cambridge: Cambridge University Press.

Bassok, M. (1990). Transfer of domain-specific problem solving procedures. *Journal of Experimental Psychology: Learning, Memory, and Cognition, 16*(3), 522–533.

Bassok, M. (1997). Two types of reliance on correlations between content and structure in reasoning about word problems. In L.D. English (Ed.), *Mathematical reasoning: Analogies, metaphors, and images. Studies in mathematical thinking and learning* (pp. 221–246). Mahwah, NJ: Lawrence Erlbaum Associates, Inc.

Bassok, M., & Holyoak, K.J. (1989). Interdomain transfer between isomorphic topics in algebra and physics. *Journal of Experimental Psychology: Learning, Memory, and Cognition, 15*, 153–166.

Beck, I.L., & McKeown, M.G. (1989). Expository text for young readers: The issue of coherence. In L.B. Resnick (Ed.), *Knowing, learning, and instruction: Essays in honor of Robert Glaser* (pp. 47–66). Hillsdale, NJ: Lawrence Erlbaum Associates Inc.

Bejar, I.I., Chaffin, R., & Embretson, S. (1991). *Cognitive and psychometric analysis of analogical problem solving*. New York: Springer-Verlag.

Bereiter, C., & Scardamalia, M. (1987). *The psychology of written composition*. Hillsdale, NJ: Lawrence Erlbaum Associates Inc.

Bernardo, A.B.I. (1994). Problem specific information and the development of problem-type schemata. *Journal of Experimental Psychology: Learning, Memory, and Cognition, 20*, 379–395.

Berry, D.C. (1983). Metacognitive experience and transfer of logical reasoning. *Quarterly Journal of Experimental Psychology, 35A*, 39–49.

Beveridge, M., & Parkins, E. (1987). Visual representation in analogical problem solving. *Memory and Cognition, 15*(3), 230–237.

Black, M. (1993). More about metaphor. In A. Ortony (Ed.), *Metaphor and thought* (pp. 19–41). Cambridge: Cambridge University Press.

Blanchette, I., & Dunbar, K. (2000). How analogies are generated: The roles of structural and superficial similarity. *Memory and Cognition, 28*(1), 108–124.

Blessing, S.B., & Ross, B.H. (1996). Content effects in problem categorisation and problem solving. *Journal of Experimental Psychology: Learning, Memory, and Cognition, 22*(3).

Boden, M. (1994). Précis of "The creative mind: Myths and mechanisms". *Behavioral and Brain Sciences, 17*, 519–570.

Brainerd, C.J., & Reyna, V.F. (1993). Memory independence and memory interference in cognitive development. *Psychological Review, 100*, 42–67.

Bransford, J.D., Arbitman-Smith, R., Stein, B.S., & Vye, N.J. (1985). Improving thinking and learning skills: An analysis of three approaches. In J.W. Segal, S.F. Chipman, & R. Glaser (Eds.), *Thinking and learning skills* (Vol. 1, pp. 133–206). Hillsdale, NJ: Lawrence Erlbaum Associates Inc.

Bransford, J.D., Barclay, J.R., & Franks, J.J. (1972). Sentence memory: A constructive versus interpretative approach. *Cognitive Psychology, 3*, 193–209.

Bransford, J.D., & Stein, B.S. (1993). *The ideal problem solver* (2nd ed.). New York: W.H. Freeman.

Brewer, W.F., & Treyens, J.C. (1981). Role of schemata in memory for places. *Cognitive Psychology, 13*, 207–230.

Britton, B.K., Van Dusen, L., Gulgoz, S., & Glynn, S.M. (1989). Instructional texts rewritten by five expert teams: Revisions and retention improvements. *Journal of Educational Psychology, 81*(2), 226–239.

Broadbent, D.E. (1975). The magical number seven after fifteen years. In R.A. Kennedy & A. Wilkes (Eds.), *Studies in long-term memory*. New York: Wiley.

Brown, A.L., & Palincsar, A.S. (1989). Guided cooperative learning and individual knowledge acquisition. In L.B. Resnick (Ed.), *Knowing, learning, and instruction: Essays in honor of Robert Glaser* (pp. 393–452). Hillsdale, NJ: Lawrence Erlbaum Associates Inc.

Brown, D.E., & Clement, J. (1989). Overcoming misconceptions via analogical reasoning: Abstract transfer versus explanatory model construction. *Instructional Science, 18*(4), 237–261.

Brown, J.S., & Burton, R.R. (1978). Diagnostic models for procedural bugs in basic mathematical skills. *Cognitive Science, 2*, 155–192.

Brown, J.S., & VanLehn, K. (1980). Repair theory: A generative theory of bugs in procedural skills. *Cognitive Science, 4*, 379–426.

Bryson, M., Bereiter, C., Scardamalia, M., & Joram, E. (1991). Going beyond the problem as given: Problem solving in expert and novice writers. In R.J. Sternberg & P.A. Frensch (Eds.), *Complex problem solving* (pp. 61–84). Hillsdale, NJ: Lawrence Erlbaum Associates Inc.

Bugliosi, V. (1978). *Till death us do part*. New York: Bantam Books.

Byrne, M.D., & Bovair, S. (1997). A working memory model of a common procedural error. *Cognitive Science, 21*(1), 31–61.

Byrnes, J.P. (1992). The conceptual basis of procedural learning. *Cognitive Development, 7*, 235–257.

Carbonell, J.G. (1982). *Experiential learning in analogical problem solving*. Paper presented at the AAAI–82: Proceedings of the National Conference on Artificial Intelligence, Los Altos, CA.

Carbonell, J.G. (1983). *Derivational analogy and its role in problem solving*. Paper presented at the Third National Conference on Artificial Intelligence, Washington, DC.

Cardinale, L.A. (1991). Conceptual models and user interaction with computers. *Computers in Human Behavior, 7*(3), 163–169.

Carey, S., & Spelke, E. (1994). Domain-specific knowledge and conceptual change. In L.A. Hirschfield & S.A. Gelman (Eds.), *Mapping the mind: Domain specificity in cognition and culture* (pp. 169–200). Cambridge: Cambridge University Press.

Carraher, T.N., Carraher, D., & Schliemann, A.D. (1985). Mathematics in the streets and in the schools. *British Journal of Developmental Psychology, 3*, 21–29.

Carroll, J.M., Smith-Kerker, P.L., Ford, J.R., & Mazur-Rimetz, S.A. (1987–88). The minimal manual. *Human–Computer Interaction, 3*, 123–153.

Ericsson, K.A., & Simon, H.A. (1993). *Protocol analysis: Verbal reports as data* (rev. ed.). Cambridge, MA: MIT Press.

Ericsson, K.A., & Smith, J. (1991). Prospects and limits of the empirical study of expertise: An introduction. In K.A. Ericsson & J. Smith (Eds.), *Toward a general theory of expertise: Prospects and limits* (pp. 1–38). Cambridge: Cambridge University Press.

Erlich, K., & Soloway, E. (1984). An empirical investigation of tacit plan knowledge in programming. In J.C. Thomas & M.L. Schneider (Eds.), *Human factors in computing systems.* Norwood, NJ: Ablex.

Eylon, B.-S., & Reif, F. (1984). Effects of knowledge organization on task performance. *Cognition and Instruction, 1*(1), 5–44.

Falkenhainer, B., Forbus, K.D., & Gentner, D. (1989). The structure-mapping engine: Algorithm and examples. *Artificial Intelligence, 41*, 1–63.

Feltovich, P.J., Johnson, P.E., Moller, J.H., & Swanson, D.B. (1984). LCS: The role and development of medical knowledge in diagnostic expertise. In W.C. Clancey & E.H. Shortliffe (Eds.), *Readings in medical artificial intelligence* (pp. 275–319). Reading, MA: Addison-Wesley.

Feltovich, P.J., Spiro, R.J., & Coulson, R.L. (1997). Issues in expert flexibility in contexts characterized by complexity and change. In P.J. Feltovich, K.M. Ford, & R.R. Hoffman (Eds.), *Expertise in context* (pp. 126–146). London: MIT Press.

Ferguson-Hessler, M.G.M., & de Jong, T. (1990). Studying physics texts: Differences in study processes between good and poor performers. *Cognition and Instruction, 7*(1), 41–54.

Flower, L.S., & Hayes, J.R. (1980). The dynamics of composing: Making plans and juggling constraints. In L.W. Gregg & E.R. Stienberg (Eds.), *Cognitive processes in writing* (pp. 31–50). Hillsdale, NJ: Lawrence Erlbaum Associates Inc.

Flower, L., & Hayes, J.R. (1981). Plans that guide the composing process. In C.H. Fredriksen & J.F. Dominic (Eds.), *Writing: The nature, development and teaching of written communication.* Hillsdale, NJ: Lawrence Erlbaum Associates Inc.

Fodor, J.A. (1985). Précis of "The modularity of mind". *Behavioral and Brain Sciences, 8*(1), 1–42.

Frensch, P.A., & Buchner, A. (1999). Domain-generality versus domain-specificity in cognition. In R.J. Sternberg (Ed.), *The nature of cognition.* London: MIT Press.

Frensch, P.A., & Funke, J. (Eds.) (1995). *Complex problem solving: The European perspective.* Hillsdale, NJ: Lawrence Erlbaum Associates Inc.

Frensch, P., & Sternberg, R.J. (1989). Expertise and intelligent thinking: When is it worse to know better? In R.J. Sternberg (Ed.), *Advances in the psychology of human intelligence* (Vol. 5, pp. 157–188). Hillsdale, NJ: Lawrence Erlbaum Associates Inc.

Gardner, H. (1983). *Frames of mind: The theory of multiple intelligences.* New York: Basic Books.

Gentner, D. (1983). Structure-mapping: A theoretical framework for analogy. *Cognitive Science, 7*, 155–170.

Gentner, D. (1989). The mechanisms of analogical reasoning. In S. Vosniadou & A. Ortony (Eds.), *Similarity and analogical reasoning.* London: Cambridge University Press.

Gentner, D., & Forbus, K.D. (1991a). *MAC/FAC: A model of similarity-based access and mapping.* Paper presented at the 13th Annual Conference of the Cognitive Science Society, Chicago, IL.

Gentner, D., & Forbus, K.D. (1991b). *MAC/FAC: A model of similarity-based retrieval.* Paper presented at the 13th Annual Conference of the Cognitive Science Society, Chicago, IL.

Gentner, D., & Gentner, D.R. (1983). Flowing waters or teeming crowds: Mental models of electricity. In D. Gentner & A.L. Stevens (Eds.), *Mental models.* Hillsdale, NJ: Lawrence Erlbaum Associates Inc.

Gentner, D., Rattermann, M.J., & Forbus, K.D. (1993). The roles of similarity in transfer: Separating retrievability from inferential soundness. *Cognitive Psychology, 25*, 524–575.

Gentner, D., & Schumacher, R.M. (1987). *Use of structure mapping theory for complex systems.* Paper presented at the IEEE International Conference on Systems, Man and Cybernetics, 14–17 October, 1986, Piscataway, NJ.

Gentner, D., & Toupin, C. (1986). Systematicity and surface similarity in the development of analogy. *Cognitive Science, 10,* 277–300.

Gick, M.L. (1985). The effect of a diagram retrieval cue on spontaneous analogical transfer. *Canadian Journal of Psychology, 39*(3), 460–466.

Gick, M.L. (1988). Two functions of diagrams in problem solving by analogy. In H. Mandl & J.R. Levin (Eds.), *Knowledge acquisition from text and pictures* (Vol. 58, pp. 215–231). Amsterdam: North-Holland.

Gick, M.L., & Holyoak, K.J. (1980). Analogical problem solving. *Cognitive Psychology, 12,* 306–356.

Gick, M.L., & Holyoak, K.J. (1983). Schema induction and analogical transfer. *Cognitive Psychology, 15,* 1–38.

Gick, M.L., & McGarry, S.J. (1992). Learning from mistakes: Inducing analogous solution failures to a source problem produces later successes in analogical transfer. *Journal of Experimental Psychology: Learning, Memory, and Cognition, 18,* 623–639.

Gigerenzer, G., & Todd, P.M. (Eds.) (1999). *Simple heuristics that make us smart.* Oxford: Oxford University Press.

Gilhooly, K.J. (1996). *Thinking: Directed, undirected and creative* (3rd ed.). London: Academic Press.

Giora, R. (1993). On the function of analogies in informative text. *Discourse Processes, 16,* 591–596.

Glaser, R. (1984). The role of knowledge. *American Psychologist, 39*(2), 93–104.

Glaser, R. (1996). Changing the agency for learning: Acquiring expert performance. In K.A. Ericsson (Ed.), *The road to excellence: The acquisition of expert performance in the arts and sciences, sports, and games.* Mahwah, NJ: Lawrence Erlbaum Associates Inc.

Glaser, R., & Bassok, M. (1989). Learning theory and the study of instruction. In M.R. Rosenzweig & L.W. Poerter (Eds.), *Annual review of psychology* (Vol. 40, pp. 631–666). Palo Alto, CA: Annual Reviews Inc.

Gobet, F., & Simon, H.A. (1996). Templates in chess memory: A mechanism for recalling several boards. *Cognitive Psychology, 31*(1), 1–40.

Graybell, A.M. (1998). The basal ganglia and chunking of action repertoires. *Neurobiology of Learning and Memory, 70,* 119–136.

Greeno, J.G. (1974). Hobbits and Orcs: Acquisition of a sequential concept. *Cognitive Psychology, 6,* 270–292.

Greeno, J.G. (1977). Process of understanding in problem solving. In N.J. Castellan, D.B. Pisoni, & G.R. Potts (Eds.), *Cognitive theory* (Vol. 2, pp. 43–83). Hillsdale, NJ: Lawrence Erlbaum Associates Inc.

Greeno, J.G., Moore, J.L., & Smith, D.R. (1993). Transfer of situated learning. In D.K. Detterman & R.J. Sternberg (Eds.), *Transfer on trial: Intelligence, cognition, and instruction* (pp. 99–167). Norwood, NJ: Ablex.

Halpern, D.F. (1996). *Thought and knowledge: An introduction to critical thinking* (3rd ed.). Hove, UK: Lawrence Erlbaum Associates Inc.

Halpern, D.F., Hanson, C., & Riefer, D. (1990). Analogies as an aid to understanding and memory. *Journal of Educational Psychology, 82*(2), 298–305.

Hasemer, T., & Domingue, J. (1989). *Common Lisp programming for artificial intelligence.* Wokingham, UK: Addison-Wesley.

Hatano, G., & Inagaki, K. (1986). Two courses of expertise. In H. Stevenson, H. Azuma, & K. Hatuka (Eds.), *Child development in Japan.* San Francisco, CA: W.H. Freeman.

Hawking, S.G. (1988). *A brief history of time.* London: Bantam Press.

Laird, J.E., Newell, A., & Rosenbloom, P.S. (1987). SOAR: An architecture for general intelligence. *Artificial Intelligence, 33*, 1–64.

Laird, J.E., & Rosenbloom, P.S. (1996). The evolution of the SOAR cognitive architecture. In D. Steier & T.M. Mitchell (Eds.), *Mind matters: A tribute to Allen Newell*. Mahwah, NJ: Lawrence Erlbaum Associates Inc.

Lamberts, K. (1990). A hybrid model of learning to solve physics problems. *European Journal of Cognitive Psychology, 2*(2), 151–170.

Larkin, J.H. (Ed.) (1978). *Problem solving in physics: Structure, process and learning*. The Netherlands: Sijthoff & Noordhoff.

Larkin, J.H. (1989). What kind of knowledge transfers? In L.B. Resnick (Ed.), *Knowing, learning, and instruction: Essays in honor of Robert Glaser* (pp. 283–306). Hillsdale, NJ: Lawrence Erlbaum Associates Inc.

Larkin, J.H., Reif, F., Carbonell, J.G., & Gugliotta, A. (1986). *FERMI: A flexible expert reasoner with multi-domain inferencing* (Tech. Rep.). Pittsburgh, PA: Department of Psychology, Carnegie-Mellon University.

Larkin, J.H., & Simon, H.A. (1987). Why a diagram is sometimes worth ten-thousand words. *Cognitive Science, 11*, 65–99.

Lave, J., & Wenger, E. (1991). *Situated learning: Legitimate peripheral participation*. Cambridge: Cambridge University Press.

LeFèvre, J.A. (1987). Processing instructional texts and examples. *Canadian Journal of Psychology, 41*(3), 351–364.

LeFèvre, J., & Dixon, P. (1986). Do written instructions need examples? *Cognition and Instruction, 3*, 1–30.

Lesgold, A., Rubinson, H., Feltovich, P., Glaser, R., Klopfer, D., & Wang, Y. (1988). Expertise in a complex skill: Diagnosing X-ray pictures. In M.T.H. Chi, R. Glaser, & M.J. Farr (Eds.), *The nature of expertise* (pp. 311–342). Hillsdale, NJ: Lawrence Erlbaum Associates Inc.

Lesgold, A.M. (1984). Acquiring expertise. In J.R. Anderson (Ed.), *Tutorials in learning and memory* (pp. 31–60). San Francisco, CA: W.H. Freeman.

Levin, J.R. (1988). A transfer-appropriate processing perspective of pictures in prose. In H. Mandl & J.R. Levin (Eds.), *Knowledge acquisition from text and pictures*. Amsterdam: North-Holland.

Levine, M. (1975). *A cognitive theory of learning: Research on hypothesis testing*. Hillsdale, NJ: Lawrence Erlbaum Associates Inc.

Lewis, A.B. (1989). Training students to represent arithmetic word problems. *Journal of Educational Psychology, 81*(4), 521–531.

Logan, G.D. (1988). Toward an instance theory of automatization. *Psychological Review, 95*(4), 492–527.

Luchins, A.S. (1942). Mechanization in problem solving: The effect of Einstellung. *Psychological Monographs, 54*(248).

Luchins, A.S., & Luchins, E.H. (1950). New experimental attempts at preventing mechanization in problem solving. *Journal of General Psychology, 42*, 279–297.

Luchins, A.S., & Luchins, E.H. (1959). *Rigidity of behaviour*. Eugene, OR: University of Oregon Press.

Luger, G.F., & Bauer, M.A. (1978). Transfer effects in isomorphic problem situations. *Acta Psychologica, 42*, 121–131.

Lung, C.-T., & Dominowski, R.L. (1985). Effects of strategy instructions and practice on nine-dot problem solving. *Journal of Experimental Psychology: Learning, Memory and Cognition, 11*, 804–811.

MacGregor, J.N., Ormerod, T.C., & Chronicle, E.P. (in press). Information-processing and insight: A process model of performance on the nine-dot and related problems. *Journal of Experimental Psychology: Learning, Memory, and Cognition*.

Maier, N.R.F. (1931). Reasoning in humans II: The solution of a problem and its appearance in consciousness. *Journal of Comparative Psychology*, *12*, 181–194.

Marcus, N., Cooper, M., & Sweller, J. (1996). Understanding instructions. *Journal of Educational Psychology*, *88*(1), 49–63.

Marshall, S.P. (1995). *Schemas in problem solving*. Cambridge: Cambridge University Press.

Mayer, R.E. (1993). The instructive metaphor: Metaphoric aids to students' understanding of science. In A. Ortony (Ed.), *Metaphor and thought* (2nd ed., pp. 561–578). Cambridge: Cambridge University Press.

McKeithen, K.B., Reitman, J.S., Rueter, H.H., & Hirtle, S.C. (1981). Knowledge organization and skill differences in computer programmers. *Cognitive Psychology*, *13*, 307–325.

McKendree, J., & Anderson, J.R. (1987). Effect of practice on knowledge and use of Basic LISP. In J.M. Carroll (Ed.), *Interfacing thought*. Cambridge, MA: MIT Press.

McNab, A. (1994). *Bravo two zero*. London: Corgi.

Meadows, S. (1993). *The child as thinker*. London: Routledge.

Medin, D., & Ortony, A. (1989). Comments on Part I: Psychological essentialism. In S. Vosniadou & A. Ortony (Eds.), *Similarity and analogical reasoning*. London: Cambridge University Press.

Medin, D.L., & Ross, B.H. (1989). *The specific character of abstract thought: Categorization, problem solving and induction* (Vol. 5). Hillsdale, NJ: Lawrence Erlbaum Associates Inc.

Metcalfe, J. (1986). Feeling of knowing in memory and problem solving. *Journal of Experimental Psychology: Learning, Memory, and Cognition*, *12*(2), 288–294.

Metcalfe, J., & Wiebe, D. (1987). Intuition in insight and noninsight problems. *Memory and Cognition*, *15*(3), 238–246.

Miller, G.A. (1956). The magical number seven, plus or minus two: Some limits on our capacity for processing information. *Psychological Review*, *63*, 81–97.

Mithen, S. (1996). *The prehistory of the mind*. London: Thames & Hudson.

Morris, C.D., Bransford, J.D., & Franks, J.J. (1977). Levels of processing versus transfer appropriate behaviour. *Journal of Verbal Learning and Verbal Behavior*, *16*, 519–533.

Müller, B. (1999). Use specificity of cognitive skills: Evidence for production rules? *Journal of Experimental Psychology: Learning, Memory, and Cognition*, *25*(1), 191–207.

Murphy, G.L., & Wright, J.C. (1984). Changes in conceptual structure with expertise: Differences between real-world experts and novices. *Journal of Experimental Psychology: Learning, Memory, and Cognition*, *10*, 144–155.

Nathan, M.J., Kintsch, W., & Young, E. (1992). A theory of algebra-word-problem comprehension and its implications for the design of learning environments. *Cognition and Instruction*, *9*(4), 329–389.

Newell, A. (1980). Physical symbol systems. *Cognitive Science*, *4*, 135–183.

Newell, A. (1990). *Unified theories of cognition*. Cambridge, MA: Harvard University Press.

Newell, A., & Rosenbloom, P.S. (1981). Mechanisms of skill acquisition and the law of practice. In J.R. Anderson (Ed.), *Cognitive skills and their acquisition*. Hillsdale, NJ: Lawrence Erlbaum Associates Inc.

Newell, A., & Simon, H.A. (1972). *Human problem solving*. Englewood Cliffs, NJ: Prentice-Hall.

Norman, G.R., Brooks, L.R., & Allen, S.W. (1989). Recall by expert medical practitioners and novices as a record of processing attention. *Journal of Experimental Psychology: Learning, Memory, and Cognition*, *15*(6), 1166–1174.

Novick, L.R. (1990). Representational transfer in problem solving. *Psychological Science*, *1*(2), 128–132.

Novick, L.R., & Hmelo, C.E. (1994). Transferring symbolic representations across nonisomorphic problems. *Journal of Experimental Psychology: Learning, Memory, and Cognition*, *20*(6), 1296–1321.

Novick, L.R., & Holyoak, K.J. (1991). Mathematical problem solving by analogy. *Journal of Experimental Psychology: Learning, Memory, and Cognition, 17*(3), 398–415.

Ohlsson, S. (1992). Information processing explanations of insight and related phenomena. In M.T. Keane & K.J. Gilhooly (Eds.), *Advances in the psychology of thinking* (pp. 1–43). London: Harvester-Wheatsheaf.

Ohlsson, S., & Rees, E. (1991). The function of conceptual understanding in the learning of arithmetic procedures. *Cognition and Instruction, 8*(2), 103–179.

Ormerod, T.C., Chronicle, E.P., & MacGregor, J.N. (1997, August). *Facilitation in variants of the nine-dot problem: Perceptual or cognitive mediation.* Poster presented at the 18th Annual Conference of the Cognitive Science Society, Stanford, CA.

Papert, S. (1980). *Mindstorms: Children, computers and powerful ideas.* New York: Harvester Press.

Papert, S. (1993). *The children's machine.* New York: Basic Books.

Partridge, D. (1987, June). *Is intuitive expertise rule based?* Paper presented at the Third International Expert Systems Conference, Oxford.

Patel, V.L., & Groen, G.J. (1991). The general and specific nature of medical expertise. In K.A. Ericsson & J. Smith (Eds.), *Towards a general theory of expertise* (pp. 93–125). Cambridge: Cambridge University Press.

Patel, V.L., & Ramoni, M.F. (1997). Cognitive models of directional inference in expert medical reasoning. In P.J. Feltovich, K.M. Ford, & R.R. Hoffman (Eds.), *Expertise in context* (pp. 67–99). London: MIT Press.

Paull, G., & Glencross, D. (1997). Expert perception and decision making in baseball. *International Journal of Sport Psychology, 28*(1), 35–56.

Payne, S.J., Squibb, H.R., & Howes, A. (1990). The nature of device models: The yoked state space hypothesis and some experiments with text editors. *Human–Computer Interaction, 5*, 415–444.

Pellegrino, J.W., & Glaser, R. (1982). Analyzing aptitudes for learning: Inductive reasoning. In R. Glaser (Ed.), *Advances in instructional psychology* (Vol. 2, pp. 245–269). Hillsdale, NJ: Lawrence Erlbaum Associates Inc.

Pennington, N., & Rehder, B. (1996). Looking for transfer and interference. In D.L. Medin (Ed.), *The psychology of learning and motivation* (Vol. 33). New York: Academic Press.

Perkins, D.N., & Salomon, G. (1989). Are cognitive skills context bound? *Educational Researcher, 18*, 16–25.

Petrie, H.G., & Oshlag, R. (1993). Metaphor and learning. In A. Ortony (Ed.), *Metaphor and thought* (2nd ed., pp. 579–609). Cambridge: Cambridge University Press.

Pirolli, P. (1991). Effects of examples and their explanations in a lesson on recursion: A production system analysis. *Cognition and Instruction, 8*(3), 207–259.

Pirolli, P.L., & Anderson, J.R. (1985). The role of learning from examples in the acquisition of recursive programming skills [Special Issue: Skill]. *Canadian Journal of Psychology, 39*(2), 240–272.

Posner, M.I. (1973). *Cognition: An introduction.* Glenview, IL: Scott, Foresman.

Postman, L., & Schwartz, M. (1964). Studies of learning to learn: Transfer as a function of method and practice and class of verbal materials. *Journal of Verbal Learning and Verbal Behavior, 3*, 37–49.

Raichle, M.E. (1998). The neural correlates of consciousness: An analysis of cognitive skill learning. *Philosophical Transactions of the Royal Society, London B: Biological Sciences, 353*(1377), 1889–1901.

Raufaste, E., Eyrolle, H., & Mariné, C. (1999). Pertinence generation in radiological diagnosis: Spreading activation and the nature of expertise. *Cognitive Science, 22*(4), 517–546.

Reason, J. (1990). *Human error.* Cambridge: Cambridge University Press.

Reed, S.K., Dempster, A., & Ettinger, M. (1985). Usefulness of analogous solutions for solving algebra word problems. *Journal of Experimental Psychology; Learning, Memory, and Cognition, 11*(1), 106–125.

Reed, S.K., Ernst, G.W., & Banerji, R. (1974). The role of analogy in transfer between similar problem states. *Cognitive Psychology, 6*, 436–450.

Reed, S.K., & Ettinger, M. (1987). Usefulness of tables for solving word problems. *Cognition and Instruction, 4*(1), 43–58.

Reeves, L.M., & Weisberg, R.W. (1993). On the concrete nature of human thinking: Content and context in analogical transfer [Special Issue: Thinking]. *Educational Psychology, 13*(3–4), 245–258.

Reimann, P., & Schult, T.J. (1996). Turning examples into cases: Acquiring knowledge structures for analogical problem solving. *Educational Psychologist, 31*(2), 123–132.

Resnick, L.B. (1989). Introduction. In L.B. Resnick (Ed.), *Knowing, learning, and instruction: Essays in honor of Robert Glaser* (pp. 1–24). Hillsdale, NJ: Lawrence Erlbaum Associates Inc.

Rist, R.S. (1989). Schema creation in programming. *Cognitive Science, 13*, 389–414.

Robertson, S.I. (1999). *Types of thinking*. London: Routledge.

Robertson, S.I. (2000). Imitative problem solving: Why transfer of learning often fails to occur. *Instructional Science, 28*, 263–289.

Robertson, S.I., & Kahney, H. (1996). The use of examples in expository texts: Outline of an interpretation theory for text analysis. *Instructional Science, 24*(2), 89–119.

Robinson, D.H., & Kiewra, K.A. (1995). Visual argument: Graphic organisers are superior to outlines in improving learning from text. *Journal of Educational Psychology, 87*(3), 455–467.

Ross, B.H. (1984). Remindings and their effects in learning a cognitive skill. *Cognitive Psychology, 16*, 371–416.

Ross, B.H. (1987). This is like that: The use of earlier problems and the separation of similarity effects. *Journal of Experimental Psychology: Learning, Memory, and Cognition, 13*(4), 629–639.

Ross, B.H. (1989a). Distinguishing types of superficial similarities. Different effects on the access and use of earlier problems. *Journal of Experimental Psychology: Learning, Memory, and Cognition, 14*, 510–520.

Ross, B.H. (1989b). Remindings in learning and instruction. In S. Vosniadou & A. Ortony (Eds.), *Similarity and analogical reasoning* (pp. 438–469). London: Cambridge University Press.

Ross, B.H. (1996). Category learning as problem solving. In D.L. Medin (Ed.), *The psychology of learning and motivation* (Vol. 35, pp. 165–192). New York: Academic Press.

Rozin, P. (1976). The evolution of intelligence and access to the cognitive unconscious. In J.M. Sprague & A.N. Epstein (Eds.), *Progress in psychobiology and physiological psychology*. New York: Academic Press.

Scheerer, M. (1963). Problem-solving. *Scientific American, 208*, 118–128.

Schmidt, H.G., Norman, G.R., & Boshuizen, H.P. (1990). A cognitive perspective on medical expertise: Theory and implications. *Academic Medicine, 65*(10), 611–621.

Schneider, W., Körkel, J., & Weinert, F.E. (1989). Expert knowledge and general abilities and text processing. In W. Schneider & F.E. Weinert (Eds.), *Interaction among aptitudes, strategies, and knowledge in cognitive performance*. New York: Springer-Verlag.

Schön, D.A. (1993). Generative metaphor: A perspective on problem-setting in social policy. In A. Ortony (Ed.), *Metaphor and thought* (pp. 137–163). Cambridge: Cambridge University Press.

Schumacher, R.M., & Czerwinski, M.P. (1992). Mental models and the acquisition of expert knowledge. In R.R. Hoffman (Ed.), *The psychology of expertise: Cognitive research and empirical AI*. New York: Springer-Verlag.

Schumacher, R.M., & Gentner, D. (1988). Transfer of training as analogical mapping [Special Issue: Human–computer interaction and cognitive engineering]. *IEEE Transactions on Systems, Man, and Cybernetics, 18*(4), 592–600.

Schunn, C.D., & Anderson, J.R. (1999). The generality/specificity of expertise in scientific reasoning. *Cognitive Science, 23*(3), 337–370.

Schunn, C.D., & Dunbar, K. (1996). Priming, analogy and awareness in complex reasoning. *Memory and Cognition, 24*(3), 271–284.

Shallice, T. (1988). Information-processing models of consciousness: Possibilities and problems. In A.J. Marcel & E. Bisiach (Eds.), *Consciousness in contemporary science* (pp. 305–333). Oxford: Oxford Science Publications.

Silver, E.A. (1979). Student perceptions of relatedness among mathematical problem solvers. *Journal for Research in Mathematics Education, 10*, 195–210.

Silver, E.A. (1986). Using conceptual and procedural knowledge: A focus on relationships. In J. Hiebert (Ed.), *Conceptual and procedural knowledge: The case of mathematics* (pp. 181–198). Hillsdale, NJ: Lawrence Erlbaum Associates Inc.

Simon, H.A. (1966). Scientific discovery and the psychology of problem solving. In R.G. Colodny (Ed.), *Mind and cosmos: Essays in contemporary science and philosophy* (pp. 22–40). Pittsburgh, PA: University of Pittsburgh Press.

Simon, H.A., & Chase, W.G. (1973). Skill in chess. *American Scientist, 61*, 394–403.

Simon, H.A., & Hayes, J.R. (1976). The understanding process: Problem isomorphs. *Cognitive Psychology, 8*, 165–190.

Simon, H.A., & Kaplan, C.A. (1989). Foundations of cognitive science. In M.I. Posner (Ed.), *Foundations of cognitive science* (pp. 1–47). Cambridge, MA: MIT Press/Bradford Books.

Simon, H.H. (1975). The functional equivalence of problem solving skills. *Cognitive Psychology, 7*, 269–288.

Simons, P.R.J. (1984). Instructing with analogies. *Journal of Educational Psychology, 76*(3), 513–527.

Singley, M.K., & Anderson, J.R. (1985). The transfer of text-editing skill. *Journal of Man–Machine Studies, 22*, 403–423.

Singley, M.K., & Anderson, J.R. (1989). *The transfer of cognitive skill.* Cambridge, MA: Harvard University Press.

Smith, E.E., & Goodman, L. (1984). Understanding written instructions: The role of an explanatory schema. *Cognition and Instruction, 1*(4), 359–396.

Solso, R.L. (1995). *Cognitive psychology* (4th ed). London: Allyn and Bacon.

Spence, M.T., & Brucks, M. (1997). The moderating effects of problem characteristics on experts' and novices' judgments. *Journal of Marketing Research, 34*(2), 233–247.

Spencer, R.M., & Weisberg, R.W. (1986). Context dependent effects on analogical transfer. *Memory and Cognition, 14*(5), 442–449.

Sperber, D. (1994). The modularity of thought and the epidemiology of representations. In L.A. Hirschfield & S.A. Gelman (Eds.), *Mapping the mind: Domain specificity in cognition and culture.* Cambridge: Cambridge University Press.

Squire, L.R., Knowlton, B., & Musen, G. (1993). The structure and organisation of memory. *Annual Review of Psychology, 44*, 453–495.

Sternberg, R.J. (1996a). *Cognitive psychology.* Orlando, FL: Harcourt Brace.

Sternberg, R.J. (1996b). The costs of expertise. In K.A. Ericsson (Ed.), *The road to excellence: The acquisition of expert performance in the arts and sciences, sports, and games* (pp. 347–354). Mahwah, NJ: Lawrence Erlbaum Associates, Inc.

Sternberg, R.J. (1997a). Cognitive conceptions of expertise. In P.J. Feltovich, K.M. Ford, & R.R. Hoffman (Eds.), *Expertise in context* (pp. 149–162). London: MIT Press.

Sternberg, R.J. (1997b). *Thinking styles.* Cambridge: Cambridge University Press.

Sternberg, R.J. (1998, June). *Abilities as developing expertise.* Paper presented at the International Conference on the Application of Psychology to the Quality of Learning and Teaching, Hong Kong.

Sternberg, R.J., & Frensch, P.A. (1992). On being an expert: A cost–benefit analysis. In R.R. Hoffman (Ed.), *The psychology of expertise: Cognitive research and empirical AI* (pp. 191–203). New York: Springer-Verlag.

Sternberg, R.J., & Nigro, G. (1983). Interaction and analogy in the comprehension and appreciation of metaphors. *Quarterly Journal of Experimental Psychology, 35A,* 17–38.

Stork, D.G. (1997). Scientist on the set: An interview with Marvin Minsky. In D.G. Stork (Ed.), *HAL's legacy: 2001's computer as dream and reality.* Cambridge, MA: MIT Press.

Swanson, H.L., O'Connor, J.E., & Carter, K.R. (1991). Problem-solving subgroups as a measure of intellectual giftedness. *British Journal of Educational Psychology, 61*(1), 55–72.

Sweller, J. (1980). Transfer effects in a problem solving context. *Quarterly Journal of Experimental Psychology, 32,* 233–239.

Sweller, J. (1988). Cognitive load during problem solving: Effects on learning. *Cognitive Science, 12,* 257–285.

Sweller, J., & Cooper, G.A. (1985). The use of worked examples as a substitute for problem solving in learning algebra. *Cognition and Instruction, 2,* 59–89.

Sweller, J., & Gee, W. (1978). Einstellung, the sequence effect and hypothesis theory. *Journal of Experimental Psychology: Human Learning and Memory, 4,* 513–526.

Tardieu, H., Ehrlich, M.-F., & Gyselinck, V. (1992). Levels of representation and domain-specific knowledge in comprehension of scientific texts [Special Issue: Discourse representation and text processing]. *Language and Cognitive Processes, 7*(3–4), 335–351.

Thomas, J.C. (1974). An analysis of behavior in the Hobbits-Orcs program. *Cognitive Psychology, 6,* 257–269.

Thorndike, E.L. (1913). *Educational psychology* (Vol. 2). New York: Columbia University Press.

Thorndike, E.L., & Woodworth, R.S. (1901). The influence of improvement in one mental function upon the efficiency of other functions. *Psychological Review, 8,* 247–261.

Thune, L.E. (1951). Warm-up effect as a function of level of practice in verbal learning. *Journal of Experimental Psychology, 42,* 250–256.

Tversky, A. (1977). Features of similarity. *Psychological Review, 84,* 327–352.

Van Dijk, T.A., & Kintsch, W. (1983). *Strategies of discourse comprehension.* New York: Academic Press.

VanLehn, K. (1986). Arithmetic procedures are induced from examples. In J. Hiebert (Ed.), *Conceptual and procedural knowledge: The case of mathematics.* Hillsdale, NJ: Lawrence Erlbaum Associates Inc.

VanLehn, K. (1989). Problem solving and cognitive skill acquisition. In M.I. Posner (Ed.), *Foundations of cognitive science.* Cambridge, MA: MIT Press.

VanLehn, K. (1990). *Mind bugs: The origins of procedural misconceptions.* Cambridge, MA: MIT Press.

VanLehn, K., Jones, R.M., & Chi, M.T.H. (1992). A model of the self-explanation effect. *The Journal of the Learning Sciences, 2,* 1–59.

Vosniadou, S. (1989). Analogical reasoning as a mechanism in knowledge acquisition: A developmental perspective. In S. Vosniadou & A. Ortony (Eds.), *Similarity and analogical reasoning.* London: Cambridge University Press.

Voss, J.F., Greene, T.R., Post, T.A., & Penner, B.C. (1983). *Problem solving skill in the social sciences* (Vol. 17). New York: Academic Press.

Ward, M., & Sweller, J. (1990). Structuring effective worked examples. *Cognition and Instruction, 7*(1), 1–39.

Waters, A.J., Underwood, G., & Findlay, J.M. (1997). Studying expertise in music reading: Use of a pattern-matching paradigm. *Perception and Psychophysics, 59*(4), 477–488.

Weisberg, R.W. (1995). Prolegomena to theories of insight in problem solving: A taxonomy of problems. In R. J. Sternberg & J.E. Davidson (Eds.), *The nature of insight*. Cambridge, MA: MIT Press.

Weisberg, R.W., & Alba, J.W. (1981). An examination of the alleged role of "fixation" in the solution of several "insight" problems. *Journal of Experimental Psychology: General, 110*, 169–192.

Weisberg, R.W., & Alba, J.W. (1982). Problem solving is not like perception: More on Gestalt theory. *Journal of Experimental Psychology: General, 111*, 326–330.

Wertheimer, M. (1945). *Productive thinking*. New York: Harper & Row.

Wheatley, G.H. (1984). *Problem solving in school mathematics* (MEPS Technical Report 84.01). West Lafayette, IN: Purdue University, School of Mathematics and Science Center.

White, B.Y. (1993). Intermediate causal models: A missing link for successful science education? In R. Glaser (Ed.), *Advances in instructional psychology* (Vol. 4). Hillsdale, NJ: Lawrence Erlbaum Associates Inc.

Winston, P.H., & Horn, B.K.P. (1989). *LISP* (3rd ed.). Reading, MA: Addison-Wesley.

Yaniv, I., & Meyer, D.E. (1987). Activation and metacognition of inaccessible information: Potential bases for incubation effects in problem solving. *Journal of Experimental Psychology: Learning, Memory, and Cognition, 13*, 187–205.

Young, R.M., & O'Shea, T. (1981). Errors in children's subtraction. *Cognitive Science, 5*, 153–177.

Zajonc, R.B. (1965). Social facilitation. *Science, 149*, 269–274.

Zajonc, R.B. (1980). Compliance. In P.B. Paulus (Ed.), *Psychology of group influence* (pp. 35–60). Hillsdale, NJ: Lawrence Erlbaum Associates Inc.

Zeitz, C.M. (1997). Some concrete advantages of abstraction: How experts' representations facilitate reasoning. In P.J. Feltovich, K.M. Ford, & R.R. Hoffman (Eds.), *Expertise in context* (pp. 43–65). Cambridge, MA: MIT Press.

Author index

Subject index

DATE DUE